FREEDOM'S COLLEGE

FREEDOM'S COLLEGE

THE HISTORY OF GROVE CITY COLLEGE

Lee Edwards

Since 1947
REGNERY
PUBLISHING, INC.
An Eagle Publishing Company ● *Washington, D.C.*

Library of Congress Cataloging-in-Publication Data

Edwards, Lee.
    Freedom's college: the history of Grove City College/Lee Edwards.
        p.cm.
    Includes bibliographical references.
    ISBN 0-89526-277-0
    1.Grove City College—History. I. Title.

    LD2073.E38 2000
    378.748'95—dc21   00-055271

Published in the United States by
Regnery Publishing, Inc.
An Eagle Publishing Company
One Massachusetts Avenue, NW
Washington, DC 20001

Visit us at <www.regnery.com>.

Distributed to the trade by
National Book Network
4720-A Boston Way
Lanham, MD 20706

Printed on acid-free paper
Manufactured in the United States of America

10 9 8 7 6 5 4 3 2 1

Books are available in quantity for promotional or premium use. Write to Director of Special Sales, Regnery Publishing, Inc., One Massachusetts Avenue, NW, Washington, DC 20001, for information on discounts and terms or call (202) 216-0600.

CONTENTS

Other Books by Lee Edwards

The Collapse of Communism (ed.)

The Conservative Revolution: The Movement That Remade America

The Power of Ideas: The Heritage Foundation at 25 Years

Goldwater: The Man Who Made a Revolution

Missionary for Freedom: The Life and Times of Walter Judd

John Paul II in the Nation's Capital (ed.)

Rebel Peddler

You Can Make the Difference (with Anne Edwards)

Ronald Reagan: A Political Biography

To Edwin J. Feulner

Foreword

By J. Paul Sticht

Throughout the last century, our nation was constantly tested by hot war and cold war, depression and recession, fiery dissent and assaults on our institutions, assassinations and demagoguery. And yet America survived all of these often mortal challenges because we are a nation rooted in religious, political, and economic liberty. "Our priceless liberty," J. Howard Pew, Grove City College's most famous graduate often remarked, "is recognized as the very cornerstone of American civilization."

Grove City College was founded one hundred and twenty-five years ago to instill in the young men and women of Western Pennsylvania an understanding of and an appreciation for this very same liberty. Under the founding president Isaac Ketler and his worthy successors, a small school in the Pennsylvania hills has become one of the most respected and honored liberal arts colleges in America.

Grove City College has succeeded because it has stuck to its mission of providing an excellent education in a thoroughly Christian atmosphere at an affordable price. When other colleges wavered or gave in, Grove City did not compromise its basic principles. It turned down the government's grants and loans because of the many intrusive regulations that accompanied them. It rejected political correctness and other pedagogical fads in favor of providing a classical liberal arts education. It kept costs down and efficiency up with a faculty dedicated to teaching and an administration that did not mind making its own coffee.

I can personally attest to the effectiveness of such an education. If I had not gone to college, specifically Grove City College, I would not have had, in all probability, the opportunities and successes I have had throughout my life. Grove City gave me far more than an excellent education. It gave me lasting values and friendships and a realization of how important it is to adhere always to your principles. Lee Edwards, one of the most respected political biographers and historians in America, presents the remarkable story of founders Isaac Ketler and Joseph Newton Pew, the enduring partnership of Weir Ketler and J. Howard Pew, the famous legal battle against the federal government that ended up in the Supreme Court, how the school handled successfully the turbulent sixties, the pressures of PC and an increasingly secular society under presidents Stanley Harker, Charles MacKenzie, and John H. Moore.

But this compelling book is far more than a history of Grove City College: It is also the history of American higher education over the last one hundred years. Dr. Edwards brilliantly juxtaposes the stories of Grove City and the American college over the past century, showing how and why Grove City has prospered while so many institutions of higher learning have declined and even fallen.

We who graduated from Grove City College have always loved her for what she gave us. There are some twenty-eight thousand of us who have taken the "less traveled path" of faith and freedom at Grove City. This wonderfully written history reminds us yet again how fortunate we are to have had leaders like Albert A. Hopeman, Jr., trustee president for twenty-six years, who summed up the college's mission as: to teach "our students what it means to be virtuous," to stress stewardship and personal responsibility, and to expose the students to "the knowledge and wisdom of the ages." Amen and amen.

Introduction

By Stephen H. Balch,
President, National Association of Scholars

Grove City College cuts a dramatic figure on today's academic landscape. Towering butte-like above parched planes, it stands as a monument to conviction's power to resist erosive change. Though unexceptional when born, Grove City College has become extraordinary through its refusal to decay.

Institutions, of course, may express, but cannot have, convictions. These belong only to men and women. It has been Grove City College's blessing to number among its leadership many such individuals. Several, like founding president Isaac Ketler, his teacher, supporter, and close confident J. N. Pew, and his son and successor, Weir, left indelible imprints on the college through their contributions to its early development, as did in later years, board president Albert Hopeman. But two seem to account for Grove City College's adamantine firmness when so much else was being swept away: J. Howard Pew, and Charles Sherrard MacKenzie. To explain why these men played such exceptional roles, it is necessary to consider the history of American higher education since mid-century.

During the two decades following World War II American higher education attained its zenith. Careers were fully opened to talents within both faculties and student bodies, and the blot of racial segregation was finally erased. As centers of research, America's universities surpassed, and sometimes eclipsed, their Old World counterparts. Motivated students, often from humble backgrounds, streamed across campuses in record numbers. One could hardly have blamed higher education's spokesmen when they exuded unbounded confidence in its ability to bestow abundance and enlightenment on nation and world alike.

To be sure, the perceptive observer might have detected troubling signs. Growing government funding, though facilitating student access, loomed as a threat to institutional independence. Mass education fostered bureaucratic bloat. At many institutions a "publish or perish" mentality undermined undergraduate teaching. And a troubling ideological one-sidedness had enveloped many faculties, particularly on the most prestigious campuses. Nonetheless, only a chronic alarmist, or one armed with the gift of prophesy (and there were several), would have been deeply concerned. The triumphs seemed too big, and the bedrock too strong, to suggest what would happen next.

That bedrock was nothing less than the belief in the power of truth; a belief that had sustained American higher education from its earliest days. It had a variety of origins. For some—including the sponsors of America's first colleges—it stemmed from a faith that God having given mankind dominion over the world, had also given him the ability to understand it. For others, it was rooted in the view that science having brought the species technological mastery, could also bring it "a final theory." Many, of course, saw in religion and science parallel paths to truth.

Then the bedrock crumbled. Some blame this on the cultural upheaval of the Sixties. Others locate deeper causes, going to the heart of modernity itself. Suffice it to say that the crisis did not mean that truth itself had become any less true. Nor did it afflict the population at large nearly as much as it did the intellectuals, literati, and professors.

Here more detail is required. To understand why Grove City College maintained its dedication to truth, one must comprehend why so many other colleges and universities didn't.

One set of the reasons can be found in the huge expansion that higher education experienced after 1945. As institutions grew bigger, faculties increasingly fragmented, weakening any sense of common enterprise, collective responsibility, or even knowledge of what was going on in the next department. Parts of institutions, just like parts of the body, will be periodically attacked by pathogenic agents. Healthy institutions, like healthy bodies, mount systemic counterattacks when such invasions occur. But internal fragmentation can prevent immune responses because sound components no longer know, care about, or have the power to influence what is happening to infected ones. Thus, when certain academic fields—mainly, those charged with exploring the deeper meanings of human existence—started to succumb to utopian fantasy or radical skepticism, few other academics evinced much concern. Whereas one might have expected academic practitioners in the natural and applied sciences, mathematics, and the more tough-minded areas of professional study, would have rushed to smother fires ablaze in the humanities and social sciences, few even smelled the smoke.

Academic elephantiasis also sapped the ability of administrators to provide remedies. They continued, of course, ostensibly to possess a large complement of oversight responsibilities. Yet the ability to exercise them effectively bore an inverse relationship to their growing scope. The bigger the institution, the less time available for examining its affairs in detail, or exercising genuine leadership, and the more that was exhausted on mediation between fractious subdivisions. In addition, as colleges and universities swelled, administrators were less and less likely themselves to be scholars with well-articulated philosophies of education. Instead they were often professional managers disinclined to risk careers for the sake of mere principle.

Moreover, colleges and universities discovered a downside to recruiting students in a mass market. The "G. I. Bill" had supported students matured in the crucible of war and as eager to learn as "make good." As time went on this healthy combination of ambitions increasingly gave way to purely vocational ones. To accommodate this pragmatism, institutions felt compelled to strip away curricular requirements having little obvious relevance to job success. Much of our civilized heritage went with them.

Burgeoning government spending on higher education and the regulation that followed, required administrators—even faculty—to shift their attentions away from the inner life of their institutions. They focused on pursuing grants, lobbying legislators, and processing paper work. Far worse, federal and state regulators began to demand that academic policy be subordinated to political objectives at odds with truth seeking, and even truthfulness.

Most corrosive in its effects was the imposition of racial, ethnic, and gender preferences through bureaucratic and judicial intimidation. By making extraneous considerations like race, ethnicity, and gender pivotal in faculty hiring and student admissions, preferences inevitably subverted intellectual standards. And once on campus, those preferentially recruited not infrequently saw themselves as charged with promoting political rather than intellectual goals, as being activists with answers rather than searchers with questions.

Seekers after truth need to be truthful. By fostering a generalized cynicism, habits of dissembling metastasize, spreading from one institutional domain to another. Accordingly, as standards were warped by quotas, or the need to kowtow to ideological factions, academic administrators felt compelled to cover their tracks, avoiding public embarrassment through a lack of candor about the multiplying consequences. And this meant they also lost the moral authority to censure untruth in others. Significant realms of academic policy, both high or low, began to revolve in vicious circles of deceit.

Ultimately, however, the commitment to truth was less eroded by structural and regulatory changes then changes in the minds of the academicians themselves.

Utopias have always had a strong appeal for intellectuals, academics emphatically included. While the actual world resists perfecting, castles-in-air are always faultless. Intellectuals, their natural architects, can acquire a following by touting their glories, and involving themselves in movements to erect them "on the ground." Utopians are, of course, sometimes interesting people and gifted teachers. In their total absence academe would surely be a duller place. Nonetheless, when too numerous, they can be immensely destructive. Captured by their certitudes and impatient with obstacles to making a heaven on earth; they readily surrender to "the totalitarian impulse." When in control of academic policy, dissent is likely to be quashed, and "thought reform" made the order of the day.

Until the '60s American higher education managed to hold its utopians in check, limiting their numbers, and keeping them away from the levers of power. To an extent this reflected the practical bent of American culture as a whole—extending even to the professorate—and discouraged excessive fantasizing. But in greater part it was attributable to American higher education's traditional forms of institutional governance, which distributed authority widely among faculty, administrators, and lay trustees.

The latter two groups—generally of down-to-earth mentality—acted as brakes on the ideological enthusiasms of the first. (Although, too often, they suppressed quite reasonable scholarly views with which they disagreed).

We have already reviewed some of the factors that undermined administrative influence over faculties. Trustee influence declined as well. Whereas in earlier times, trustees felt they had both the responsibility and the capability to oversee the intellectual health of their colleges and universities, by the 1960s they had lost their nerve. To be sure, they continued to function as major institutional boosters and fund-raisers, and often offered good business advice. But serious concern for the cultural climate on their campuses had, for the overwhelming majority, become a taboo.

In the aftermath of the '60s, these power shifts had massive consequences. On campus after campus radical egalitarians and ethno-gender separatists rapidly expanded their influence. Some created research institutes, student centers, instructional programs, and even whole new fields to pursue their ideological objectives, while others worked to overawe established disciplines. Unlike their less politicized colleagues they relentlessly exploited the hiring process to bring in fellow-thinkers.

With respect to the curriculum they eliminated requirements deemed too "traditional," or too difficult, and then pressed to add others debunking whatever of tradition remained. Hostile to anything tainted by "elitism" they favored student recruitment processes that abjured standards, and grading (or non-grading) practices that did the same.

Following a logically tortured path, they discovered that equality required admissions and hiring quotas based on ancestry and sex. Important areas of extracurricular activity were turned by them into agencies of New Age proselytization, most notably student life and freshman orientation programs.

Virtually invisible to non-activist faculty, these programs worked overtime to instill correct thought and behavior. Needless to say, correct behavior in utopian eyes didn't involve adherence to traditional moral norms and practices. Thus, while many colleges and universities increasingly sought to capture students' minds and spirits, policy and preachment were unleashed to "liberate" their passions.

Reality allows ideals but not utopias, a conclusion modern history has written out in blood. As a result, by the twentieth century's end, utopian theorists were driven to take refuge in relativism—the denial of an objective reality. If truth is not found but "constructed," we can have whatever "truth" we please. If verification is just an exercise of power; the repeated failure of utopian projects—of large-scale social engineering in all its forms—need never be taken as conclusive. "Truth" triumphs through the exercise of will, so we only should will the harder.

Postmodernism is the portmanteau term covering the varied applications of this epistemological conceit, and its greatest influence has been felt in the humanities. Its signature is an intellectual leveling sweeping away distinctions between high and popular culture, knowledge and current opinion, art and lurid sensation. Its end product is a sophistical cynicism that corrodes respect for learning in virtually all its forms, except insofar as they facilitate rhetorical manipulation or further ideological goals. Once this cynicism is sufficiently pervasive, the classic mission of liberal education, fostering the love of reason and truth becomes impossible.

A discussion of broad trends like these is necessarily couched in generalities. But all generalization rests on particular instances shaped by the decisions of flesh and blood human beings. Making generalizations about a large category of objects, such as colleges and universities, suggests a determinism that never exists. Trends may take hold because similarly placed parties are subject to similar desires, fears, opportunities, or misconceptions, but however many are carried away there is always the possibility of holding fast or steering a contrary course. What robustness of individuality, then, allowed Grove City College to chart its distinct path? One that arose out of the very love of truth that so many other institutions were making it their business to mock.

By 1971, J. Howard Pew would have been viewed by many as a relic of a bygone age, his eighty-nine years being the least of it. What really marked him as a man out of time was his marriage of a staunch belief in individual liberty to a powerful sense of social responsibility. Like many Americans born in the late Nineteenth Century, though far fewer today, he understood freedom not as an indulgence but as an opportunity to serve, with service devoted in substantial measure to passing this understanding of freedom and obligation along to others. As an integral part of his Christian faith, the cherishment of freedom could not be divorced from responsibility. And it was for precisely this reason that he retained, so late in life, an intense dedication to the well-being of Grove City College: it too was transmitting the principles of responsible freedom and Christian service to future generations. When most trustees were fading into the woodwork, ignoring the progressive demoralization of their institutions, Pew, despite his years, remained keenly aware of what was happening both in the world at large, and in the smaller one of Grove City. At the critical moment this alertness moved him to action.

As Lee Edwards's illuminating history reveals there were many signs during the late '50s and '60s the long-standing consensus about the college's mission was challenged by some faculty and students, as well as by representatives of the counter-culture invited to speak on campus. The college's receptivity to challenge was, to be sure, a sign of its intellectual vitality and openness to the world, each indispensable to providing a serious liberal education.

The question was whether the college's leaders would bring its ideals intact through this period of testing.

When Grove City College's presidency was vacated in 1971, board president J. Howard Pew, now entering the last year of his life, fully realized what was at stake. By happy circumstance he had, some years earlier, made friends with Charles Sherrard MacKenzie, an experienced educator and Presbyterian minister. Recognizing Mackenzie as a man to whom the college's ideals could be safely entrusted, Pew advanced his candidacy and, against some opposition, secured him the post. Though few, other than Pew, might have guessed it, with the hiring of MacKenzie, Grove City's future as an honorable exception to so much that was wrong with American higher education was assured.

Soon after commenced the great crisis of Grove City's history, its courageous battle, begun in 1976, to affirm its independence from government control. Except for some training programs during the First and Second World Wars, Grove City had scrupulously avoided direct entanglement with, or subsidy from, government. For many years this was also the policy of many other private colleges and universities, and so long as government spending on higher education stayed small, it was not a difficult one to maintain. Once government began offering assistance on a wholesale basis, however, seemingly firm resolves started to crumble. Grove City College long resisted temptation, at least as far as direct subventions were concerned, but it did not object to its undergraduates individually soliciting them in the form of federal scholarship grants or guaranteed student loans. This, it assumed, was not the college's affair but theirs alone.

The government thought otherwise. Thus, when president MacKenzie received from the U.S. Department of Education a letter demanding that he sign an "assurance of compliance," pledging that Grove City College would not violate Title IX of the

Education Amendments Act of 1992, a moment of truth had arrived. The provisions of Title IX forbid discrimination against women, something Grove City College, by everyone's admission, had never engaged in. But MacKenzie knew that if he put his pen to the "assurance" the college would be ceding ultimate control over its policies to the machinations of bureaucrats and politicians, something to which he could never consent.

The story of Grove City College's gallant defense of its independence is vividly recounted below. Eventually a split Supreme Court would rule against its position that the freedom of a private college should not be forfeit through the decisions of third parties (i.e., students deciding to accept federal aid), but by bravely asserting this position it won an enormous moral victory, not only for itself, but for American higher education and the larger cause of liberty.

The victories for higher education and liberty were won first by the sterling example Grove City set; that of a small college speaking the truth to power that there were freedoms too precious to sell. And second, by Grove City's demonstration that it could not only survive but flourish without the subventions upon which virtually all other institutions depended. Although few other institutions have been bold enough to adopt Grove City's course, its proven feasibility is of major significance.

Perhaps even more important was Grove City College's inner victory, which accomplished, in a sense, its second founding. Throughout most of its history, Grove City's leaders had thought of themselves as conservators of a precious heritage. It was only after they had weathered the federal storm that they fully realized that they were not just conservators but a saving remnant. As such they gained a renewed and deepened commitment to hold their flame aloft, to rededicate themselves to truth and freedom, and to reject anything unworthy of the heroic act of self-assertion that had made their college famous. There could be no thought of turning back.

Grove City College has thus become a national leader. But an institution's character, like that of an individual's, rests as much on what it does at home as abroad. In other words, Grove City's national leadership depends on its internal life matching its public stance, on the consistency between the education it provides and the message it sends to the world. There could be no better way of ensuring this consistency than by graduating young people formed in the mold of Charles Mackenzie and J. Howard Pew, sharing their zest for the freedom to serve the truth. Readers of *Freedom's College* will be left in little doubt of Grove City College's capacity to continue to fulfill this exacting but critical charge.

Preface

For more than seventy years he had been coming to Grove City College in western Pennsylvania, and although he felt the weight of his eighty-nine years, J. Howard Pew was happy to be on campus that beautiful spring day of May 1, 1971. All that he saw was a fulfillment of his father's injunction many decades ago to "make the college... beautiful."[1] The bright sun illuminated the stained-glass windows of the Gothic-style Harbison Chapel and bathed the red brick and sandstone buildings that lined the main quadrangle. Flags rippled in the light wind. The young men and women flowing up and down the sidewalks talked quickly and laughed easily, filled with hope and promise for themselves and their country.

Pew felt confident about the future of the college. While many other schools had strayed from or even abandoned their mission, Grove City had remained true to its original charter—providing an excellent education in a thoroughly Christian atmosphere at a reasonable price. And he felt good about the new president, Charles S. "Sherry" MacKenzie, an outstanding scholar and man of faith whom he had personally persuaded to lead the college into its second century.

Pew was looking forward to the ceremonies of Parents' Day, which, he had been told, had drawn the largest crowd in its thirteen-year history—some four thousand visitors. He had given careful thought to the remarks he would deliver as president of the board of trustees. What he said might surprise those who only thought of him as a very successful businessman. He had firm ideas about what was important in this life, ideas he hoped would set all those present, especially the young people, to thinking.

Many colleges and universities across America were still recovering from the disruptions of the student rebellion of the 1960s. One school where there had been no seizure of the president's office, no burning of books, no bombing of buildings—no violence of any kind—was Grove City College. A central reason was the mutual respect of the students, faculty, administration, and trustees for each other and for the mission of the school, so often articulated by its longtime number one benefactor, J. Howard Pew.

Pew was "a solid rock of a man," six feet two inches tall and weighing over two hundred pounds.[2] He had thick bushy eyebrows and a deep resonant voice that easily filled a room. He wore old-fashioned frameless glasses and a dark blue suit regardless of the season, often with a white carnation in the lapel. Despite his considerable wealth, his wants were simple: a good cigar, meat-and-potato meals (roast beef was a favorite), a game of golf every Wednesday afternoon, and a Bible close at hand. He was a self-confessing biblical Christian and had been ordained a ruling elder in the United Presbyterian Church. What attracted him most to the Westminster Confession was its unequivocal defense of liberty under biblical authority. Again and again (including his last will and testament), he proclaimed the interdependence of

Christianity and freedom: "We must first have faith in God before we can enjoy the blessings of liberty."[3]

Pew's message that sunny May afternoon to the parents and guests who overflowed Hicks Hall and the main dining room of Mary Anderson Pew Hall was unadorned and direct, the essence of the college's and his own philosophy.

First and foremost, he said, Grove City was a Christian college. Its "prime responsibility" was to inculcate in the minds and hearts of young people "those Christian, moral, and ethical principles without which neither our College nor our Country can long endure."

Second, Grove City was determined to adhere to a policy of balancing its budget each and every year, not simply to save money, but to demonstrate that it was a reliable steward. "If the College is unable to make a good accounting of its stewardship," Pew stated, "is it competent to be entrusted with the training of our youth?"

Third, the primary issue before every American citizen today was freedom. "If the taxers, the planners, the equalizers and the socialists," he said, "can be prevented from further encroaching on the freedoms of the people, then the opportunities which lie ahead for you are infinitely greater than at any time in history." But without freedom, Pew warned, "neither Grove City College, our church, nor any of our other institutions can long exist."

He then concluded with an admonition to the young people in the audience that surprised those who could not get beyond the fact that he was one of the wealthiest men in America. Do not strive to be successful or powerful or wealthy, he urged, but to live by the Gospel and help make America "a place of which our children, and our children's children, may well be proud."[4]

Faith and freedom, freedom and faith. They had been J. Howard Pew's tenets as an undergraduate at Grove City College in the late 1890s, as president of the Sun Oil Company through two world wars and a great depression, and as one of the most generous and self-effacing philanthropists in American history. No one will ever know how many millions of dollars Pew gave to a multitude of institutions, causes, and individuals during his lifetime (the Pew Memorial Trust donated more than $7 million in 1970 alone to various educational, religious, and charitable organizations). As far as he and the other members of his independently minded family were concerned, it wasn't anyone else's business what they did with their money. But the presidents, trustees, and closest friends of Grove City College knew what J. Howard Pew and his father Joseph Newton Pew before him had given the college in spirit as well as in treasure almost from its founding in 1876.

Warm applause erupted when Pew finished speaking, and there was more applause when he announced that the new women's dormitory would be named in honor of Helen Harker, the enormously popular wife of President Stanley Harker, retiring after fifteen years at the helm of the college. J. Howard Pew returned to Grove City the following month to deliver a brief tribute to President Harker during commencement exercises, but that would be his last visit.

In August, he suffered a heart attack while on vacation in Canada. Poor health prevented him from attending the inauguration of Charles MacKenzie, Grove City College's fifth president, in November. It was the first major function he had missed in forty years as head of the board of trustees (he had first joined the board in 1912, nearly sixty years before). J. Howard Pew died at Knollwood, his fifty-nine-acre estate in suburban Philadelphia, on November 27, 1971, two months short of his ninetieth birthday. It was, remarked one observer, like "a great tree falling."[5]

Attending the brief, simple memorial services in Ardmore, Pennsylvania, were evangelist Billy Graham, who read Psalm 112, one of Pew's favorite biblical passages ("Blessed is the man who fears the Lord, who greatly delights in his commandments!"); Senator Barry Goldwater of Arizona, who had been the presidential candidate of the Republican Party in 1964; Senate chaplain Edward L. Elson; Sun Oil officials like retired chairman Robert G. Dunlop; and many others, high and low, who had known J. Howard Pew. They recalled his personal integrity, his religious convictions, his commitment to moral values, his dedication to freedom, his unfailing generosity, "his willingness," as Dunlop put it, "to speak out for what he believed in."[6]

More than one described Pew as a master builder of companies, colleges, and churches who loved to recite "The Bridge Builder" by the nineteenth-century poet Will Allen Dromgoole. When an old man is asked why he has bothered to build a bridge over "a sullen tide" that he himself has easily traversed, he replies that some youth is sure to follow him who may find crossing the deep water daunting:

> He, too, must cross in the twilight dim.
> Good friend, I am building this bridge for him.[7]

One of the most enduring bridges that J. Howard Pew helped to build in his long productive life was Grove City College.

CHAPTER ONE

A Modest Beginning

As America celebrated its one hundredth birthday in July 1876, anything seemed possible to the confident citizens of a still young, vibrant nation. After all, they had recently fought and won a great civil war to preserve the Union. Under the impetus of the Industrial Revolution, they were building factories and starting businesses at an astonishing rate. With the help of the transcontinental railroad, they were moving ever westward across a seemingly endless land, establishing new towns and cities wherever they went.

It was the age of inventors, entrepreneurs, and builders—of Alexander Graham Bell, Thomas A. Edison, John D. Rockfeller, and Andrew Carnegie. Never before, it seemed, had any nation been in such a hurry to expand, develop, and prosper. In the last third of the nineteenth century, America moved from kerosene to electricity for its lighting, from the telegraph to the telephone for its communication, from the horse to the automobile for its transportation, from steam power to electric power, from a rural to an increasingly urbanized society. Grievous conditions nevertheless persisted: mill and factory employees, many of them underage, worked sixty hours a week; and fewer than ten percent of American farm houses before 1900 had plumbing.

But overshadowing such grim conditions was the great symbol of nineteenth-century progress—the railroad. In 1840, it was believed a human being could not withstand exposure to a speed of thirty miles per hour; in 1893, a New York Central locomotive reached 120 miles an hour. America was covered from coast to coast with bands of shining steel. According to historian Samuel Eliot Morison, there were 35,000 miles of steam railroad in the United States in 1865, "more than in all Europe."[1]

Millions of immigrants from Europe poured into America, becoming its miners, factory workers, and farmers. Although not everyone enjoyed the American Dream, everyone believed he might one day. Russian immigrant Mary Antin called her autobiography *The Promised Land*. Progressive leader Herbert Croly would write a book titled *The Promise of American Life*. Freedom and promise, wrote historian Page Smith, were "talismanic words" for the new and old citizens of nineteenth-century America.[2]

The First College

At the very center of the American Dream was the schoolroom. From the very first—in the 1630s—Puritan settlers had evinced a strong desire to found institutions of learning in the New World. The Massachusetts Bay Colony required towns of one hundred families or more to set up a grammar school on the English model. These schools took in boys of six or eight and kept them for six years, during which they studied Latin and Greek grammar, and literature, and arithmetic.[3] And when some 130 alumni of the universities of Oxford, Cambridge, and Dublin emigrated to New England, they wanted the same advantages for their children that they had had in the old country. The result was the founding, in 1636, of what would become Harvard College.

With no rivals in the English colonies until William and Mary College was founded in 1693 and Yale in 1701, "Harvard set both the pace and pattern for higher education in North America."[4] It offered a traditional four-year liberal arts course, emphasizing the study of Latin, with instruction primarily by lecture and recitation. Students lived in dormitories and dined with their tutors. Although half of its graduates in the seventeenth century became ministers, Harvard was not a divinity school. Its purpose, education historian Christopher J. Lucas points out, was twofold: to raise up "a literate and pious clergy" and to prepare the men "destined to positions of responsibility and leadership in society."[5] Still, there was no disputing Harvard's Christian character as its earliest printed rules made clear: "Every one shall consider the mayne End of his life & studyes, to know God and Jesus Christ, which is Eternall life."[6]

For a century and a half, the colonial college[7] preserved an academic tradition based upon character as much as erudition and on "civic virtue over private advantage."[8] Harvard and the others were never popular institutions but rather "served the aristocratic elements of colonial society."[9] They were not, however, exclusively private schools but creatures to some extent of the state. Harvard, for example, was supported by the General Court from the moment of its birth through the grant of two thousand acres of land and later through tax levies and even rents from the Charlestown Ferry.

At the close of the American Revolution, the future of the American college seemed uncertain to some national leaders. Benjamin Rush, the revolutionary patriot, argued that American higher education should be modified to serve the new democratic order while Noah Webster, lexicographer and author, wrote that the minds of American youth should be inspired "with just and liberal ideas of government, and with an inviolable attachment to their own country."[10]

In a letter to Samuel Johnson, Benjamin Franklin revealed his conception of the purpose of educational institutions: "I think with you, that nothing is of more importance for the public weal, than to form and train up youth in wisdom and virtue." For Thomas Jefferson, according to historian Henry J. Perkinson, education was the ultimate safeguard of liberty—only an educated people could maintain and use the institutions designed to protect them against tyranny.[11] Both Founders were convinced of the high value of the classics. Jefferson, education historian John S. Brubacher has pointed out, wished to supplement the classical curriculum with more modern subjects such as government and modern languages, while Franklin suggested a parallel and more utilitarian curriculum for those who "could not profit from studying Latin and Greek."[12]

A Land of Colleges

The people agreed that education was essential to the new republic. There was such a rush to start new institutions of higher learning following the winning of independence that by the eve of the Civil War, 250 colleges had sprouted in America, leading one observer to comment, "Our country is to be a land of colleges."[13] Ohio, with a total population of three million, boasted thirty-seven colleges and universities while England with a population of twenty-three million had only four universities. Rivalry among religious denominations (led by the Congregationalists and the Presbyterians), state pride, increasing wealth, and a rapidly growing population all furthered the educational flowering—as well as one more factor: the American college was attracting the sons and even daughters of middle-class families. No longer the exclusive redoubts of the aristocracy, colleges were increasingly recognized as a means of getting ahead as well as getting an education.

And yet the colleges of the mid-nineteenth century would have been quite familiar to the founders of Harvard two hundred years earlier. School began with chapel services. The curriculum depended largely on classical texts. Professors and tutors taught a variety of subjects—there were no specialists. Student piety was a major concern. Student behavior was strictly controlled. Almost all of the college students were white, male, and upper class. Within a few short years, however, American higher education would undergo revolutionary changes.

Centennial Symbol

The most dramatic symbol of the nation's one hundredth birthday celebration in 1876 was the Centennial Exposition in Philadelphia. The focus of the fair was gigantic Machinery Hall, a 1,402-foot by 360-foot wooden building covering thirteen acres. In it was a dazzling display of American inventions, including the telephone, the typewriter, the mimeograph, and the 2,500-horsepower Corliss engine later bought by George Pullman for his sleeper-car factory. Almost ten million people—nearly a third of the nation—visited the exposition during the six months it was open, attracted by the display of great things accomplished and the hope of greater things to come.

Due west of the Philadelphia Exposition was one of the nation's burgeoning regions, western Pennsylvania, with its huge deposits of coal and a new railroad system to carry the fuel to the waiting furnaces of the rapidly expanding iron and steel industry. And there was oil too, first discovered in 1859 in Titusville, located about halfway between Erie and Pittsburgh. In a few short years, oil for America's lamps and lubricants for its machinery would create a billion-dollar national industry.

Scots-Irish Presbyterians—hardworking and God-fearing—along with English and German immigrants had first settled the western part of Pennsylvania, and they were now joined by willing workers from southern and eastern Europe. Regardless of origin, they wanted what new communities always want—stores, churches, and schools for their children. Indeed, one observer wrote, "Wherever Presbyterians went, they carried a demand for education."[14] It has been estimated that from 1802 to 1870, the Presbyterian Church founded fourteen academies, ten parochial schools, and five female seminaries in the upper Ohio valley. The most famous and earliest of the Presbyterian academies was William Tennent's "Log College" at Neshaminy, Pennsylvania, founded in 1727, out of which grew the College of New Jersey (later renamed Princeton University).

The Civil War, wrote historian Frederick Rudolph, cemented the East and the Middle West into "a formidable alliance of resources"—natural, human, industrial, and financial.[15] Western Pennsylvania lay in the very center of that great alliance.

Grove City's Origins

The settlement of what is now Grove City, located some sixty miles north of Pittsburgh, occurred in April 1798, when the Cunningham family, traveling from central Pennsylvania, built a log hut and later a grist mill on Wolf Creek.[16] In about 1844, two Cunningham brothers laid out a village they called Pine Grove; visitors could purchase supper, lodging, breakfast, and a shoeshine for fifty cents. Almost four decades later, in January 1883, an area of about six-hundred acres became the borough of Grove City, a somewhat pretentious name for a community of only five hundred. Coalmining remained Grove City's main industry right into the mid-1900s with as many as two thousand men employed in and around the city, although dairy farms dotted the countryside. Miners' wages were low, but so were prices: around the turn of the century, milk went for five cents a quart, bread for five cents a loaf.

The Methodists were the first to organize a church, followed by the Presbyterians who built a frame church at the corner of Broad and Main streets in about 1847. The Reverend W. T. Dickson served as pastor and also conducted a select or private school in his home and the church. In good weather church services were held in a grove down by the creek.

The town steadily grew, but urban renewal, historian David Dayton writes, was often the inadvertent result of fire. In May 1890, sixteen downtown buildings were destroyed by fire, followed in June 1898, by ten other buildings in the business district that were also gutted by fire. Each time, Grove City's citizens, inspired perhaps by Chicago's determination following its great fire of 1871, built and rebuilt. Schools were invariably at the top of the list.

The First Schools

The early schools in western Pennsylvania were established because the local community demanded them. But since the state had limited responsibility for education, people who wished to educate their children subscribed money to pay a teacher, most often a young man "with fair education and interest in teaching as a stepping stone to professional studies."[17] Such neighborhood schools had no grades and accepted students from six to twenty-one years of age, moving them up as fast as possible. Bibles, catechisms, and hymnals served as the first schoolbooks.

But the widespread demand for free common, or public, schools persuaded the state legislature in 1834 to pass the Free School Act, setting up county divisions and local school districts. By 1880, fifty-eight public high schools dotted the state. In the interim private academies had been established to fill the vacuum. Now, as the number of public high schools increased, the popularity of the academies declined. But there were still significant educational gaps. As late as 1889, western Pennsylvania had only eighty-seven teachers with college degrees.[18]

Many towns, including Pine Grove, felt strongly that there was a need and a place for both public and private schools in their community. Although a new public school was being built in 1875, Pine Grove leaders wanted to retain the select school, which had been run by Reverend W. T. Dickson until he moved away. They collected $800 and, to confirm their decision, added a second story to the school building to be used for instruction in higher learning. A search was initiated for a new principal.

By a vote of four to three, the city fathers, in early 1876, selected twenty-three-year-old, redheaded Isaac Conrad Ketler, then studying Latin and Greek at National University in Lebanon, Ohio. They chose him because, first of all, he was one of them, a native Pennsylvanian, born in the central part of the state in Northumberland County, but reared in Blacktown, just four miles from Pine Grove, in the heart of western Pennsylvania. The young educator had a "wide circle of friends among its people, and was proud of its schools."[19] Second, he was a devout Presbyterian with a passion for education that had been encouraged by his grandmother and by Joseph Newton Pew, one of his grade school teachers. J. N. Pew, wrote Isaac Ketler's son Weir, "was a man of marked ability" with a "striking and forceful personality."[20] He and Isaac Ketler would ultimately forge a remarkable relationship that would profoundly influence the purpose and character of Grove City College.

Young Ketler was also selected because he so clearly wanted the job. Asked later in life why he had chosen to come to Pine Grove when there was no guarantee of salary (he was presently making $80 a month), the number of students was uncertain, and he might have to rent his schoolroom (for $20), Ketler replied, "I knew the community and its interest in education; and a railroad had recently been completed into the town. I thought there was an opportunity to develop a school there."[21] At the time Pine Grove was barely a town, but rather a community of some twenty homes and a mere two hundred citizens.

The odds did not deter Isaac Ketler, who had always been disciplined and determined. When his father objected to his seeking advanced schooling, he left home at age seventeen and earned enough money in the lumber camps of western Pennsylvania to enter college.

A Select School

The energetic new principal wasted no time. In March 1876, a flyer was distributed in town and the surrounding countryside announcing that the spring term of a "Select School at Pine Grove, Pa." would begin on April 11. The "design of the institution" was "to fit young men and women for College, and to prepare those who desire to teach to do good work in the school room." Classes would be held in "the new and lately furnished brick School Hall." Tuition would run from $4.00 to $6.50 for a twelve-week session. Room and board would be with private families "at reasonable rates"—$2.50 to $3.00 a week.[22]

Sometimes the male students would get together and rent an unfurnished house that they would fill with an assortment of used chairs, desks, beds and mattresses, and sometimes a large bureau. As for food, most of them were farm boys and found it more economical to bring a bushel of potatoes, a barrel of flour, or a quarter of beef from home, than to pay the regular boarding house charges. But whether they made their own arrangements or boarded with a private family, they were all instructed about the school's firm rules regarding "study, sports, and courtship."[23] Number one was that they were expected to be in their rooms and studying by 7:00 P.M.

The school was an unquestioned success from its opening day, when thirteen students enrolled. A total of twenty-six young men and women—Grove City College has always been coeducational—signed up for the first term, eager to further themselves and attracted by the dynamic principal who gave as many as fourteen recitations a day in the classroom, visited students' boarding rooms to affirm they were morally conducive, recruited students on his horse-and-buggy visits to farms, oversaw school finances, and presided over all school functions, academic and social. The new principal was so eager to get started that he furnished the school with the necessary equipment at his own expense.[24]

Young Ketler was already demonstrating the essential elements of a leader. He had remarkable vitality and stamina, enabling him to maintain an arduous daily schedule that would have felled most people. A man of ideas and action, he shifted easily from the intellectual demands of the classroom to the managerial skills of the principal's office. And he had a grounded belief in God and His providence that was unshakeable. He felt certain that what he was doing was God's will.

One observer has suggested that Isaac Ketler was a spiritual heir of the New England Puritans. In his 205-page epic poem *The Pilgrims*, Ketler declares his "sincere conviction that the Pilgrim movement is the greatest epic-action of the modern world, a theme well-worthy of a Homer, or a Milton." He warmly praised the Pilgrims' determination to order everything—personal lives, worship, business, politics—in accord with God's plan. The Puritans "forged Isaac Conrad Ketler's character," and his German heritage and Scots Presbyterian faith reinforced it.[25]

In the fall of 1876 the name of the school was changed to "Pine Grove Normal Academy," and its academic program strengthened with the addition of advanced classes in Latin and Greek and in the theory and methodology of teaching. The community responded enthusiastically: sixty-seven students registered the first day of the fall session, another seven on the second day. A year later, the school catalogue revealed that the student body had almost doubled, with a roster of sixty young men and fifty-five young women. Three new teachers were added for a total faculty of nine. The ambitious two-year course of study combined the classical and the practical, with classes in Latin, Greek, and English, history and political geography, bookkeeping and mathematics, physical science, vocal and instrumental music, and teacher training. The latter course attracted the largest group of students.

The word quickly spread throughout western Pennsylvania that the new school in Pine Grove was offering quality education at bargain prices. By comparison Allegheny College in Meadville was charging a contingent fee of $10 per term, Westminster College in New Wilmington, $37 a year. Tuition at Pine Grove Normal Academy in 1884 (when it formally became a college) was $10 per twelve week session (there were three sessions in the school year). It rose slowly to $12 per session in 1890, $15 in 1900, and only $25 in 1913, on the eve of World War I.

In reality, longtime Grove City College professor Hans Sennholz points out, the academy was three schools in one: an academy that offered a curriculum for boys and girls not going to college; a high school that included college preparatory studies; and "a Normal School or School of Pedagogy" that provided training for elementary school teaching.[26]

From the beginning, a Christian environment was ensured. School started every morning with about forty-five minutes of Scripture reading, prayers, and singing. The catalogue stressed that prayer meetings were held at the Presbyterian and Methodist churches, and students were expected "to attend preaching at least once on [the] Sabbath."[27]

The academy's objectives were tailored to the nineteenth-century needs of western Pennsylvania and the upper Ohio valley and yet were consistent with the liberal arts traditions of American higher education. As set forth in the catalogue, they were to prepare students of western Pennsylvania for college, teaching, or business; to create "a thirst for knowledge;" to form correct habits; and—echoing the words of the classical Greek philosophers—to "incite love for the true, beautiful, and good."[28]

In just two years Pine Grove Normal Academy had become so popular that a group of citizens decided to apply for a charter of incorporation for the academy and to purchase land for a school building. Although they were men of "small financial resources, living in a small village," wrote one historian, they wanted young people to have "opportunities for growth in mind and spirit."[29] Grove City, moreover, maintained a close relationship between town and gown, with little of the tension and none of the hostility found in many college towns.

Members of the Pine Grove community acquired stock in the new corporation, raising sufficient capital to buy four acres and erect the first building owned by the academy. Lacking cash, but wanting to be part of the enterprise, several citizens paid in labor and material, hauling stone and making brick for the new school. One man, who later contributed many thousands of dollars to the college, often recalled with pride that, as a young farmer, he had put two silver dollars in the collection plate for the school. Later known as Recitation Hall, the three-story building with its handsome bell tower was first occupied in December 1879. The total cost of the building, furniture, bell, stoves, and grounds was $8,607.33, a large sum for so small a town.[30]

Reflecting the principal's no-nonsense attitude and the school's Christian focus, the 1880 catalogue set forth "what the faculty expect of students" and in turn "what students may expect of the faculty." Students should be "earnest, honest, energetic and truthful" and have "a teachable spirit." In response, the faculty were expected to "labor zealously for the moral, intellectual and physical welfare of the students," always seeking "to lead them to a higher plane of living and... to the Lamb of God."[31]

A New College

The ever restless Ketler now set in motion plans to transform the academy into a college, a longtime ambition of his. Even before moving to Pine Grove, he had told a friend that he felt a college might well be established in the community. Thus, over the next several years, Ketler began offering four-year courses of study, built a boarding hall for women, enlarged the board of trustees, erected a twelve-room Music Hall, and assured inquiring students and their parents that there were "no saloons nearer than nine miles" of the campus.[32] He also found time to improve his own education, adding a Master of Arts degree from Allegheny College in 1882 and a Doctor of Philosophy degree from the College of Wooster in Ohio in 1884.

When over five hundred students attended classes during the academic year of 1882-1883, the trustees appointed a committee to "take steps toward securing university powers" for the academy.[33] And on November 21, 1884, just eight years after the founding of the Pine Grove Select School, the Mercer County court approved the change of the school's name to "Grove City College." That same year, the catalogue stated that "Grove City College is a Christian but undenominational institution of learning."[34] An official seal with an open Bible at its center was designed. The motto stretching across the Bible's pages was *Lux Mea*, taken from the verse of Psalm 119 that reads, "Thy word is a lamp unto my feet and a light unto my path."

Isaac Ketler personally reinforced the college's Christian character by enrolling part-time at Western Theological Seminary in Allegheny, Pennsylvania, from which he graduated in 1888. He was ordained by Butler Presbytery that same summer. While he was at the Presbyterian seminary, most of the school's business was conducted by two early stalwarts of the college, James B. McClelland, who had been instrumental in hiring Isaac Ketler, and Dr. W. J. McConkey, pastor of the city's Presbyterian church. The partnership of these three men reflected the unique and enduring relationship at Grove City College between city, church, and school.

Ketler and the college would need the prudent counsel and steady support of men like McClelland, McConkey, and Pittsburgh industrialist J. N. Pew in particular, as they negotiated the turbulent waters of American higher education in the last quarter of the nineteenth century.

The Age of Isms

It was a time of revolutionary ideas, such as evolution and scientism, which affected, not merely the teaching of biology and philosophy, but challenged the traditional curriculum and the Christian core of the American college. Teachers increasingly favored a monistic rather than a multilayered explanation of truth and reality. All life, evolutionists argued, could be explained through the "law" of natural selection. There was no need for the metaphysical, only the physical. Man had evolved from the apes, without any help from God. Charles Darwin, the author of *The Origin of the Species*, was hailed as the "Newton of natural history," and his theories were tirelessly promoted by prominent educators like Yale's William Graham Sumner and Harvard's Asa Gray. It was the age of ideology, the birth of the isms that shape our lives to this day. According to historians R. R. Palmer and Joel Colton, the word liberalism first appeared in English in 1819, radicalism in 1820, socialism in 1832, and conservatism in 1835.[35]

But the dominant ism of the post-Civil War period in America was Darwinism, which had some paradoxical consequences. While promoting natural history as a logical replacement for philosophy and theology, Darwinism led to an increasingly narrow notion of history, even to its rejection. After all, if things were always changing so rapidly, of what use was past experience to the solution of current problems? Rhetoric, along with tempers, flared as evolutionists and creationists waged a fierce war over their origins. Not even a Texas Methodist, wrote one Darwinian sarcastically, "would think of taking his car to Moses, Joshua, Luther or George Washington to have the carburetor adjusted or the valves ground."[36]

It was during this period of intellectual ferment that Johns Hopkins University was founded. In 1876 America's first true university adopted the model of the German research university with its commitment to academic freedom for professors, the "free" selection of courses by students, and the substitution of the natural sciences for the classics in the curriculum. Its trustees, however, never aimed at the curricular variety that characterized Cornell University, rejecting courses in music and military science. The cost of living in Baltimore was reasonable: a Johns Hopkins student could "live off the fat of the land for $500 a year." Tuition was $80 for the academic year.[37] Johns Hopkins, with its abiding belief in the world of the Enlightenment, was the academic model for such new schools as Stanford University (1891), the University of Chicago (1892), and the land-grant state universities created by Congress with the Morrill Act of 1862.

The direction of the land-grant schools had been determined as early as 1848 when U.S. Congressman Justin Smith Morrill of Vermont suggested that American colleges should "lop off" the "antique" studies based on European scholarship and replace them "with those of a ... more practical value."[38] The Morrill Act created in every state, at least one college or university devoted to agricultural and mechanical training. Their success encouraged other colleges to add technical and mechanical training to their curricula. A century later land-grant colleges would be enrolling more than 20 percent of all college students. They were not, however, strictly secular institutions. In the 1890s, according to historian George M. Marsden, almost all state universities still held compulsory chapel services and some required Sunday church attendance. State-sponsored chapel services "did not become rare" until World War II.[39] Even Harvard's arts and sciences faculty in 1898 offered four courses on church history and three on American history.[40]

A passion for academic reform permeated American higher education in the late 1800s as the enrollment of students increased four times as fast as the population. A major challenge was how to strike the right balance between academic learning and professional training. Charles W. Eliot of Harvard and Andrew D. White of Cornell strongly supported more practical education, but disagreed with those who saw no use for any education "beyond that which enables a man to live by his wits and to prey upon his neighbor." A broader vision was needed, White insisted, an ideal of the university as a place offering instruction in both humane and scientific disciplines for a wide variety of occupations.[41] A onetime Quaker turned Unitarian, White asserted that he was not anti-Christian but antisectarian, explaining that Cornell was dedicated to high moral values and free scientific inquiry. His ecumenical vision captured the imagination of many young Americans: the 1871 freshman class at Cornell topped 250, the largest freshman class in the history of American higher education.

Like the philosopher Herbert Spencer, White promoted the "new individualism" and freedom from authoritarianism. But this freedom, historian John S. Brubacher points out, did not extend to "Marxists, anarchists, and other radical disturbers of the social order." Cornell's president sought an intellectual elite that would lead the nation and ensure rational reforms.[42]

White believed that higher education should be supported and even controlled by government, although recognizing the dangers of such control. As early as 1874, writes Cornell historian Morris Bishop, White insisted that "advanced education must be provided by the state legislatures" with the help of private donors.[43] Here, too, White's beliefs had a major influence on higher education in America.

Eliot's personal crusade was the adoption of the elective system. In his inaugural address as president of Harvard in October 1869, Eliot announced that from then on students would have more freedom to select from among different classes and courses of study. "The young man of nineteen or twenty," he declared, "ought to know what he likes best and is most fit for." For the individual, Eliot argued, the only prudent course was "the highest development of his peculiar faculty."[44] Thus not only election but a vast expansion of the curriculum was justified. By the 1880s Harvard students had unlimited free choice in course selection. Traditionalists called the idea of curricular choice a "fraud" and a "monstrosity." James McCosh of Princeton (the mentor of a future president of Grove City College) asserted in 1885 that the elective system was not "an advance in scholarship" but "a bid for popularity." He asked pointedly, "Has there been of late any great poem, any great scientific discovery, any great history, any great philosophic work, by the young men of Cambridge?"[45]

The American University

But the elective principle swept across higher education (what could be more American than the freedom to choose?), although few schools adopted the radical Harvard version. The elective principle, argued Frederick Rudolph, moved the individual to the center of the university and declared that not all educated men had to have mastered the same subjects and to know the same things. It freed the curriculum from the past and "enabled colleges to become universities. It transformed the English college in America by grafting upon it German ideals and in the process created the American university."[46]

The elective system flourished from about 1870 to 1910, historian John S. Brubacher has written, because it met the needs of American culture during that period. A rural society was being transformed into a great industrial nation. Science was perceived as the key to material progress and intellectual enlightenment. The traditional liberal arts college with its clerical faculty and prescribed curriculum was on the way out. Eliot's system, "with all its revolutionary implications," reflected the spirit of the time.[47]

At Johns Hopkins University in Baltimore, the professor, not the student, was king. President Daniel Coit Gilman insisted that the faculty be given only students who could challenge and stimulate them intellectually. Nothing could have been more remote, wrote Frederick Rudolph, from the spirit of the old-time college where the teachers were "busily engaged in stimulating the students."[48] Johns Hopkins also substituted a search for scientific truth for the acceptance of revealed religious truth. In fact, according to one historian, "Johns Hopkins elevated man's reason to a position it had not before attained in the United States."[49]

Thus, wrote George Marsden, the course of the modern American university was set. Religion would have almost no say in any aspect of the enterprise, including graduate, professional (except for theology), and technical education. Since virtually all university teachers would eventually be trained in graduate schools built on the Johns Hopkins model, "the forces eroding

Christian influences, even in the undergraduate classrooms, were destined to be immense."[50] The dominant educational principles of the late nineteenth century were defined by "a synthesis of Enlightenment ideals" (reason and the individual above all) and "an enlightened Christianity, or religion of humanity" (the progenitor of twentieth-century secular humanism).[51]

Alarmed academic traditionalists responded by insisting that piety and morality were the chief ends of a college. "The great aim of every great teacher, from Socrates to Hopkins," declared W. W. Strong, the president of Carleton College in 1887, "has been the building of character."[52] But such arguments had scant impact on the majority of school presidents and professors who bowed to the wishes of a utilitarian populace and adjusted to students seemingly uncertain about their careers. Under such circumstances, why not let a hundred courses bloom? Oberlin College was an extreme example of Midwestern populism, combining manual labor (poor students could work for their education), evangelical religion, coeducation, the Graham-cracker diet, and abstention from alcohol, tobacco, tea, coffee, and pepper.[53]

The idea that a fixed body of knowledge defined an educated person began to fade and disappear from many campuses replaced by the democratic notion that each person should control his own education and his own destiny. "The age of radical curricular egalitarianism," wrote Christopher Lucas, "was at hand."[54]

A Different Path

But not at Grove City College. It firmly rejected the notion that no subject was more important than another. There, as at other small traditional colleges throughout America, a renewed dedication to an academic climate where morality and character were nurtured, where mind, heart, and will were focused on the needs of society as well as self, was voiced. President Ketler believed that the main

business of the college was to make good citizens, not great scholars. And to that end, Grove City College had to be, without apology or equivocation, a Christian and nondenominational
institution of learning. There was no denying, however, its close
connection with the Presbyterian Church. In the 1880s half of the
teaching staff, including Dr. Ketler, were ordained Presbyterian
ministers. In keeping with his somewhat austere personality,
Ketler's faith was intellectual rather than emotional. According to
the eminent Scots scholar and educator W. M. Ramsay, who came
to know him, Isaac Ketler had "a certain distrust for religious
methods which appealed too much to the emotions."[55]

In a sermon to the graduating class of 1894, President Ketler
warned the young men and women of Grove City College against
a "childish sentimentalism" that anticipated God's love and favor
"without restitution." "We want a God," said the president sternly,
"who will punish the sinner." After praising Abraham, Moses,
Isaiah, Daniel, Paul, Augustine, Calvin, and Wesley as "the highest
embodiment of human worth and genius," Ketler urged his young
audience to let "faith in God and humble dependence upon the
Holy Spirit" guide them to the truth that "will make you strong for
the battle of life."[56]

But for all the emphasis on obeying a sovereign God, there
was no banning of controversial books or ideas at Grove City. The
students read and discussed Darwinian theory extensively. Dr.
Samuel Dodds, a minister who taught physics and chemistry,
"determined to lead [his] students as far as they wanted to go in
these lines, carefully and wisely guiding them into the truth."[57] At
the time, most church-affiliated colleges asked teachers to instruct
their students in the Bible one class a week. At Dodds's suggestion, the Bible was made a Grove City College textbook. So central to the spirit of the school was the Bible that it was taught as a
separate but optional course.

The Sacral Character of All Life

Reflecting Calvinist doctrine, the college stressed the sacral character of all life, the actions of the state, as well as the activities of the
church. The perception that there was no major gap between the
two realms was "the dominant view," historian George Marsden
wrote, of the first three centuries of American higher education. It
has remained the prevailing attitude at Grove City College.[58]

Striving for a balance between the old and the new, President
Ketler methodically developed the school's scientific curriculum.
Science teachers, even on the early faculties, held at least baccalaureate degrees. In 1883, the college added a course in phonography
(a system of shorthand still in its early development) and included
a chemistry laboratory in the new building completed in 1888.

At first the curriculum was compulsory, with each student
required to pass every regular course before graduation, particularly President Ketler's senior class in mental and moral science.
The first experiment with electives came in the 1888–1889 academic year. It was far from President Eliot's radical approach at
Harvard, but it did recognize that young men and women should
be given some choice. In the classical course, Grove City students
could elect to take Latin, Greek, or German in place of calculus.
Reflecting the American fascination with Germany, students were
also allowed to take three terms of German instead of two terms of
either Latin or Greek. In the scientific course, students could
choose three terms of German instead of two terms of Latin.

Borrowing from the mission of the historic American college, as well as that of the new "common" or state-grant schools,
Grove City College declared that its purpose was to "popularize"
the idea of attending college "without lowering the standard of
college education." Of special concern to President Ketler was the
area of teacher training. The first six-week summer school for
teachers was held in 1887. It was designed for teachers already on

a college faculty who wanted to improve their teaching methods or complete their work on a baccalaureate degree. (Many college teachers had only a high school degree.) The summer school also offered regular courses for undergraduates who desired to make up a course or obtain a degree in less than four years. The Christian environment of Grove City College was reinforced by the addition of a six-week summer Bible school in the late 1890s.

The college was hard pressed to service adequately the ever increasing student body. And so in 1888 the charter was amended to raise the amount of stock from $25,000 to $50,000, and an impressive three-story brick building (Founders' Hall) was built. It contained classrooms, a chapel that could accommodate the entire student body, offices, two gymnasiums, a museum, and several laboratories.

As Grove City College approached its fifteenth anniversary, it seemed as if the school would continue to grow in size and reputation in western Pennsylvania and beyond. But major crises were on the way. First, in 1890, Isaac Ketler was invited to become president of prestigious Macalester College, located between St. Paul and Minneapolis. Most Grove City citizens were pessimistic about persuading President Ketler to remain at their little college. How could they compete with the attractions of two great midwestern cities? Several of Ketler's closest friends urged him to accept the offer, and when he visited Macalester College, he was strongly impressed by what he saw. He was, moreover, promised a salary three times that offered by Grove City College and use of the handsome President's House. (In Grove City the Ketlers owned a comfortable but modest-sized house on Main Street.)

"I never saw in all my life," Ketler wrote his wife Matilda, "a place half so lovely for a college nor a more desirable place to live."[59]

And yet he decided to stay in Grove City, motivated, almost surely, by his abiding love for and pride in the little academy he had built into one of the outstanding small colleges in the region. No less important must have been the steadfast support of the faculty which had formally said of Ketler when he had once been challenged by some in the community about his stewardship: "It was his highest and holiest ambition, as far as his life's work was concerned, to serve his God and to bless the World by establishing a school in this place that, in the good done, might not only equal but, if possible, excel that of any other school."[60]

In his determination to improve the college, Ketler expanded the curriculum—he established a Business Department, replaced Latin and Greek with French and German in the modern classical course, instituted a Department of Telegraphy, and started a Military Department. To that end, all male students were organized into a battalion known as the Grove City College Corps of Cadets, which took one hour a week of theoretical instruction and two hours of drill using small arms. Within a year, the school declared that the Military Department had been of "incalculable benefit ... making college discipline one-half easier."[61] It was also an important precedent for the Student Army Training Corps, which during World War I ensured a high level of student enrollment at Grove City College when many other schools struggled to exist. The school catalogue's claim that "no other college in Pennsylvania furnishes so wide a scope of work as is found in this institution" was not mere boosterism.[62] The constant flow of new students and the school's growing reputation, particularly in the fields of teacher training and music, confirmed that Isaac Ketler was building a notable small college.

The Crisis of 1893
And then came the economic panic of 1893 and a national depression. By the end of 1894, 642 banks had gone under and 22,500 miles of railway were in receivership. One-fourth of America's

industrial plants were closed, and hundreds of thousands of workers were without jobs. From 1891 to 1895 the index of farm produce
plummeted from $14.70 to $9.71. Wheat cost more to grow than the
farmer could sell it for. The bad times hit Grove City hard.

President Ketler and the college faced a mounting burden of
debt while the stockholders saw little likelihood of dividends. For
some fifteen years there had been sufficient money to hire instructors, acquire land, erect buildings, and even pay interest on the
debt, but no record shows that the owners (that is, the stockholders) ever received a penny of compensation. Clearly, help from
outside the Grove City community had to be secured if the college were to survive.

Through a mutual friend, President Ketler met with Joseph
Newton Pew, his boyhood teacher, now a wealthy businessman in
Pittsburgh. The educator recalled a meeting he had with the
industrialist in Parker City, an early center of the oil industry,
twenty years earlier. Pew had then remarked to his young friend
that he could see no future in teaching, but he could see one in
oil. "Why don't you give up teaching," he had asked Ketler, "and
go into the oil business with me? I think we can make some money
in it." The teacher had respectfully declined.

Now, with just a hint of a smile, Dr. Ketler said to the successful oil executive, "Years ago you asked me to go into business with you. Now, I have come to ask you to go into business
with me."[63]

Pew agreed to consider helping Grove City College if other
prominent citizens of Pittsburgh would join the effort and then
practically ensured they would by giving Ketler the names of
leaders whom he knew in the business, religious, and civic affairs
of the city. The two men created a unique partnership of college
president and board of trustee president that lasted as long as
they lived and then continued with their sons, J. Howard Pew

and Weir Ketler. Aside from their firm belief in the importance of education, J. N. Pew and Isaac Ketler were bound by their strong Presbyterian faith. Together the millionaire and the educator saved Grove City College from going under and enabled it to continue its mission of offering a good education in a Christian environment at a fair price.

One of the first men that President Ketler called on was Pittsburgh businessman Samuel P. Harbison, who immediately remarked, "I know about the work of the college, and I approve it." Ketler left Harbison's office with a substantial check which Pew quickly "more than duplicated."[64] In exchange for their support, Pew, Harbison, and the other new trustees (like Major A. P. Burchfield, W. A. Shaw, Edward O'Neill, Dr. Joseph Gibson, and Dr. William H. McMillan) requested that the structure of the college be changed from that of a commercial stock company to a charitable not-for-profit institution. As they had from the founding of the school nearly two decades earlier, the citizens of Grove City demonstrated their unselfish spirit and good will. At a special meeting in the college chapel on November 4, 1894, the 256 stockholders agreed without one dissenting vote to surrender their stock to the college so that its mission could be continued.

A new charter, modeled on that of the University of Chicago, was adopted. It stated that Grove City College would be "an undenominational but evangelical Christian school," but with no mandatory test of religious belief for the students or faculty of the college. With only minor amendments through the years, the charter has remained the school's basic governing document.[65]

The new board of trustees quickly made their presence and their pocketbooks felt, providing funds for a series of physical improvements, including new sewers, steam heating, and the addition of a chemistry wing to the administration building. The library was improved, and then, through a $30,000 gift from philanthropist

Andrew Carnegie, a new library was built. A Department of Mechanical and Civil Engineering was added in 1902 through a generous appropriation of $20,000 by the state legislature, i.e., tax-payer funds. It was the last direct government aid that Grove City ever accepted. The college's land holdings were then enlarged with financial help from the trustees. At the turn of the century the school contained six buildings and forty acres of land in the center of Grove City below Wolf Creek (the "lower campus").

A modest endowment fund was created, but the Pew philosophy—that the student should essentially pay his own way without financial help from the college—still prevailed. On its twenty-fifth anniversary, in 1901, Grove City College had an enrollment of 662 students, eighteen faculty members, and one administrator, President Ketler, who shared a secretary with the professor of Greek. There was no dean. Grove City was known for keeping overhead to a minimum in an era when the median number of administrative officers in an American college was four. Most of the college's graduates went into teaching or business, but the school was proud that some twenty-six of its five thousand alumni had traveled overseas to undertake religious and charitable work.

The life of a faculty member at the college was rewarding in many ways, particularly in the relationships forged with students. There was more than one Mr. Chips at Grove City. Perhaps the best loved teacher was Alva John Calderwood, who had excelled in the classroom and played halfback on the football team for three years before graduating from Grove City College in 1896. Except for his time at Harvard in advanced study, he spent the next five decades on campus as professor, friend, mentor, and finally dean of the college. Other popular faculty members included the scientist-minister Samuel Dodds, the historian Frank Hays, and the mathematician John A. Courtney. All were excellent scholars, but above all they were teachers.

On the other hand, a Grove City College teacher had no tenure, no union, no health insurance, and no formal pension plan, although President Ketler approved sick leave, pensions, and bonuses for teachers who performed well. A faculty member was expected to teach Monday through Saturday (and continued to do so throughout the twentieth century) and in all four school sessions—fall, winter, spring, and summer. For a Gilded Age, the financial rewards were modest. In 1896 President Ketler received a salary of $2,500 while the three highest paid faculty members were paid $1,000 each. Some of the instructors received as little as $360 a year. The trustees made it clear that they expected the faculty and administration to devote their full time to the school, stating that "no outside work will be permitted to interfere with each one's duties in the class room." All members of the college were also expected to practice "total abstinence" from alcohol.[66]

The life of a Grove City College professor was little affected by the new wave of learned societies that sprang up in the late nineteenth century, such as the American Philological Association in 1869, the American Chemical Society in 1877, the Modern Language Association in 1883, the American Historical Association in 1884, the American Economic Association in 1885, and the American Mathematical Society and the Geological Society of America, both in 1888. Their annual meetings, historian Frederick Rudolph wrote, enabled educators to read and discuss papers, establish the parameters of their discipline, enjoy "the pleasures of life off the reservation," and populate a hiring hall for college and university presidents and department chairmen.[67]

The Principle of Academic Freedom

These associations helped establish the principles of academic freedom and tenure in American higher education. Borrowing from the German concept of *lehrfreiheit* (the right of the university professor to freedom of inquiry and freedom of teaching), the American professor added the right of free speech guaranteed under the First Amendment to the doctrine of academic freedom. No one disputed that a professor could use his professional competence and scientific knowledge to discuss controversial subjects in the classroom as long as he did not attempt to indoctrinate his students. But when a professor sought to apply his economic, political, and social findings to the outside world, he often collided with the businessmen who served as trustees and benefactors of their schools. An economist at the University of Chicago was dismissed when he attacked the railroads in the 1890s, as was a political scientist at Marietta College for criticizing monopolies.[68]

President Ketler (and subsequent Grove City College presidents) avoided such conflicts by appointing faculty who either endorsed the free enterprise ideas of Pew, Harbison, and other trustees, or were discreet in their public statements about the vices as well as the virtues of capitalism. Academic tenure—the guarantee of a permanent job to a professor—became an issue in higher education in the early decades of the twentieth century, particularly after 1915 when the American Association of University Professors (AAUP) was founded. But tenure was never a problem at Grove City College because it never existed there—although one unhappy faculty member, with the cooperation of the AAUP, made it an issue in the early 1960s.

Amid all the intellectual Sturm und Drang, Grove City students found time and energy for extracurricular pursuits, particularly in the literary and debating fields. In those pre-Internet, pretelevision, preradio days, young people delighted in writing and reading essays and poetry. Grove City men formed debating societies named Webster, Shakespeare, and Henry, and literary clubs like Conabor, Bryant, Ossoli, and Lowell. The women started their own literary society, Speedwell, in 1881. When the New

College Building was completed in 1888, Webster, Shakespeare, and Speedwell were given rooms that were among the finest in all Pennsylvania, "furnished with rare elegance and taste."[69] Soon thereafter, in 1891, the women formed a second literary society, Philokalian, and until the mid-twentieth century, the four clubs were a central part of student life on campus.

One of the more active campus organizations in the 1880s, according to school historian David Dayton, was the College Temperance Union, a reflection of the school's Presbyterian roots and the city's historic prohibition of beer, whiskey, and other spirits. A historical sketch published in 1897 boasted, "There is not and never has been a licensed hotel in the town or community."[70] Another center of student activity was the Christian Union, an organization of young men contemplating a career in the Gospel ministry. They spent much of their time running Sabbath schools in the surrounding coal-mining villages. And there was also the Missionary Society which encouraged young men and women to consider joining the missions and financially supported foreign missionaries. Grove City College students took the idea of missions seriously, pledging $250 annually (a significant sum in the late nineteenth century) to support the Reverend Mr. J. H. Martin, class of '88, in his work in India.[71]

And then there was the Young Men's Christian Association (YMCA) and the Young Women's Christian Association (YWCA), both supported by the board of trustees. When several young men returned from a summer Bible program in Minnesota brimming with Christian zeal, the administration decided to sponsor a summer Bible school at Grove City College in the summer of 1897. It would continue every summer for the next half century. Bible study classes were held in the morning and afternoon, with public meetings in the evening featuring Christian leaders from America, Canada, and Great Britain.

Although a popular program with an enrollment of more than two hundred, the Bible school lost money every summer. Each year President Isaac Ketler would send an identical financial statement to J. N. Pew and Samuel Harbison, and each year the two men would make up the deficit equally between them. President Weir Ketler would depend on the same generosity from J. Howard Pew when the annual deficit of the summer Bible school became his responsibility.

The dress as well as the morals of Grove City College students were emphatically Victorian. The women wore long, dark, full-skirted dresses and long, dark stockings with high-button shoes, and stiff-brimmed hats. The men wore dark suits with a vest, white shirt, and tie. Nearly every man wore a hat. Professors wore stiff-collared white shirts, five-button coats with matching dark trousers and vest, usually with a gold watch chain strung across their stomachs. Small-town virtues were emphasized. An 1897 brochure boasted that the student was protected "from the vices and allurements of a large city."[72] Among the vices not allowed on campus, according to alumnae Marian McConkey, whose great, great grandfather was one of Grove City's first settlers, were dancing and cardplaying.[73]

Beginning with the Lord

Each day began with a chapel service that every student was required to attend. Along with a Bible lesson, prayer, and singing, visiting speakers often addressed the student body and sometimes left a lasting impression. There was the veteran of the Civil War who explained that his Bible had stopped a bullet from killing him. When he added that the Bible had been in his hip not his front pocket, the students erupted into laughter, inspiring the quick-witted Dr. Ketler to remark, "Well, now, young people, you can see that the Bible can save you coming or going."[74]

The first Greek-letter social fraternities in America appeared at Union College and Hamilton College in the late 1820s and 1830s and spread so quickly that few American colleges were left untouched by a social movement that was the exclusive invention of the undergraduate. Fraternities, wrote Frederick Rudolph, offered an escape from the typical "collegiate regimen which began with prayers before dawn and ended with prayers after dark."[75] They largely replaced the literary societies that had served as a center of social life on most campuses. Their class-laden message, added Rudolph, was clear: Among the barbarians, we are the Greeks.

Fraternities institutionalized the worldly diversions that college students have engaged in since the founding of the first universities in the early Middle Ages—"drinking, smoking, card playing, singing, and seducing." College presidents and chaplains resisted as best they could, but fraternities survived every criticism (one college president referred to their "evil" influences), every attempt at abolition.[76] They represented, in truth, the new secular values that now dominated most colleges—prestige and success—rather than the old Christian virtues—humility and morality—that had guided the traditional American college.

Accordingly, Greek-letter fraternities made a very late start at Grove City College. The faculty uncovered an underground fraternity in 1904—the "Possum Club"—and expelled twelve members, including the editor in chief of *The Collegian* and the son of a faculty member. The club had been in existence for at least a decade and is credited in 1894 with placing Isaac Ketler's horse and buggy on the rostrum of the chapel.[77] Grove City's first local fraternity, Pan Sophic, was not formed until 1911, the Adelphikos in 1913. Four years later the first sorority, Sigma Sigma Sigma, was organized as was the Delta Iota fraternity. They were not, however, officially recognized as fraternities and sororities by a skeptical administration, but rather as "clubs." Not until 1927, did the faculty vote to recognize the Pan Hellenic Association of Sororities. Two years later they approved the constitution of the Inter-Fraternity Council. Even then the administration would not allow fraternity housing, insisting that the regular dormitory housing provided by the college was less expensive and more "democratic."[78] To this day national fraternities are not allowed on the campus of Grove City College.

The first football game in America was played between Princeton and Rutgers in 1869, but it was a far cry from the modern game: young men took turns kicking a cow's bladder between the two schools. The sport seemed ridiculous to many school authorities. Cornell president Andrew White, asked to arrange a game in Cleveland, replied: "I will not permit thirty men to travel four hundred miles merely to agitate a bag of wind."[79] But within twenty years the game had become so popular that for the first time since the founding of Harvard College in 1636, colleges began to accept the idea of intercollegiate relations.

At Grove City, baseball was initially the most popular sport. The first recorded game was in 1884, with Grove City defeating Westminster College by 4 to 3. The following year both the students and faculty cut classes one sunny day to lay out a new athletic field on the brush-covered swamp land between Recitation Hall and Wolf Creek. At sundown, however, the amateur builders discovered that the batter's box was so near the creek that any foul ball would wind up in the water. Sunburned but undeterred, they returned the next morning and cleared away the brush for a sports field which serves the college to this day.

The school's first official football team was organized in 1892; the players had to let their hair grow long as they did not wear helmets. By 1897, the school was playing a seven or eight-game season with opponents like Westminster, Geneva College,

Thiel College, Allegheny College, and the University of Pittsburgh. The wolverine was selected as the school's official mascot; in later years, a student dressed as "Willie the Wolverine" prowled the side-lines. Grove City's first basketball team was formed in 1898 and played under oil lamps. In the early 1900s, when the Carnegie Library was built, the basement was used for basketball. But the ceiling was so low that long shots were impossible, necessitating some of the best passing teams in Pennsylvania and, it was said by Grove City partisans, in the nation. President Ketler laid down a core principle at the beginning: Grove City athletics was amateur athletics. No Grove City College student could suit up unless he had first declared that he had received no direct or indirect financial aid for playing.

By now it was generally agreed throughout western Penn-sylvania that Grove City was a good college, although not really a pretty one. The campus grounds had limited landscaping with no broad green lawns or sculptured trees. The campus was poorly lit except for an occasional gas light outside a main building. Sidewalks were mostly dirt paths except near the buildings. All roads were unpaved—the students traveled to and from school by horse and buggy and/or railroad. They cheered quietly in 1895 when the board of trustees approved the installation of bathing rooms and toilets in the basement of the New College Building, which housed the gymnasium and chemistry labs, the president's office, an auditorium, and club rooms. Indoor plumbing was gradually installed in most of the old buildings; until then, like most of small-town rural America, members of the college com-munity were obliged to use an outdoor facility.

At the center of the students' peaceful, well-ordered lives was a dynamo of a president who filled his long days with teach-ing, administering, and passing out school flyers on his frequent trips to the countryside that proclaimed: "Every young man or woman who desires an education can obtain it. The way is open to all."[80]

The flyer's ebullience reflected the spirit of optimism that still prevailed in most of America at the turn of the century. But the nation and its people had changed so much and so fast in the last two decades that reaction and reform were inevitable.

CHAPTER TWO

Crisis and Change

They called themselves progressives and pragmatists. They proposed a New Nationalism and a New Freedom. They called for, and got, a federal income tax, the direct election of U.S. senators, antitrust laws, and women's suffrage. Their political leaders were Theodore Roosevelt and Woodrow Wilson. A "welfare state" (to use progressive journalist Herbert Croly's phrase) was their end, and a beneficent government—federal, state, and local—was their means. To reassure the defenders of the American ideals of freedom and faith, they explained that the new state would be controlled by Congress and staffed by an efficient and dedicated bureaucracy.[1]

Few Americans denied that the Industrial Age had produced economic inequities and political corruption. Politics needed to be cleaned up and the giant trusts busted. Unrestrained individualism—and profits—was not what America was all about. "Real" weekly earnings in all American industries between 1900 and 1914 were significantly less than the average earnings of the 1880s. The problem was striking the right balance between prudent reform and radical change. Theodore Roosevelt, for example, shifted from advocating the outright dissolution to judicious regulation of the giant corporations during his presidency as he came to understand that big business was not only here to stay but served a positive function in the American economy.

But his philosophy, historian Samuel Eliot Morison points out, was Hamiltonian not Jeffersonian. Not for him, Jefferson's vision of a nation of small businesses, small farmers, and states' rights. He believed, as Hamilton had, that the federal government should be truly national and take decisive action when the states would not. "The New Nationalism," TR explained, "puts the national need before sectional or personal advantage." Roosevelt used the "general welfare clause" of the Constitution to promise a "square deal" for the farmer, worker, and small businessman, all of whom were being "victimized" by big business.[2] The Square Deal was effective politics and guaranteed dramatic headlines. TR was the darling of the new journalists—the muckrakers—who exposed the malefactions of Standard Oil, the meatpacking industry, the railroads, the stock market, and life insurance. By 1906, however, even Roosevelt, who had coined the term "muckruckers," was denouncing these early investigative journalists, such as Lincoln Steffens, for having turned into muck-makers.[3]

Forty-three-year-old Teddy Roosevelt became America's youngest ever president in 1901. Virile and vital, he changed America's mores as well as its politics. One journalist never forgot his first visit to Roosevelt's library: on his desk were a gold miner's pan, a silver dagger, and piles of books; animal skins decorated the walls and covered the floor. Roosevelt suddenly appeared—"robust, hearty, wholesome, like a gust of wind," dressed "in knickerbockers, a worn coat, and a disreputable pair of tramping shoes."[4]

College students were inspired by TR's irrepressible optimism, they adopted his casual dress, they participated in sports with an equal fervor. He was a man of a thousand interests and a hundred hobbies—rancher, biographer, historian, naturalist, Rough Rider, hunter—who built the Panama Canal, transformed the United States into a great naval power, persuaded Congress to pass the Pure Food and Drug and Meat Inspection Acts, and created five national parks, two national game preserves, and fifty-one wild bird preserves.

He was easy to admire, but his presidency marked the true beginning of big government in America. As political historian Matthew Spalding writes, "TR favored central control of the economy for the sake of efficiency, and his ultimate goal was a benign collaboration of mammoth institutions."[5] His program, the New Nationalism, was used as a starting point by his cousin, President Franklin D. Roosevelt, for the New Deal of the 1930s. Some eighty years later, Vice President Al Gore praised Theodore Roosevelt and Woodrow Wilson for having "invented the modern bureaucratic state."[6] For all his many admirable personal qualities, TR and his view of progress conflicted sharply with the nation's founding ideal of a limited constitutional republic.

John Dewey and Progressive Education

Reform fervor inevitably affected American higher education. Leading the way was John Dewey, pragmatist and founder of the progressive education movement. Dewey believed, writes historian Page Smith, that students should explore all issues with an open mind, set aside all rote learning, question all authority, and realize they could direct the evolution of human society. The fundamental question for Dewey was, not whether any action was morally good or bad, but whether its results were socially useful or harmful. "Growth itself," he declared, "is the only moral 'end.'" He had come a long way from his early years as a practicing Christian; now he admitted that he could not think of "any large idea about the world being independently generated by religion."[7]

Under Dewey's influence, and that of his disciples at Columbia Teachers College in New York City, higher education became ever more secular and results-oriented at the turn of the century. Antioch College, Sarah Lawrence College, and Bennington College, for example, called themselves "Progressive Education Colleges" and offered such courses as cooking, vocational training, and teacher education.[8] The humanist trends in the American university accelerated when the University of Chicago was started with much fanfare and Rockefeller money.

Armed with John D. Rockefeller's millions and directed by President William Rainey Harper, Chicago came to epitomize American pragmatism and enterprise. Conspicuously missing was any idea of the importance of faith and religion in life. Universities, it was argued, should be responsive only to social and economic trends. *Cosmopolitan* magazine charged in 1909 that American colleges were consistently teaching that "the decalogue is no more sacred than a syllabus... there are no absolute evils... the change from one religion to another is like getting a new hat... moral precepts are passing shibboleths."[9]

But secular trends notwithstanding, in hundreds of denominational colleges traditional Christianity still played a prominent role. Approximately half of all undergraduates in the pre-World War I period attended church-related schools. But even among these colleges, many featured majors for students, faculty specialization, and "practical" training.

A Less Traveled Road

Grove City College was satisfied to take the more traditional road, not caught up in the fervor of change for the sake of change. Beginning his fourth decade as president in 1907, Isaac Ketler was full of energy and plans for Grove City. His long-held ambition was to expand the college to the upper campus above Wolf Creek. Creig Hoyt (later dean of the college) remembered how, as a student, President Ketler had walked with him all over the Washabaugh farm, pointing to sites where the new men's dormitory would be located, as well as other buildings, walks, and drives. To a remarkable degree, Grove City College historian David Dayton points out, the new campus of the 1930s "matched the dream of the founder."[10]

In the meantime a women's dormitory, "The Colonial," was constructed and received some sixty "student guests" in the fall term of 1904. It was modern, even luxurious, with steam heat, electric lighting, and a marble-lined bathroom in each suite or single room. Room and board for such comfort was $60 dollars for a full term. President Ketler assured the women students that he had instructed Dean Arabelle March "to have no rules but to make it a happy beautiful home for the girls." But there were rules. When he learned that a public dance had been held in The Colonial, the president lost no time in reprimanding Dean March and the housekeeper: "You... should have stopped it immediately, if in no other way by turning out the lights."[11]

The United Presbyterian Church helped by selling its old building for $7,000 to the college, which named it Ivy Chapel and used it as a classroom until the 1950s. And after years of placing gymnasiums in various buildings—first the New College Building and then the Carnegie Library—the trustees approved the construction of a physical education building (including a swimming pool and a basketball court) that was completed in 1913. Outdoor facilities for baseball, football, and a field track were also developed. In keeping with the college's long-standing policy of cooperation with the local citizenry, Grove City residents were invited and encouraged to attend the school's sporting events. At the direction of the trustees, an area known as the College Park was kept open to the public.

Since the founding of Pine Grove Normal Academy in 1876, men had lived off campus in private homes sanctioned by the administration. In 1910 the trustees decided, with the stimulus of a $25,000 pledge from J. N. Pew, to build a men's dormitory. Memorial Hall would not be completed until 1914, but it had the distinction of being the first building on the Upper Campus, over-looking Wolf Creek and the Lower Campus. The total cost of $85,000, including landscaping and furniture, was paid by the Pew family. Unfortunately, neither Joseph Pew nor Isaac Ketler would be there to celebrate its opening.

Although it remained rooted in the classical liberal arts, the college's curriculum was modified when necessary to serve the modern needs of the students. When more and more young men and women attended Grove City in order to receive college teacher training, a chair of education was established. Telegraphy and the three-year normal scientific course were dropped. A Department of Civil and Mechanical Engineering was added. The School of Philosophy, however, a special interest of President Ketler, was retained, and doctoral degrees in philosophy were awarded. Professor Alexander T. Ormond of Princeton, a future president of Grove City College, and Sir William M. Ramsay of Oxford, a dis-tinguished Scots educator, were frequent lecturers at the philoso-phy school. The Department of Military Science and Tactics, which required every able-bodied male student to join a "cadet battalion," was discontinued in 1910 when the number of appli-cations declined sharply and many students in the battalion went "AWOL."[12]

While steadfastly maintaining its Christian character, Grove City College emphasized that it was nondenominational and required no religious test of its trustees, faculty, or students. It readily acknowledged its close ties to a largely Presbyterian community but declined to be formally affiliated with the Presbyterian Church.

President Ketler systematically renewed the faculty. Among the new teachers was Herman Poehlmann, who headed the music department until retiring in 1939. A former chorus director at the Dresden Conservatory of Music in Germany, Poehlmann conducted the college orchestra and found time to direct a Grove City chorus that traveled extensively throughout western Pennsylvania. He composed the official college song "Mid the Pines in columns growing" and some two hundred other songs. And he brought with him his beautiful young wife and singer, Johanna, who, after seven years of teaching voice at Grove City College, became a star soloist at the Metropolitan Opera in New York City before suffering an early, tragic death.

Johanna Poehlmann was in San Francisco on a national concert tour with the famed Italian tenor Enrico Caruso when the terrible earthquake of 1906 leveled the city. While saving the life of another singer about to jump out of a window, Johanna suffered serious injuries from which she died at the age of thirty-eight. The press mourned her death as a "loss to the musical world." Unhappily, there are no recordings of her magnificent voice.[13]

Such outstanding musical talent drew students from all over the Midwest. Indeed in 1909 the enrollment at the Grove City Conservatory of Music exceeded that of the college: 219 students in the college and 254 in the conservatory. The campus was filled every day with the sound of music, to such an extent that some even wondered about the future of Grove City College: would it be a liberal arts college or a school of music?[14]

Another professorial pillar was Herbert William Harmon, who taught physics at Grove City College from 1906 to 1946 and also coached football and baseball. Harmon was a pioneer in radio broadcasting, installing in 1914 the first radio station in America operated in code. In April 1920 he produced the first scheduled radio broadcast—an address by President Weir Ketler to the Rotary Club of New Castle, Pennsylvania. With Harmon's help, Station WSAJ at Grove City College received its license in 1921 and has been on the air ever since.[15]

Even the indefatigable Isaac Ketler could not sustain forever a workload of fifteen- and sixteen-hour days, and at last asked various members of the faculty to be his part-time assistants. James McClelland was named vice president in 1894, and James F. Ray registrar and assistant to the president in 1907. Three years later Otto Sieplien was placed in charge of student registration, and resident managers took up residence in the women's dormitories. To this day every dean at Grove City College teaches at least one course. By 1913 there were thirty faculty members.

Undoubtedly guided by the Holy Spirit, President Ketler seemed to have a knack for turning up wherever he was needed. In the early years of the college, a favorite prank of the male students was to roll up the wooden sidewalks of the city after dark. One night they had just finished rolling up a block-long sidewalk when the president suddenly appeared and personally supervised the unrolling. Another time, a resourceful junior, having raised his class's flag over the administration building before dawn, discovered that President Ketler had removed his ladder and left him stranded on the third-story roof. Only when the student agreed to lower the flag did Ketler put back the ladder.[16]

And then there were the two male students who got hungry for chicken one evening and decided to visit the president's hencoop. One of the boys caught a plump, tender bird and was handing it over the fence when his accomplice impatiently remarked, "Give it to me quick." "You had better give it to me," interrupted another voice. "It's my chicken." Recognizing President Ketler's voice, the stricken boys dropped their booty and ran off as fast as they could. The next morning Dr. Ketler called the two students into his office but made no mention of the night before, instead inviting them to dinner at the president's house that evening. The young men were cordially received and dined well—on chicken. "I know that you are away from home," said the president, "and sometimes get tired of the food. So if you ever feel hungry for a chicken dinner, just tell me and I will be only too glad to have you dine with me." The presidential hencoop was never again visited by the students.[17]

Isaac Ketler could also be a stern disciplinarian, once sending a young man home for excessive profanity. But he tempered justice with mercy. If students damaged property belonging to the college, President Ketler would not bring them to court but would fine those responsible.

Amid the constant stress and strain of running a college, Isaac Ketler also found the time to help his wife Matilda raise three sons—a fourth son, Conrad, died in infancy. William became an executive for Peoples Natural Gas in Pittsburgh; Weir taught at Grove City College and then succeeded to the presidency of the college; and Frank became a superintendent of schools near Philadelphia.

For the college and the city, the climax of the school year was the weeklong graduation festival that included candlelight banquets by the literary and other clubs, a full-scale recital by the students of the music department, a colorful display of student art, and festive, punch-laden class reunions. The social highlight of the week was President and Mrs. Ketler's formal reception, given the night before commencement, at which the faculty passed around dishes of rich ice cream and heaping plates of cookies and cakes.

On commencement day the citizens of Grove City and the nearby countryside came to town early to join in the celebration. The livery stables were filled with brightly polished buggies for the visitors. The brassy town band led a procession down Main Street, newly sprinkled with water to subdue the dust, across the bridge over Wolf Creek, and onto the College Park. President Ketler proudly "led his seniors up onto the pine-decked pavilion erected for the occasion."[18] The program began at 9:30 A.M. and lasted into the late afternoon, with almost every graduate offering remarks. The 1894 commencement program listed thirty-eight speakers, a tribute to the compelling oratory of the speakers and the good nature of the audience used to making its own entertainment. Longtime resident and Grove City College graduate Marian McConkey recalls her mother's descriptions of the "beautiful, long, voluminous" dresses that the girls wore. "A graduation dress," McConkey explains, "was just as important as a wedding gown."[19]

By 1912 some ten thousand young men and women had attended Grove City College. More Grove City graduates had become teachers than those of any other Pennsylvania college. About 250 of its young men had gone into the Christian ministry, and more than sixty men and women had entered the foreign missions. In nearly four decades of existence, Grove City College had not deviated from its calling: to produce good American citizens and strong Christians and resolutely to defend the twin principles of freedom and faith.

In the brief span of just five years, the college was hit hard by the death of its most important benefactor, the loss of not one but two presidents, and the coming of a great world war that required the service of millions of young American men. Any one of these heavy blows would have crippled an ordinary institution.

Petroleum and the Pews

"No single industry has been more important to the American economy in the twentieth century," wrote historian Arthur M. Johnson, "than the petroleum industry." It provided the inexpensive energy that fueled startling economic growth, helped win two world wars, and produced an unequalled standard of living in the world.[20] One of the most successful and innovative petroleum companies for more than a century was the Sun Oil Company. At the heart of the company's history were two men— founder J. N. Pew and his son J. Howard Pew.[21]

Joseph Newton Pew was a true Pennsylvanian, born in July 1848 in the Pew family farmhouse located seven miles northwest of Grove City. The Pews were Bible-centered Presbyterians brought up "to pray unshamedly, to weigh their behavior against the Ten Commandments." Consequently when the "Old School" Presbyterian Church declared that keeping slaves was not a bar to Christian communion, the Pews withdrew and helped found the Free Presbyterian Church. Their opposition to slavery was not limited to Sundays. For many years the Pew farm was a way station on the underground railroad to Canada. On more than one occasion Newton Pew and his siblings were awakened at night to convey escaping slaves to the next station.[22]

At the age of eighteen Newton Pew began teaching in London, four miles west of Pine Grove; one of his brightest pupils was Isaac Ketler. But in a few years, the self-reliant, ambitious, young teacher was drawn to the world of business and moved to Titusville in northwestern Pennsylvania (site of the first commercial oil well in 1859) where he ran, simultaneously, a real estate office, an insurance agency, and a loan service. Brimming with self-confidence, he placed an advertisement in the local paper in June 1872 proclaiming, "I am always prepared to sell the best

Business Property, Building Lots, Dwellings, Oil Lands, Oil Wells, and Unimproved Lands."[23]

In the mid-1870s Pew and Edward O. Emerson began supplying natural gas to drilling sites in western Pennsylvania. Until then, drillers had considered natural gas a "waste" product and had abandoned wells when they hit gas. Pew and Emerson, however, recognized the potential of natural gas as a fuel for drilling and illumination and for residential use. In 1882 they incorporated Penn Fuel Company and began piping natural gas into Pittsburgh, the first major American city to be supplied gas for industrial and home use.

The 1885 oil strike in Lima, Ohio, inspired Pew to enter the oil business. He and Emerson organized the Sun Oil Line Company to lease wells, transport petroleum, and store oil. In the final decade of the nineteenth century, Pew and Emerson began working to create an integrated oil company, buying a refinery in Toledo, Ohio, and a small railroad company. Then in 1899 Pew bought out Emerson and took full control of Sun Oil, by now one of the most profitable oil independents in America. Its success can be measured by the fact that it successfully resisted absorption by John D. Rockefeller and the giant Standard Oil Company of Indiana.

When the 1901 Spindletop discovery spawned the Texas oil rush, J. N. Pew sent his nephews Robert C. and J. Edgar Pew to the area to explore the possibilities and negotiate for leases. (Until the 1960s the Sun Company was strictly a family-run company.) J. Edgar Pew remained in Texas to manage the properties and the drilling and distribution operations. But Robert C. Pew returned to the Toledo refinery where J. Howard Pew was hard at work searching for ways to make the thick Texas crude oil more profitable. At this time J. N. Pew moved to Philadelphia where he oversaw the construction of the Marcus Hook refinery, incorporated the Sun Company (of New Jersey), and established a solid marketing foundation with national and even international customers.

Throughout all of these intensely competitive and demanding years, J. N. Pew never forgot Grove City College. Shortly before his death, he wrote President Ketler that he was "more interested in the College" than in the business enterprises that were demanding so much of his strength and time.[24] Over a period of nearly twenty years, he and his former pupil Isaac Ketler led their school into the first rank of liberal arts colleges in western Pennsylvania. And then on October 10, 1912, following two heart attacks, Joseph Newton Pew died at the age of sixty-four. He had succeeded in his profession, as so many Scots-Irish Presbyterians had, by combining high moral idealism with a zeal for capitalism and progress. He had been a superb organizer who lived by the Golden Rule, gladly sharing his wealth with those in need. And always on his mind and in his heart had been the college about which he had once urged Isaac Ketler: "Make [it] healthful, for that is essential. Make it beautiful, for that is an education."[25]

He also ensured a Pew presence at Grove City College, suggesting at the last commencement he attended in June 1912 that his son J. Howard, who had graduated from the college in 1900, and his nephew John Glenn be added to the board of trustees. Thirty-year-old J. Howard Pew was named chairman of the building committee, a post he would hold for nearly six decades. Following J. N. Pew's death, Fred R. Babcock of Pittsburgh, who had become a trustee only two years earlier, but had led the successful fundraising drive for the new gymnasium, was elected president of the board. Babcock was cut out of the same Presbyterian cloth as his predecessor and was imbued with the same admiration for the self-made man and woman.

In his first public address on campus, Babcock leader declared that "the desire for quick and easy wealth is the source of half our troubles." The Pittsburgh business leader cautioned his young listeners to prepare themselves for a long, hard pull in life but reassured them that nature was just: "For industry, she pays in wealth and comfort; for integrity, in respect and honor; for ability, in fame; for folly, in distress; for loyalty, she returns the same superb quality multiplied a hundred-fold and it then becomes affection. Therefore let it be one of our duties to spread the bonds of affection and thereby increase the power and influence and efficiency of our institution."[26]

It was J. Howard Pew who suggested that the new men's dormitory, dedicated to his father, be erected on the high ground overlooking the existing lower campus. President Ketler was enthusiastic about the new location. As he viewed the site, he talked excitedly to friends about the future, calling the proposed new building the beginning of "a fifty-year program."[27] But for Isaac Ketler it would remain only a dream.

The Passing of the Founder

Although he had been told for some months that he should have his appendix removed, the always busy president never found the time, wrapped up in the needs of the college. But in late June 1913 the pain became so intense that he entered the hospital for surgery—but it was too late. As the end approached, President Ketler dictated messages to old associates and friends. To the citizens of Grove City, he wrote, "Whatever success I have had in life was not due to myself, but to the good people of Grove City who stood back of me." To the trustees and faculty, he said, "I commit the interests of the College to [you]... It was a labor of love. Let it always stand for the best things." With almost his last breath and secure in his faith, he said, "It is Providence."[28]

At his funeral, W. L. McEwan, vice president of the board of trustees, stated that "the aim of all [Isaac Ketler's] services" to Grove City College was "to make Christian men and women, qualified to do their work in the world." Dr. Robert Calder, the college pastor, revealed a conversation he had had with President Ketler shortly before his death. Asked how he maintained such a busy schedule, Ketler replied, "My philosophy and theology unite in teaching me the sovereign goodness of God, and I do not worry after I have done my best." His longtime friend Sir William M. Ramsay summed up his educational success by saying that President Ketler "knew well... that he had to adapt his College to the needs of the moment and to the opportunities of the people. He knew he must begin on a humble level, and work up to a higher standard."[29] And so he had for nearly four decades.

In 1912–1913, the last school year of the Isaac Ketler administration, Grove City offered the degrees of bachelor of arts, science, and philosophy (and a Ph.D. in philosophy). Under Ketler's guidance, the members of the faculty sought to impart ethical principles in harmony with evangelical Christianity. They were an impressive group—graduates of Harvard, Princeton, Yale, Johns Hopkins, Cornell, Northwestern University, and Bonn University. Seven of them had Ph.D.'s, three had master's degrees, five had B.A.'s. They worked long and hard, ten hours a day, six days a week, forty-six weeks a year, "on any level of instruction wherein they were competent and needed."[30]

Isaac Ketler left behind a Christian institution of higher learning well known and deeply respected throughout the Ohio Valley. Who could follow the dedicated founder of so successful an enterprise? The trustees (and everyone else at the college) were confident they had found their man in sixty-five-year-old Alexander T. Ormond, chairman of the Department of Philosophy at Princeton University and a nationally known educator. Ormond was a large man with a thick walrus moustache, expansive in nature and girth, resembling former President William Howard Taft, who tipped the scales at over three hundred pounds.

Author of three well-received books on philosophy, Ormond was a colleague and friend of Woodrow Wilson, Princeton's former president, who had just been elected president of the United States. Ormond knew the region well, having been born in Punxsutawney in western Pennsylvania, and he knew the college: he had been coming to Grove City every summer since 1908 to teach in the Bible School and the School of Philosophy. Sir William S. Ramsay went so far as to say that Ormond "is the man whom [Isaac Ketler] himself probably would have chosen."[31] There was no question about his intellect and educational experience, but did he have the necessary managerial skills?

The Ormond Administration

At his inauguration in November 1913, President Ormond emphasized his commitment to the principles of faith and freedom, principles that had characterized Grove City College from its founding, and stressed the importance of providing an education "that is at once sound, liberal and practical."[32] As Robert S. Calder, the college chaplain, put it, the aim of the college under the new president would be to produce "scholars with character."[33] President Wilson sent a warm letter of congratulations to his old friend, describing Ormond as "a man of pure conscience, extraordinary intellectual power, and a [loveable] character."[34]

He was also a man full of grand plans for Grove City College which, he said, "must grow or it must die." He proposed to raise $1 million for a new recitation building, a new science building, a college chapel, a bigger library, more teachers, and higher faculty salaries.[35] The trustees approved the expansion but reminded the new president that the college had always operated on a pay-as-you-go basis, depending on tuition rather than endowment income. Ormond, determined to expand the facilities, improve the academic standards, and modernize the administration all at the same time, suggested that the extra costs be borne by the trustees and friends of the college, not by the students and their families. The trustees were impressed by the breadth of Ormond's vision but still concerned about its cost. There was certainly no denying the new president's personal commitment to the school. Ormond, a widower, and his daughter Margaret lived in an apartment in The Colonial dormitory and took their meals with the female students in the dining hall.

In his two short years as president, Alexander Ormond was responsible for important academic changes at Grove City College. All applicants were now required to pass a rigorous English examination: A new bulletin warned that "special stress will be placed upon... Spelling, Capitalization, Punctuation, Grammar, the proper division of thought into sentences and paragraphs, orderly arrangement and expression of ideas."[36] To improve standards, students were not allowed to take more than fifteen hours of classes in a term unless they had all A and B grades. Even honor students were not permitted to take more than twenty hours.

Total student enrollment including the summer school rose during the Ormond administration from 797 in 1913 to 962 in 1915 (nearly 21 percent), while the faculty grew from 21 to 29 (some 38 percent). The new student-teacher ratio reduced the student load per instructor but inevitably raised instruction costs. One of the new students was a Parsi from India who had studied under Dr. Ormond at Princeton and followed him to Grove City. He wore a long Nehru jacket and carried a cane with a silver head, causing some Grovers to wonder whether he was a German spy.[37]

To improve the administration, young Weir C. Ketler, professor of mathematics and son of Isaac Ketler, was appointed, in 1914, to the new position of assistant to the president. "I find in Weir Ketler great possibilities," Ormond informed the president of the board of trustees. "He is a remarkable young man."[38] Weir had wanted to become a lawyer and had enrolled at Yale. But he had obediently returned to Grove City when his mother told him, "You have to help your father."[39] There were other key appointments. In 1915, A. J. Calderwood was named dean of the faculty. Creig S. Hoyt joined the chemistry department, allowing O. J. Sieplein to concentrate more on his expanding duties as registrar. In response to the many technical advances in farming, a School of Agriculture was created, and not only for those attending the college. Selected agricultural courses were offered free of charge to anyone in the area.

To encourage greater campus spirit, the student-run *Collegian* was converted from a monthly magazine into a weekly newspaper. A book entitled *Songs of Grove City College* was published and helped establish a new tradition—Friday morning sings—at which students sang popular songs led by a male quartet. Commented President Ormond, "There is nothing that will bind the students and Alumni together better than a book of college songs."[40] An Athletic Association of Grove City College, made up of students, alumni, and faculty, was organized and put in charge of sports activities. And after several years of informal meetings, usually in Pittsburgh, graduates formed the Alumni Association in June 1913 and set annual dues at fifty cents.

The changes drew favorable comment from visitors, including Governor-elect Martin Brumbaugh of Pennsylvania. A member of the state's College and University Council for fifteen years, Brumbaugh revealed in the summer of 1914 that Grove City College had been rated "A-1" by the council. He added that the school "has sent more of its graduates into the profession of teaching than any other similar institution in the State."[41]

On November 14, 1914, the thirtieth anniversary of the college charter, Memorial Hall was dedicated. At the alumni luncheon, the endowment fund was officially named the Isaac C. Ketler Memorial Foundation, its income to be used "for general college purposes as shall be hereafter determined." But unbeknownst to the alumni, the trustees had already reacted to the school's rapidly rising debt by postponing and effectively ending Ormond's ambitious million-dollar fund-raising campaign. Then as now, the president of Grove City College could propose, but the board of trustees disposed. In truth, the board was so worried about finances that it authorized a campaign to seek "state aid" from Pennsylvania, despite its cherished tradition of fiscal independence. But it added a caveat—if the state "should attach any unusual condition to a grant," the matter would be referred to the finance committee or the board of trustees.[42] In those arcadian years, before the coming of the Leviathan state, Americans still believed that government might not attach "unusual" conditions to a grant.

In the meantime the trustees, after consultation with the assistant to the president, Weir Ketler (acting for an ill President Ormond), concluded that they could trim the faculty by seven members without affecting "the high standard" of the college. Informed of the board's decision the seven teachers generously offered to resign, reducing the faculty to its pre-Ormond level and saving the college $6,765.00 per annum.

After his many years at Princeton, President Ormond was adjusting, good-naturedly as always, to the limitations of a small liberal arts college. On December 18, 1915, he became ill while traveling to visit his brother in Elderton, Pennsylvania, and died following a heart attack. Although sudden, his passing was not totally unexpected, as Ormond suffered from diabetes, for which there was then no effective treatment, and ate far more than was wise for someone with his poor health and excessive weight.

Another Ketler

Still, Alexander Ormond's death stunned the campus, coming so soon after the grievous losses of Isaac Ketler and J. N. Pew. The college had lost yet another experienced and highly regarded leader. In this crisis the board of trustees turned to someone whom it knew and had already come to admire for his calm demeanor, his sure administrative hand, and his genuine care for the institution—Weir C. Ketler. Just two days after Ormond's death and two-and-a-half years after the death of his father, Weir Ketler was named acting president of Grove City College "with the full duties and powers of the office of President." The following June, the trustees unanimously elected him president of the faculty and the college. The students were enthusiastic, hailing him as "the crowned Prince who from the Founder sprung."[43] He was twenty-seven years old, one of the youngest college presidents in America, and a layman, not a clergyman like his father. It was a harbinger of the future. In 1860, 90 percent of all college presidents had trained for the ministry, by 1933, no more than 12 percent had theological preparation[44]

At the annual alumni meeting in February 1916, and while still only acting president, Weir Kelter presented his vision of Grove City College, placing the student body at the center. He stated that the students must have "ample and adequate facilities," the college should stand for "thorough and accurate scholarship," and the faculty should provide the necessary stimulus so that the students "do their work honestly and well." Then he got to the heart of the matter: "The aim of our college should be to send out young men and women who not only have well-trained and efficient minds but who possess well-rounded personalities, who respond to high motives and who follow high ideals. Their lives should exemplify solid, vigorous, aggressive Christianity. We want no smug self-sufficiency, or critical hypocrisy. We believe in constructiveness, in men and women who have courage, who believe in right and who are not afraid to make a stand for the right in the moral and civic issues of life."[45]

Isaac Ketler would have vigorously applauded.

It seemed to many observers that Weir Ketler had been destined to head Grove City College. Indeed, the college and the town were very nearly all he had ever known. He was born on March 14, 1889, in Grove City, the second of four Ketler boys, and attended the local public schools. He graduated from the college in 1908 with a B.A. and immediately joined the faculty as an "assistant in Algebra, Geometry, and General History." A year later he went to Yale University where he earned a second B.A. in 1910. Weir intended to practice law and had already passed a preliminary examination in Pennsylvania. He returned to Grove City, however, after his mother informed him that his father "needed" him. Weir Ketler taught mathematics for two years and then moved to the Department of History and Politics; he also coached basketball. In the spring of 1914 the young professor added a further duty when he became assistant to the president. In December 1915, just seven years after his graduation, he was elevated to the post of acting president. Despite his youth and lack of administrative experience, the trustees decided that Weir Ketler was the man who could lead the college in the ensuing years. No one guessed how successful—and tumultuous—they would be.

President Ketler inherited a modest domain of fifty acres, nine buildings (eight on the lower campus), and a plant valued at about $700,000. The academic faculty numbered twenty, the student body totaled just over one thousand, but only one-third were regular students. The rest were enrolled in the School of Music, the summer school, secretarial courses, and preparatory and special classes.[46] When Ketler retired in 1956, four decades later, Grove City College had 1,200 full-time undergraduates, a devoted faculty of seventy-six, and twenty-one buildings on what was widely considered one of the most beautiful campuses in the nation.

Growth and Reaction

Ketler began his tenure as president at a time of change but also of reaction in American higher education. Colleges like Harvard, Yale, and Princeton had become great universities. What had been, for the most part, elitist institutions were now open to all classes and sexes. In response to public demand, state legislatures were pouring huge sums of money into public education. The people took full advantage of the changes: between 1890 and 1925 enrollment in institutions of higher education grew 4.7 times as fast as the population.[47]

But various observers felt that some profoundly important things had been left behind in the rush, so typically American, to build a new and better academy. "It is a hard saying," summed up Harvard's official historian, Samuel Eliot Morison, "but Mr. Eliot, more than any other man, is responsible for the greatest educational crime of the century against American youth—depriving him of his classical heritage."[48]

Former President Theodore Roosevelt asserted stoutly that the colleges should turn out "young men with ardent convictions on the side of right." William Jennings Bryan, a frequent political adversary of Roosevelt, on this occasion agreed with his old foe, setting forth the need for morality, conviction, and a regard for the whole man.[49] Philosopher Irving Babbitt and his colleagues, who came to be known as the New Humanists, disputed the university's emphasis on the practical and on scientific materialism. Let us hear less about service and power, said Babbitt, and more about wisdom and character.[50] Harkening back to an earlier age, the general education movement was launched at Columbia University in 1919, advancing the idea that "there is a certain minimum of... [the Western] intellectual and spiritual tradition that a man must experience and understand if he is to be called educated."[51] The movement spread as chastened educators (although not all) cooled on curricular specialization and the elective principle. Even Eliot's successor at Harvard, Abbott Lawrence Lowell, declared that "the college ought to produce, not defective specialists, but men intellectually well rounded, of wide sympathies and unfettered judgment."[52]

The general education movement, however, was scarcely noted at Grove City College because Weir Ketler, like his predecessors, had never wavered from his understanding that Western heritage, particularly Christianity, was vital to the education of a college student and a good citizen. The students agreed. "Other colleges may be older and boast of greater wealth," proclaimed *The Collegian*, "but none can excel in the Christian atmosphere which pervades Grove City College."[53]

The Guns of 1917

Any sense of self-satisfaction at Grove City was abruptly abandoned when on April 2, 1917—during Holy Week—President Woodrow Wilson asked Congress to declare war on Germany. Cast aside were such considerations as campus spirit, faculty reform, curricular review, and the other daily problems of a liberal arts college. Ketler and the trustees were confronted with two fundamental questions: How should the college contribute to the war effort? And would the school survive if every able-bodied young man in America were drafted? A judicious mixing of patriotism and pragmatism provided the answers.

Although the college's military training program had been eliminated from the curriculum in 1912, the board of trustees had reestablished a military department in June 1916 as the fighting in Europe grew fiercer. The action was undoubtedly inspired by General Leonard Wood and the War Department which had organized in the summer of 1915 the first Plattsburgh training camp, at which some 1,200 civilian volunteers were instructed in modern warfare by regular army officers; the volunteers paid for their own food, uniforms, and travel expenses. The following summer, some 16,000 young American men were enrolled in "Plattsburghs" across the country, providing a cadre of trained army officers.

Early in 1917 President Ketler reported to the trustees that the War Department had "assured" him the college could begin a Department of Military Science and Tactics "on or about the first of April." Around the same time the faculty affirmed its "thorough-going support of President Wilson and whatever measures he may deem it advisable to take in the present crisis." *The Collegian* concurred, reporting "great enthusiasm" among students for the introduction of military training, mixed "with a grim determination... to do their part, when called upon, in this great world war."[54]

Such commitment reflected the patriotic spirit of the region whose sons had fought and fought well in every national conflict since the Revolutionary War. Several Grove City College students, for example, were enrolled in the Pennsylvania National Guard that participated in the 1916 border campaign against Mexican rebel leader Pancho Villa. Upon their return these students aroused "a preparedness spirit" on campus.[55]

Many "Grovers" (as students of the college often called themselves) answered the call. For the 1915–1916 academic year, 217 male students were enrolled full-time at Grove City College.

The number plummeted to less than half—just ninety—for the 1917–1918 academic year. The patriotic undergraduate spirit was captured in a *Collegian* editorial that declared, "No red-blooded American youth should make any plans for the future which will not aid directly in strengthening the resources of our nation."[56] Amid rising concern about increasing costs and decreasing income, President Ketler argued strongly that the college should stay open and promised to keep the deficit to a minimum. He reported what the secretary of war and other government officials had said at a meeting of college and university presidents in Washington, D.C.: "They emphasized the fact that if the War were long, we would need a constant stream of trained men and women to carry its responsibilities and in any case we would need a host of highly educated men and women for the period of rebuilding after the War."[57]

To prevent a drop in student enrollment that would produce a shortage of needed scientists, technicians, and medical personnel, the federal government took several steps. It gave deferments to students receiving training in these fields. It established a Student Army Training Corps "to prevent unnecessary and wasteful depletion of the colleges." It signed contracts with over 525 institutions for the "subsistence, quarters, and military and academic instruction" of college students who enlisted as cadet officers and who would be called into active service if the War Department gave the order.[58] (By October 1918 more than 140,000 students had enrolled in the corps.)

In the spring of 1918 the secretary of war announced that the government would establish a military training unit at Grove City College. All men over eighteen would be enrolled in the army reserve but would not be called into active service until they reached the age of twenty-one. The government would pay for the uniforms and the training but nothing more. Until then the college, led by the Pew family, had dutifully borne all the expenses of the military department. J. N. Pew, Jr., for example, arranged for the purchase of 125 rifles from the U.S. Training Rifle Company of Philadelphia. J. Howard Pew, chairman of the committee on military affairs, backed by the board of trustees, had agreed to pay the costs of the uniforms and the salaries of the instructors.

In August 1918, as American troops assumed an ever greater role in the European fighting, the draft law was changed to encourage more young men to join the Students Army Training Corps. They would now be housed, clothed, and receive pay of $30 dollars a month. As a result, in the fall term of Grove City College's 1918–1919 academic year, 234 enlisted men were preparing to become officer candidates. The campus took on a martial air—176 young men were housed in Memorial Hall and the others were placed in private homes in town. By the end of October all the men had been inducted, and the special classes, drills, and other elements of the military program were "running smoothly."[59]

The Grove City College students who were not in uniform strove to do their part. "Success in this crisis," stated *The Collegian*, "depends upon the cooperation of everyone.... We must command every resource in this supreme effort to 'the world safe for democracy.'" Such patriotic rhetoric was inevitable, given the vast propaganda campaign conducted by the American government, which was calculated, states historian Samuel Eliot Morison, "to make people love the war and hate the enemy."[60]

Meanwhile, the commitment of Grove City students to their college was tested in October 1917 when thirteen upperclassmen were suspended by the administration for hazing freshmen. Although the hazing was an annual fall occurrence, President Ketler had expressed his strong disapproval of the practice on several occasions, but to no avail, and thus decided to take action. At emotion-charged mass meetings, usually docile Grove City students, male and female, threatened to boycott classes. But calmer heads prevailed, and everyone involved in the hazing agreed to appear before the disciplinary committee and accept their punishment. Another seven men were suspended, but a week later, all twenty students were allowed to return to class. "They have taken their punishment like men," commented *The Collegian* with pride.[61]

On November 11, 1918, an armistice finally ended "the war to end all wars"—which had turned out to be the bloodiest conflict the world had ever seen. (The number killed and dead of wounds totaled almost 8 million.) One month later, the Students Army Training Corps at Grove City College was demobilized, but the school was so proud of its contributions to the war effort that the 1918–1919 catalogue stated: "If the emergency had continued longer the [corps] would have fully justified the efforts to bring it into existence."[62] At least in wartime Grove City College and the federal government had demonstrated that they could work together effectively and harmoniously.

President Ketler was so pleased with the esprit de corps produced by the military training that he proposed the formation of a Reserve Officers Training Corps unit on campus. Grove City College's ROTC unit—one of 150 at colleges across the country—was launched in the spring of 1919 with uniforms and equipment provided by the government. A military inspector subsequently reported that Grove City "was a model college of its class" and its ROTC unit "had a better spirit and was better trained than any unit he had visited."[63]

But in only one year student interest in military training declined sharply, accentuated by the fact that many of the incoming freshman and sophomores had been on active duty during the war. They felt they had done their duty. By the spring of 1920 the college concluded it could not maintain a ROTC unit that met government regulations, and so the faculty, with the president and the board of trustees' approval, discontinued the program. There would be no military presence on campus until the 1940s and World War II.

Keeping the College Going

In the wake of World War I and throughout the 1920s, Weir Ketler used every bit of his managerial skills and ingenuity to keep the college going. Debt had escalated to over $150,000 because of the sharp drop in the student body during the war years. Attendance at the summer school had declined significantly as public schools opened their doors in summertime to elementary school teachers. Prices of everything from food to fuel soared, forcing the college to raise room and board from $69 dollars in 1917 to $99 in 1918. Tuition was also increased from $28 dollars to $40 dollars for a twelve-week term two years later. Although there was a clear need for a new science building and a chapel, the board of trustees was reluctant to add to the already sizeable debt. In the last half of 1918 the board and other supporters of the college conducted a fund-raising campaign that raised $105,360, but total indebtedness was still a formidable $133,946.18.

Grove City College's endowment continued to lag far behind other colleges in Pennsylvania. In 1920, with a full-time enrollment of 450, the college's endowment was only $261,398. By contrast, Allegheny College, with 500 students, had an endowment of $2.25 million; Washington & Jefferson College, with an enrollment of 368, had an endowment of over $1 million; and Swarthmore College, with 507 students, had $2 million.[64]

Unlike many other college presidents, Weir Ketler refused to become a "financial drummer" for the college to the exclusion of virtually all other duties. He was aided in his resolution by the largesse of the board of trustees, the support of the Grove City community, and the growing participation of the alumni. During Christmas of 1919, however, he decided to visit the General Education Board (more familiarly known as the Rockefeller Foundation) in New York City and received the impression that "the College just now is in a strong position in which to make an appeal."[65]

To trim costs President Ketler discontinued the Graduate School of Philosophy, started in 1897, which offered a Ph.D. It was the first of several steps that the president would take to hone the academic mission of the college. In 1918, the college offered for the first time, the degree of Bachelor of Science in Chemical Engineering. The following year Grove City instituted a four-year course leading to a bachelor of music degree—the school had long had one of the most popular music departments in western Pennsylvania. Ketler also suggested the addition of classes in accounting and business administration, but the board's Committee on Faculty and Curriculum demurred. Engineering and music were familiar disciplines—accounting and business administration were new and unknown. Who could say how many students they would attract? (Today the single largest department at Grove City College is the Department of Business Administration, Economics and International Management.)

Intent on serving families of modest means, the college refused to keep raising tuition and other costs to balance its budget. The average annual cost of attendance at twenty-seven Pennsylvania colleges in 1920 was $422.00. Grove City charged $375.50, eighteenth on the list.[66] The school strove to conduct its affairs as much like a business as possible, but also agreed that the college's "distinguishing ear-marks. . . are its moral purpose, its scientific aim, its unselfish public service, its inspirations to all men in all noble things, and its incorruptibility by commercialism."[67]

The Ketler reforms clearly helped improve the financial position and academic performance of the college. But they usually occurred ad hoc, in reaction to a particular problem. Gradually, Ketler and the board of trustees decided that what Grove City College needed was a "master plan" for all aspects of the school—financial, academic, and physical. The idea appealed strongly to their orderly, businesslike minds, but it contrasted sharply with the national zeitgeist of unbridled optimism based on the naive notion that what goes up will never come down.

CHAPTER THREE

The Master Plan

In his campaign speeches for the presidency in the fall of 1920, Republican candidate Warren G. Harding insisted that "America's present need is not heroics but healing; not nostrums but normalcy; not revolution but restoration."[1] The voters emphatically agreed and gave Harding a landslide victory of 61 percent over Democrat James A. Cox—the widest margin in American history until 1964. But what was normalcy in 1920s America? Was it national Prohibition or machine-gunning bootleggers? Female emancipation or the Ku Klux Klan? Iconoclast H. L. Mencken of the *American Mercury* or Henry ("American Century") Luce of *Time* magazine? Aviation hero Charles A. Lindbergh or evangelist Billy Sunday? Stock market bulls or bears? Normalcy kept changing.

One constant factor was the car. Indeed, historian Samuel Eliot Morrison has credited the socio-economic transformation in America during the first four decades of the twentieth century to the automobile, which enabled the long-isolated farmer to carry his crops to market, the skilled worker to live miles from his job, and the segregated southern black to head north to seek a job.

In their efforts to put a car in every garage, Henry Ford and his rivals even spawned a new business—"high-powered" salesmanship and advertising.[2]

National policymakers were enthusiastic about freedom of movement within America's borders, but not across its borders. Unlimited immigration, except for Asians, had been U.S. policy until World War I, but organized labor, fearing competition, and America-firsters, fearing a "mongrelization" of American society, persuaded Congress to assign strict quotas to various countries. After trying and failing to make the world safe for democracy, a disillusioned nation turned inward and stayed there for the next two decades.

In those postwar years, the women's movement pushed through the two constitutional amendments of the era—the Eighteenth, outlawing alcoholic beverages, and the Nineteenth, giving women the vote. The latter was a long overdue application of the "equality" principle of the Declaration of Independence. The former was a well-meaning but ham-handed experiment in social policy. Temperance had been proceeding steadily—twenty-seven states were dry by 1917—but its federalization produced disastrous results. It encouraged lawbreaking and created a criminal class that smoothly switched to gambling and drugs when the Eighteenth Amendment was repealed in 1933. Many young people, rebelling against authority, drank who otherwise would not have. College students who used to gather around a keg of beer singing their alma mater song now got drunk on illegal gin and hot jazz. The double standard—almost every public official had his favorite speakeasy—encouraged hypocrisy in politics and other American institutions.[3]

After three centuries in which Christian morals had been maintained by law, religion, and custom, wrote Samuel Eliot Morison, "permissiveness [became] a dominant principle in education and sexual relations."[4] Romance shifted from the front parlor to the back seat of a car, the waltz gave way to the bunny hug, and the patriotic songs of George M. Cohan and Irving Berlin were drowned out by the syncopated beat of jazz, which the Reverend Henry Van Dyke called "a sensual teasing of the strings of sensual passion."[5]

This social revolution was led by America's intellectuals who scorned middle-class order and convention. They came out of World War I, novelist F. Scott Fitzgerald wrote, "to find all gods dead, all wars fought, all faiths in man shaken."[6] Their alienation had its certain impact on young Americans looking, as they always are, for a cause. Ex-communist Whittaker Chambers, author of the magisterial work *Witness*, has recounted how as a student at Columbia University in the 1920s it was liberalism in its modern guise as socialism that swept away his "immature and patchwork beliefs."[7]

Progressives like John Dewey visited the Soviet Union and proclaimed that the Soviet Union was already providing "a searching spiritual challenge" as well as an economic challenge.[8] Their enthusiasm for "a tomorrow that works" (to paraphrase Lincoln Steffens) helped lay the ideological foundation for the big-government philosophy of the New Deal a decade later.

In these restless days, wrote historian Frederick Rudolph, it was not surprising that Dewey's experiential theories made significant headway in the colleges. Dewey insisted that education must be free from "the grip of authority of custom and traditions as standards of belief."[9] In their place he offered a progressive education dedicated to the proposition that the classroom experience must be relevant to the problems of the day and hold the interest of the student. Dewey's disciples eagerly went to work and began producing doctoral dissertations like *A Study of the Achievement of College Students' Beginning Courses in Food*

Preparation and Serving and Related Factors. This prompted one observer to wonder whether such scholarship was "the final pay-off" from the mix of the elective principle, German scholarship, and the marriage between science and equality.[10]

Some educators were roused to action. Robert Maynard Hutchins of the University of Chicago led a revolt against progressive education in the 1930s, calling for a return to the old scholastic curriculum and the Great Books of Western Civilization. President Ketler and the other leaders of Grove City College applauded Hutchins and congratulated themselves that no such revolt was needed on their campus: they had never abandoned traditional Christian education, and they never would.

Staying on Course

Amid all the national educational tacking to and fro, Grove City's board of trustees carefully and methodically proceeded with a master plan for the school. In 1922 a planning committee recommended the purchase of land on what is now the Upper Campus, the erection of various buildings, and a campaign to raise $1 million in new endowment. The Pew family again led the way with a $17,500 gift for the purchase of property behind Memorial Hall.

But the college did not wish to become totally dependent on Pew generosity. Reaching out to the foundation world, the board submitted a $250,000 proposal for the endowment fund to the General Education Board, founded and funded by billionaire John D. Rockefeller. It also approached the Presbyterian Board of Christian Education for major support. To improve its acceptance among such sophisticated donors, Grove City adopted in May 1923 a formal budget system. Soon thereafter the Reverend Arthur Boyd was hired as "a financial agent" for the endowment campaign, followed by Dr. H. V. Comin, who reported directly to trustees president F. R. Babcock. The more professional approach produced results almost immediately. The Rockefeller Foundation (more formally, the General Education Board) pledged $100,000 in 1924, and the Presbyterian Board promised to contribute 8 percent of the college's $750,000 challenge fund, some $60,000. President Ketler informed the board of trustees that the Rockefeller grant was recognition of Grove City's "stability and permanence."[11]

The students also did their part, led by J. Stanley Harker, chairman of the undergraduate campaign for endowment and a future president of Grove City College. Seniors, it was suggested, should give $5 while in school and pledge $100 a year for three years when they started receiving a salary. The 1925 Yearbook reported that students pledged $30,000, a sizeable commitment even in that golden year. Students also led a Poster Parade through town and held meetings with Grove City citizens inspiring them to exceed the town's endowment goal.

By 1928 the Grove City College endowment had reached more than $600,000, two-and-a-half times that of a decade earlier. But President Ketler informed the board that the school would need to raise $3 million to build a new science building, chapel, dormitories for men and women, and a second gymnasium. Although many other schools were happily spending government funds, Grove City's president and board stood firm: they would seek and accept money only from private sources.

The college's determination to maintain a wall between school and state was reflected in the faculty's position regarding the creation of a federal Department of Education. When asked by the American Council on Education for its views about such a department, along with the issues of federal aid to education, federal setting of standards, and federal inspection of educational institutions, the faculty replied: "There is nothing to be

gained by the creation of a Department of Education in the place
of the present Bureau of Education.... [Moreover,] unifying the
educational systems of the various states would be a detriment
rather than a help to the development of our high schools and
colleges."[12]

Grove City College did not, however, isolate itself from the
rest of American society. It adapted when and where necessary,
while still agreeing with conservative historian Russell Kirk that
change and reform are not identical. Indeed, as President Ketler
put it in his January 1923 report to the board of trustees, the college would resist "any rapid or radical change that has not proved
its worth in the school of experience."[13]

In that same report Ketler discussed the essential qualities of
a college education, starting with the development of a positive,
wholesome character and the encouragement of sound scholarship. He revealed that the dean of men, A. J. Calderwood, personally consulted with every student who was failing or doing less
than satisfactory work. The objective was not just to produce a
passing grade but to develop "the mind of the student" so that
he could "do useful work in the world."[14]

Nor would the college ignore the educational importance of
the students' extracurricular activities, wrote Ketler, conceding
that he was treading on "dangerous ground." He insisted, nevertheless, that things like athletics, literary societies, religious organizations, publications, and class activities "give avenues for the
full play of initiative and leadership." They develop, he believed,
"that liberal, broad-visioned type of man or woman which the
world so much needs."[15] And so it was that throughout the twenties, Grove City's administration, faculty, and student body
worked together to produce a balance of the curricular and the
extracurricular consistent with the conservative, Christian character of the college.

In November 1923, for example, a student delegation pressed President Ketler for the institution of a student council and a more active social life, including dancing on campus. The following year the faculty approved the formation of a student council, and although it had minimal impact at first, the principle of giving students a say in the affairs of the college was established. Dancing turned out to be more problematic: it was not until 1926 that the board of trustees permitted dancing on Saturdays and before holidays if chaperones and a responsible student committee were present.[16]

Jazz Age or no Jazz Age, Grove City College coeds were expected to behave like ladies, according to a handbook written by the dean of women Lois Cory-Thompson: no "clinging" to the arm of a man, no standing in "conversation" at the dormitory entrance, and no walking with men in the "byways" of Grove City. Men could smoke a pipe in the dormitory, and it was known that they drank at stag parties, but prohibition was generally enforced on campus and in town. And there were so few cars at the school that the yearbook editor had to hitchhike back and forth to Butler to proofread the publication.[17]

Although intercollegiate debate had been discontinued during World War I, a Debate Club was organized at Grove City College in 1920. A chapter of the national forensic honorary, Pi Kappa Delta, was formed two years later, the first national honorary on campus. The topics debated ranged from the place of the closed shop in American industry to whether Great Britain and the United States "should join in alliance to protect France from invasion."[18] The American Chemical Society, for its part, had a campus organization of nine members, "the largest body of any college in the state."[19] By 1924, there were six fraternities and ten sororities at the college, although fraternity housing was still not allowed. The college took its role as in loco parentis seriously:

men and women sat on opposite sides of the chapel during morning devotions, women on the left, men on the right. Faculty members checked attendance daily and on Sunday until 1956.

Expect Great Things

It was at one of the chapel services that President Ketler proposed
a motto for the college. He described a visit to the General Motors
show room in Detroit where a new Cadillac was on display. A sign
read: "Expect great things of the new Cadillac. Ride in it and realize your expectations." Ketler suggested that Grove City take as
its slogan for the coming year, "Expect Great Things."[20] The suggestion was warmly applauded, and the phrase, so typical of the
optimistic twenties, was adopted by the college for use in its promotional literature.

Sometimes criticized for being too formal (even when raking
the leaves in his yard, he wore a white shirt and tie), Ketler was also
praised by students for displaying the essential qualities of a college president: "firm in his purposes, kindly in disposition, keen in
judgment, [and] a lover of fair play and hard work." When
the young president celebrated his thirty-fifth birthday, the
students presented him with thirty-five American Beauty roses
during chapel.[21]

Like his father, Weir Ketler worked long and hard at managing the affairs of the college, and like his father he also raised,
with his wife Ellen Bell, who had been a student of his at Grove
City, four children. They were Eleanor, who married R. Heath
Larry, a vice chairman of U.S. Steel and longtime vice chairman
of the college's board of trustees; George, who became the business manager of the state school at Polk, Pennsylvania;
W. Richard, who died after serving in World War II; and David,
a successful Grove City lawyer. In the words of a longtime
trustee, Ketler was "a devout man, indeed," and when he spoke in

the chapel, the depth of his Christian faith was clear.[22] Because Weir and Ellen Ketler lived off campus in their own house (there was no President's Home until the 1950s), they were not able to entertain faculty or students as the first families of Grove City College later did.

Knowing that good things did not just happen, President Ketler began initiating important curricular changes at the college. Grove City became one of the first institutions of higher learning in Pennsylvania to offer a degree in commerce. Its program to train teachers for certification was approved by the State Department of Public Instruction in 1921. The same year, the first two Grove City students graduated with a BS degree in chemical engineering. And in June 1922 the college was accredited by the Association of Colleges and Secondary Schools of the Middle States and Maryland.

Such regional associations were an outgrowth of the national groups—such as the National Association of State Universities, the Association of American Universities, and the Association of Land-Grant Colleges—that had been formed around the turn of the century, accepting "the inevitability" of seeking common standards on problems like admission.[23]

At the June 1926 commencement exercises marking the fiftieth anniversary of Grove City College, Dr. Francis B. Haas, Pennsylvania's superintendent of public instruction, discussed the college's signal contributions to public education. He pointed out that more than half of the county school superintendents and eighty-four of the school principals in western Pennsylvania had attended Grove City, which was only one of thirteen colleges in the region.

Toward the end of the decade, the faculty decided that Grove City College should eliminate the master's degree from its curriculum. After studying fifty years of experimentation with higher degrees, the college concluded it would henceforth function as a college, pure and simple. At the same time, the faculty restructured the school's course of study, introducing the concept of majors (sixteen for the B.A. degree, nine for the B.S. degree) and offering a two-year premedical course.

When asked (during American Education Week) what they expected from a college education, members of a sociology class responded with a revealing list of twenty-five "benefits," including: "A morality based on the Golden Rule;" "a knowledge of important current events. (This doesn't include divorce scandals, batting averages, nor Paris styles.);" "a sound knowledge of sane, sound, and liberal economics;" "a training in subjects which can be used directly in earning a living, as science, business, teaching, etc.;" "a spirit of optimism," and "the habit of depending upon yourself. (One of the great weaknesses of college students.)."[24]

The innate strength of the college was confirmed yet again when Frederick Raymond Babcock, who had served as president of the board of trustees since 1913, died unexpectedly in January 1928. In a moving letter to the trustees, President Ketler expressed his personal gratitude for Babcock's "energetic leadership" and "personal interest" in a young and inexperienced college president. Without Babcock's "unfailing support," Ketler said, his task would have been "infinitely more difficult."[25]

He pointed out that during Babcock's tenure, the endowment had increased from $81,000 to more than $600,000; the campus had been enlarged; important additions had been made to buildings; the faculty had increased; and the student body had almost doubled. Babcock was a deeply committed board president, Ketler said and had personally telephoned trustees to make meetings. He had made it a point to attend a wide variety of Grove City College activities, including sports events. "It remains for us," Ketler stated, "to take up the tasks that he has laid down and carry them forward."[26]

The board of trustees thought that J. Howard Pew, a trustee since 1912, was the perfect successor and elected him president of the board. But Pew explained that while honored by the board's action, his responsibilities as president of Sun Oil took too much of his time. William L. Clause was therefore chosen and served as president of the board of trustees with distinction until 1931 when he died. It was then that J. Howard Pew finally agreed to become board president and forged a remarkable relationship with President Ketler for the ensuing twenty-five years.

The growth of Grove City College, as well as that of American higher education during the twenties, could be traced, Weir Ketler stated in his June 1929 report to the board of trustees, to the increased number of high schools, the nation's prosperity, the spread of junior colleges and branch campuses, and the state teachers colleges that offered tuition-free four-year degrees. "[Our] record of growth in the past few years," Ketler stated, "is, I think, an encouraging sign for the future. It is an indication of vitality and I believe we can face the future with some confidence."[27]

For the college and for the nation, it had been a decade for which to give thanks. Although there were a few clouds in the sky—the stock market seemed prone to unpredictable ups and downs—Grove City College along with the rest of America expected that the thirties would be as peaceful and prosperous. And then on October 29, 1929 (Black Tuesday), the bottom fell out of the stock market, and of America.

Undeterred by the Depression
Blue chip stocks like American Telephone & Telegraph fell from 304 in September 1929 to a low of 70¼ in 1932. Investment

capital slowed to a trickle. Foreign trade declined drastically. American exports fell from more than $4.5 billion in 1929 to less than $1.5 billion in 1932. In less than a year, industrial production fell by 26 percent. The only number that kept going up was the number of unemployed: 3 million in April 1930, 4 million in October 1930, 7 million in October 1931, 11 million in the fall of 1932, and over 12 million in 1933, about one-fourth of the labor force.

Starting in 1930 consumer buying declined sharply, and the public, wary of banks, hid its money in mattresses. In the cities, soup kitchens, breadlines, and shantytowns sprang up where the jobless gathered. Small towns in the farm belt were almost empty. Some farmers resisted eviction from their homes with guns. Even the wealthy were affected: New York apartment houses offered five-year leases for one year's rent, while entire Pullman trains rolled along without a passenger. Commented former President Calvin Coolidge with typical understatement, "The country is not in good condition."[28]

Yet J. Howard Pew and the other trustees and the officials of Grove City College refused to panic and moved ahead calmly with a master plan—a striking display of courage and confidence in the future of the college and the country. In March 1930, just five months after the collapse of the stock market, the board of trustees formally approved a fund-raising campaign for a new science building and a dormitory and accepted a proposal by trustees William A. Harbison and Ralph W. Harbison to build a chapel as a memorial to their father, Samuel P. Harbison, a long-time member of the board. The board's decision was undoubtedly influenced by a December 12, 1929, letter from J. Howard Pew, who said he thought he could persuade the Pew estate "to contribute $150,000" toward the campaign target of $300,000 for the science and dormitory buildings.[29] After more than a decade of campaigning for money and discussing expansion to the Upper Campus, wrote one observer, the board of trustees "approved the construction of three major buildings in one day!"[30]

President Ketler later explained that the Depression was a positive, rather than a negative, factor in the decision to proceed with construction: by proceeding without delay "the building costs could be kept at a reasonable figure, unemployment would be relieved, and the use of the buildings by the College would not be deferred."[31] It is a rare man indeed who can be so rational when nearly everyone else around him is losing his head.

It also seemed to more than a few that divine providence was hard at work. When the Depression deepened, the trustees informed the Harbisons that they would understand if the family delayed building the chapel until the economic picture brightened. The Harbisons responded that a commitment was a commitment, and they wanted to proceed with the memorial to their father.

At the Center of the Campus

The inspiring result was a beautiful chapel of Gothic design surmounted by a tall pointed flèche or spire in the French tradition. The exterior walls were made of Briar Hill sandstone in warm buff and tan shades and trimmed with buff Indiana limestone. In the interior all of the molded arches and truss supports were of the same Indiana limestone. The floors were wood laid on concrete, the pews were of hand-decorated oak, the great lanterns hanging from the ceiling of hand-wrought bronze. The high arched roof was made of slate with wooden beams and cork, with star-shaped designs on a background of purple and blue. Imported stained-glass windows portrayed Reformation heroes like John Wycliffe, John Knox, John Calvin, and Martin Luther—

beneath them was the inscription, "There is no other Head of the Church but the Lord Jesus Christ." In the great nave window was a figure of Christ the Great Teacher. The side aisle windows presented key events of the early Christian church, as well as the religious and educational history of America. The chapel had a capacity of nine hundred, including a balcony that could accommodate 150 people. The Frances St. Leger Babcock Memorial Organ, a magnificent four-manual Kimball organ of thirty-four stops with a cathedral type stop-key console, was made possible through a $20,000 bequest of Fred R. Babcock, the late president of the board of trustees.

The prominent position of the chapel on the Upper Campus and its visibility to the Lower Campus and to Grove City were traceable to the recommendation of the Olmsted Brothers, the prestigious landscape architects who had designed New York City's Central Park, and the willingness of J. Howard Pew to pay their handsome fee. But Pew would have it no other way, remembering his father's injunction to make the campus "beautiful."

In his dedication address, Reverend W. L. McEwan, the vice president of the board of trustees, explained that the Harbisons' generosity was intended to help the school "maintain its Christian standards." He added, with justifiable pride, that it was "no light achievement for a small Christian college [like Grove City], emphasizing character as well as culture, to have lived through these [last] fifty years." That commitment was making an ever greater impression. Christian men and women everywhere, McEwan asserted, were coming to regard Grove City College, not as just a good regional school, but as "one of the best agencies [in the nation] for the extension of the Kingdom of God."[32]

The Hall of Science was a handsome, three-story red brick building with a square clock tower jutting up another three stories. Along with class and lecture rooms, laboratories, offices, a museum, and a library (no more converted coal bins), the science building contained the campus radio station on the third floor. The station's antenna spouted from the top of the tower, ensuring good reception and good music for every Grover. The new men's dormitory—accommodating 115 and with dining facilities for all the men on campus—would be dedicated the following June and named in honor of Isaac C. Ketler, the school's founder. In discussing the first Ketler's greatest contributions to Grove City College, the new president of the board of trustees, J. Howard Pew, suggested that it lay "in increasing our capacity for the enjoyment and appreciation of those finer things without which life is but a barren existence."[33] It was not what the president of one of the most successful corporations in America would be expected to say, but J. Howard Pew was not your typical American corporate executive.

Summing up a momentous day in the history of Grove City College, W. Scott Bowman, the moderator of the Presbyterian Church of the Synod of Pennsylvania, pointed out that the three buildings—the chapel, the science building, and the dormitory—represented the spirit, the intellect, and the body of man—the "indispensable instruments of culture."[34]

Meanwhile, the spirit, intellect, and body of America at large were being sorely tested.

The New Deal

Harvard historian Samuel Eliot Morison has described the New Deal as "American as a bale of hay—an opportunist, rule-of-thumb method of curing deep-seated ills." In the famous First Hundred Days, President Roosevelt shepherded thirteen major pieces of legislation through Congress, including insurance for all bank deposits, refinancing of home mortgages, Wall Street reforms, authorization for nearly $4 billion in federal relief,

legalization of beer, and laws creating the National Recovery
Administration (NRA), the Civilian Conservation Corps (CCC),
the Agricultural Adjustment Administration (AAA), and the
Tennessee Valley Authority (TVA). "It was all improvised,"
insisted historian William Manchester. "Take a method and try
it," the president told his aides. "If it fails, try another. But above
all, try something."[35]

They even borrowed freely from a much maligned predecessor. Columnist Walter Lippmann asserted that the New Deal
continued the innovative corporatism, or progressivism, of
Herbert Hoover, using public money to bolster private credit
and activity, albeit on a far grander scale.[36] Conservatives argued
that the New Deal was driven by the idea of a nationally planned
economy rather than America's traditional market economy. All
historians, regardless of their philosophical persuasion, agree that
Roosevelt made the White House *the* center of governmental
power for the first time in American history. An anxious and even
desperate people applauded the president and his actions. An
overwhelmingly Democratic Congress rubber-stamped FDR's
every proposal. The Supreme Court was silent, for the while.

The New Deal was a radical break with American tradition—nothing less than a new contract between the government and the governed. Presidential candidate Roosevelt had
explained that the New Deal was not a political slogan but "a
changed *concept* of the duty and responsibility of Government."
Government, FDR declared, now "has a final responsibility for
the well-being of its citizens."[37]

With those words, "a final responsibility," and Roosevelt's
subsequent election, America began a fifty-year experiment in
ever larger government and ever less individual responsibility that
produced a swarm of executive agencies, a thicket of federal
statutes and bureaucratic regulations, and a 90 percent solution

to almost everything, from taxes to subsidies. And because the confidence of the nation had been so profoundly shaken by the Great Depression, most people happily accepted the government's new prominent role in their lives.

Like most revolutions the New Deal went too far. The National Recovery Administration was to be "a partnership in planning" between business and government, with the government having the right to prevent unfair practices and to enforce agreements. The intention was to eliminate unfair competition and sweatshops, but the industry-by-industry codes "inevitably meant the end of trust-busting and the return of price-fixing."[38] Of the more than seven hundred codes, nearly six hundred had price-fixing clauses. The NRA was apparently determined to protect every business in America: Code 450 regulated dog food, Code 427 took on curled hair, Code 262 ruled on dress shoulder pads. General Hugh Johnson, NRA's ebullient, barnstorming administrator, said of the blue eagle that appeared on every NRA code, poster, and decal, "May God have mercy on the man or group of men who attempt to trifle with this bird."[39]

As it turned out, the nine men who made up the Supreme Court did more than trifle with the NRA—they ruled it unconstitutional. Beginning in January 1935 and over the next sixteen months, the high court struck down eight major Rooseveltian measures, including the central legislation of the New Deal— the National Recovery Administration and the Agricultural Adjustment Act. Chief Justice Charles E. Hughes declared that "extraordinary conditions do not create or enlarge constitutional power. The Constitution established a national government with powers deemed to be adequate."[40] In a sense, wrote New Deal historian Alonzo Hamby, "it was remarkable that the New Deal was able to break through these carefully devised constitutional barriers for so long."[41]

Nevertheless, the New Deal was an unqualified political success: President Roosevelt constructed a grand coalition of organized labor, the South, women, ethnic minorities, big city bosses, and blacks that elected him four times and kept Congress predominantly Democratic between 1932 and 1980. Tax, spend, and elect was a winning mantra for the Democratic Party for nearly five decades. But the New Deal was far less successful in ending the Depression and putting the nation on the road to sound economic recovery. In 1937 the stock market crashed again, although not so resoundingly, and unemployment in 1938, according to some surveys, climbed back to almost eleven million. It was World War II, not the New Deal, that finally put America back on its economic feet.

But the Democratic hegemony, wrote British historian Paul Johnson, enabled FDR and his associates "to lay the foundations of an American welfare state," which would grow and grow and grow into a mighty Leviathan.[42] With its seductive offer of "entitlements," the federal government would even invade the field of education, traditionally a local responsibility. The money went to students rather than to the colleges and universities themselves, but the practice was "a departure in federal policy."[43] The National Youth Administration from 1935 to 1943 spent over $93 million on the higher education of 620,000 students.

The money was hard to resist because most college students of the 1930s faced an uncertain future. In January 1935 several million youths between sixteen and twenty-four were on relief. One college president commented that the 150,000 students being awarded degrees that June were entering a society that "did not want them." *Fortune* polled twenty-five universities and concluded that undergraduates hoped for "a job that is guaranteed to be safe and permanent."[44] But what kind of higher education would help them get such a job?

Even staying in college was a study in survival. Many under-graduates worked forty hours a week when school was in session and twice as many hours during their "vacations." One student at Duquesne University held twenty-seven odd jobs on campus and in adjacent Pittsburgh. Working your way through college has never been easy, and it is a tribute to their grit that so many young Americans managed it during the hard-pressed 1930s.

Some educators were unhappy with what they regarded as higher education's surrender to a society "defined by its trade-school, finishing-school qualities." They were led, as mentioned, by President Robert Maynard Hutchins of the University of Chicago, who cried, "Down with vocationalism!" and proposed a return to the traditional curriculum. Great books and general education programs, suggested historian Frederick Rudolph, were part of the search "for order in a society and world torn by chaos."[45] But while many in academe agreed with Hutchins's diag-nosis, they did not accept his prescription.

Grove City College sought a Golden Mean between extremes. It was neither a trade school nor a finishing school but a liberal arts college committed to providing a good education and turning out good citizens. According to President Ketler the college aimed "to meet the needs of its students and the commu-nity which it serves rather than to exploit any new or experimen-tal education theories."[46]

Navigating the Stormy 1930s

Grove City College sailed safely through the stormy seas of the 1930s, with two experienced captains sharing the helm: Weir Ketler, a deft administrator and quietly caring president; and J. Howard Pew, an enormously successful businessman and com-mitted Christian. They were not just colleagues and collabora-tors in an enterprise of high purpose, but close friends. They shared their vacation plans, stories about their families, and, when appropriate, concern for each other's health. Ketler suffered from severe migraine headaches throughout his years at Grove City. When his secretary Adele Armstrong privately expressed deep worry about her boss's health to J. Howard Pew, Pew immediately wrote Ketler that he should "arrange to get away for at least a couple of weeks, as I feel this is vitally important [to] the interests of the College." Inasmuch as it was late January, Pew suggested that his friend think about going "at least as far south as Augusta" to find a decent climate.[47]

J. Howard Pew had always been a hands-on manager at the Sun Oil Company. Now as chairman of the building committee, as well as president of Grove City's board of trustees, he was interested in everything connected with the college. Once, while discussing the cost of constructing a new administration building—which became Crawford Hall—Ketler reported that two large laboratories had been installed on the third floor of the Hall of Science, the service areas of The Colonial had been improved at a cost of $2,500, and new lighting fixtures had been installed in Memorial Hall. He ended his letter by promising to show Pew the plans for the new men's dormitory when he was in Philadelphia "for Mary Pew's wedding."[48]

When the question of Social Security for the faculty and employees of the college arose, Pew expressed his firm opposition, calling the program "a scheme of the Government to get the money and squander it for its own purposes" and predicting that "it is quite likely" that the people who contribute to the system "will never receive the benefits."[49] Pew's skepticism has been fully justified as politicians now scramble to save the father of all entitlement programs.

In another area, although he believed that the college should not make a practice of offering scholarships to students for reasons of need or merit. J. Howard Pew personally underwrote the expenses of several Grove City students every year. Usually they were the children of current or past employees of the Sun Oil Company. Every spring President Ketler personally sent the oil executive a statement of charges: they totaled $1,252.50 in the 1938–1939 school year. Sometimes Pew was persuaded to extend his charity, as when the pastor of the First Presbyterian Church of Ardmore, Pennsylvania, asked him to help a church member who was "a splendid Christian young woman." When Pew learned that the girl's father could contribute $200, he responded that he would be willing to give the pastor $50 "to help defray her expenses provided my name is not used in connection with it."[50]

While opposed to any comprehensive scholarship program, Pew did support the principle of student loans. The board of trustees, he once explained to an alumnus, had endeavored to direct the college's activities in such a way "as would not inculcate in the minds of the students the idea that the world owed them a living," but "to teach them that they must make their own way in life."[51]

Pew and Ketler often discussed politics and increasingly in the late 1930s the situation in Europe. Once, while thanking Pew for covering the deficit of the Bible School in the summer of 1939, Ketler expressed his doubt that England and France would "press the war long," particularly if Poland should fall quickly. Drawing on his sources of information in and out of Washington, Pew quietly set his friend straight. "The rank and file of the people in [England and France]," he reported, "are determined to have a showdown with Hitler." Saving "a revolution in Germany," he wrote, "in all probability the war will last for several years."[52]

Even with two such leaders it was not always smooth going for the college during the Depression years. The school had to borrow money for part of the cost of several new buildings. And many students were hard pressed to meet their obligations, although Grove City maintained tuition at $85 a semester; room and board was an additional $153 to $190 a semester. Often students were unable to pay their bills until after the term was completed, but the school was sympathetic: there was no suggestion to pay up or else. Some students paid their tuition and other charges in coal or potatoes, which were then served in the dormitory dining halls.[53]

The college even permitted some indirect and very limited federal assistance: under the Federal Relief Administration, seventy-five students held a variety of campus jobs, ranging from working in the library and the alumni office to painting fences and building a road from Pine Street in Grove City to Harbison Chapel.[54] But no compromise was allowed with regard to student attendance at daily chapel which remained compulsory. *The Collegian* newspaper retaliated one year by publishing which members of the faculty attended chapel during the course of a month. Dean Calderwood was commended for his almost 100 percent attendance, but according to a reporter who wisely preferred to remain anonymous, half the faculty was absent more than 50 percent of the time.[55]

Public approval of the school's solid academic performance and its Christian emphasis came in 1937 when Grove City College became the largest liberal arts college in Pennsylvania with 842 full-time students, ranking behind only the state universities and two state teachers colleges. That year Thiel had an enrollment of 257, Allegheny 645, Westminster 530, and Slippery Rock 659. The Grove City faculty also rose steadily, increasing from forty-one in 1931 to fifty-three in 1939. But salaries remained modest: Dean Calderwood, who continued to teach Latin, topped the list with $4,266.62. Most professors received between $2,500 and $3,500 per annum. Weir Ketler's annual salary in 1941–1942, after nearly thirty years as president, was still only $8,499.96. J. Howard Pew supplemented that in the summer of 1944 with a $1,000 check to "help defray expenses" of Ketler's summer vacation in Canada.[56]

While religion remained at the core of Grove City College, it was barely present on many campuses in America during the 1930s. The sharp decline of the collegiate YMCAs was telling: in 1921 YMCAs reached a numerical peak with 731 campus chapters and approximately 90,000 members—one in seven of a total student population of 600,000. By 1940, just before World War II, the number of colleges and universities had climbed to 1,700 with 1.5 million students. But the number of YMCAs had dropped to 480 with an enrollment of only 50,000, about one in thirty of the college population. At Grove City, however, the YMCA and the YWCA continued to hold a favored position. By the mid-1930s, when new extracurricular activities were competing for the students' time, President Ketler reminded everyone that Wednesday evenings were "reserved" for the weekly meetings of the YMCA and the YWCA.

Certainly the board of trustees had no difficulty in answering "yes" when asked by the Board of Christian Education of the Presbyterian Church whether the college had an educational program for its students that accepted "Christianity as the highest philosophy of life."[57] The official school catalogue declared, the college was "a Christian college" at which "the study of the Bible is an integral part of the curriculum."[58]

It seemed natural enough that a forceful rebuttal of the Modernists, who dismissed most of the Bible as myth and filled with errors and contradictions, would appear on the front page of *The Collegian*. The unsigned article argued that instead of sponsoring dances, card parties, movies, and dinners to increase their membership, the churches ought to "get back to the Bible." "Give us more of the great teachings of the Word," the student writer demanded.[59]

The American college student of the day, according to liberal commentator Harold Laski, had a "hostility to politics and an aversion to public service."[60] Neither was true of the Grove City student, who formally debated a wide spectrum of subjects, ranging from the Kellogg Peace Pact and free trade to presidential powers and the National Recovery Act. In 1935 alone, Grovers participated in thirty-seven intercollegiate debates. But they were not part of the left-wing "revolt on the campus" described by socialist writer James Wechsler in his highly subjective analysis of higher education.

Wechsler called for "a more fruitful order" based on "industrial democracy," i.e., socialism. He was delighted when hundreds of Princeton students turned out on a sunny April day in 1935 to listen to socialist presidential candidate Norman Thomas and to protest against what the *Daily Princetonian* called "the black pall of war that today enshrouds the world."[61] Wechsler would not have been pleased with the more rational approach of Grove City students who, nonetheless, reflected the passive isolationism of the majority of Americans.

In November 1936, for example, on the eighteenth anniversary of Armistice Day, *The Collegian* editorialized against the "arrogant militarism and dominating imperialism" of newspaper publisher William Randolph Hearst and suggested in their place "a policy of purely defense armament" and a rejection of "jingoism."[62] The paper noted approvingly that stage, screen, and radio star Eddie Cantor had offered a $5,000, four-year scholarship to the college or university student who wrote the best letter (only five hundred words) on "How Can America Stay Out of War."[63]

Of little interest to the crusading editors was how the college, always coed, consistently favored men over women. All of the cheerleaders at athletic events were male. Invariably, the student council president was male. It was not until 1933 that a Women's Athletic Association was organized, although it quickly made its presence felt. The first state convention of the Pennsylvania Athletic Federation of College Women was held at Grove City College, which also provided the federation's first president, Barbara Snow. On the academic side, it was 1935 before the Science Club awarded its outstanding science award for the first time to a coed, Wilda Asplund.

The importance of women in the life and economy of the college was dramatically recognized in 1936 when the $300,000 Mary Anderson Pew Dormitory for women, all buff limestone and brick like the Harbison Chapel, was completed. Dedicated to the memory of J. N. Pew's wife, the Gothic-style building was a gift of the Pew family.

The male tendency to place the female student on a pedestal and keep her there was probably reinforced by such events as the annual "May Pageant Program" which featured the crowning of the May Queen, usually attended by three pages, six flower girls, and four ladies in waiting. The program also offered dances, frolics, and revels in the "same spirit of joy" that animated "wood nymphs and fauns... centuries ago."[64]

Large or small, all of the decisions regarding student life had to be approved by the administration and the faculty, unimpressed by John Dewey and other progressives. A 1933 resolution, for example, declared that any student who got married during the school year would "thereby sever his relationship to the College." All student organizations, except for fraternities and sororities, had to have their financial records audited twice a year. And while students urged the imposition of an activity fee to support student publications and other activities, no such fee was approved until the late 1950s.[65]

Dormitory life was strictly enforced: no drinking, gambling, dishonesty (theft), or hazing. There was no need to mention that on a campus where men and women slept in separate dorms, "overnights" were forbidden. The school's Christian code contributed to a general, although not total, sobriety and chastity. It helped that the college reserved the right to dismiss any student "whenever, in its judgment, such action seems advisable."[66] The possession of automobiles was limited to the few commuters. The student dress code was conservative: the men wore suits and the women skirts and sweaters to class which began promptly at 7:40 A.M. And, remembers Alice Ketler, a future daughter-in-law of President Ketler, "we had to wear long dresses for dinner."[67]

The campus, however, was not a monastery. Local and even nationally known "swing" bands played at the proms—a tuxedo could be rented for $3.50 from Reynolds Summers McCann in New Castle—and radio or record hops were held when funds were not available for live music.[68] Playing cards, especially bridge, was popular, as were the movies. Girls in the dorms were given special late hours when "a notable movie"—like Paul Muni in *The Story of Louis Pasteur*—was showing at the local theater, although "everyone must attend the first show, coming home immediately afterwards."[69] Homesick students could call home in the evening—only thirty-five cents for three minutes, courtesy of the Bell Telephone Company of Pennsylvania. If they had been studying too hard and needed a break, students could visit Isally's where sundaes or milk shakes were ten cents, hot chocolate with whipped cream, five cents. "Nobody," recalls Alice Ketler, "had a lot of money." She was happy to receive twenty-five cents an hour working as an assistant to a professor of business.[70]

There was also politics. A presidential poll in the fall of 1936 gave the Republican candidate, Kansas governor Alf Landon, a commanding 3-1 margin over incumbent President Roosevelt. A Student Republican League was formed, with Dean Calderwood as faculty adviser. When FDR trounced Landon in November, carrying forty-six out of forty-eight states, *The Collegian* began its front-page news story, "Tears for the passing of the Republican party drenched the land today." Even rock-ribbed Republican Mercer County had voted Democratic.[71]

Reaching for Higher Standards

President Ketler and Dean Calderwood worked together closely to raise Grove City's academic standards, earning the school, in the fall of 1937, a notice from the accrediting commission of the Association of American Universities that Grove City College had been placed on its accepted list. The honor rested on such improvements as new courses in the engineering and business majors; more individual student counseling; and comprehensive examinations that emphasized the acquirement of "a usable body of language." The classes were small, averaging about twenty-five. Ketler suggested to the board of trustees that the college should not try to increase its numbers "indefinitely" but be more concerned with a careful selection of students and "higher standards of achievement." His seriousness about the pursuit of academic excellence was underscored by his telling the board, in a subsequent report, that fifty students had been advised in the past year they would not be allowed to return because of unsatisfactory grades.[72]

The board responded to Ketler's leadership by approving the construction of a new administration building, Crawford Hall, made possible through gifts of trustees Harry J. Crawford and J. Howard Pew totaling $375,000. It was the fifth major building erected on the Upper Campus since 1930. The total cost of the buildings was close to $2 million, a remarkable showing for a small college of fewer than one thousand students during the Depression years. The students showed their appreciation by stealing the cornerstone of Crawford Hall when it was first laid, but returned it, somewhat abashed, in time for the construction to proceed.

The administration's success depended upon committed faculty members like the multitalented Creig Simmons Hoyt, who taught chemistry from 1913 until 1957, published widely, and served as dean of the college after Calderwood's death in 1951; tall, slender Elinor M. Caruthers, who taught German, French, and Spanish from 1908 to 1940 and led over twenty student tours to Europe; and dynamic Daniel Carroll McEuen, a member of the English department from 1920 to 1958, who also coached track, football, and debating, and directed plays.

There was also gruff, tough H. O. White, who was college registrar for forty-two years, from 1918 to 1960, and the only faculty member (he taught classical languages for several years prior to becoming registrar) to serve under Grove City College's first four presidents. Jacob P. "Jake" Hassler, an auditor in private life, was the college's bursar from 1924 to 1964. In 1930 energetic R. G. Walters was appointed director of teacher training and then put in charge of publicity for the college. Like so many other faculty members, Walters added to an already heavy burden by establishing a placement bureau for students and acting as a vocational adviser.

All of this work paid off in a very tangible way: 70 percent of the graduates were placed in "good teaching or business positions," an admirable showing when millions of Americans were still without a job and the memory of the Great Depression figured in the decisions of every business, large and small.[73]

Grove City students knew how fortunate they were to attend a college that combined so skillfully the practical, the idealistic, and the religious in its curriculum and extracurriculum. "The college students of today," commented *The Collegian*, "are thinkers and practicalists. Their philosophy is humanistic and religious from [which] they can establish a secure life."[74]

As the dark decade drew to a close, Dean Calderwood would declare with justification that Grove City College had survived and even thrived in the face of historic adversity. Its survival was due in no small measure, he insisted, to the intimate relationship between the college and the town, summed up in the slogan, "Grove City—Where Education and Industry Unite."[75]

The school and the city and the nation would have cause to unite even more closely in a short while when the German Panzer divisions swept across Western Europe and the Japanese Imperial Navy set sail for Pearl Harbor.

CHAPTER FOUR

War and Peace

It was the first truly global war. World War I had been long, brutish, and bloody, with 7.7 million men killed on both sides, but the fighting had been concentrated in Europe. World War II was fought everywhere: On the beaches and in the fields, in small towns and great cities, on land and sea and in the air, on the continents of Europe, Africa, Asia, and off the coasts of North America. And the human cost was far greater, with a terrible total of 57 million military and civilian dead. The Soviet Union suffered the most casualties—an estimated 21.3 million—but Nationalist China also paid an awful price—1.32 million dead. In America there were 295,000 military dead and almost no civilian casualties.

Even prior to Pearl Harbor, historian Samuel Eliot Morison points out, America had been preparing for the conflict—Lend-Lease and the big defense appropriations of 1940–41 added 6 million workers to the payrolls, almost eliminating unemployment. But the Japanese attack on December 7, 1941, galvanized American industry—including the Sun companies under J. Howard Pew—into "high-speed planning and production."[1]

During the war American factories and shipyards poured out a cataract of materiel and weapons: 296,000 planes, 102,000 tanks, and 88,000 ships and landing craft. A unique production miracle was the construction of the mammoth Pentagon building, with its sixteen miles of corridors and 600,000 square feet of office space, in just fourteen months.

All remaining traces of American isolationism disappeared with Pearl Harbor. Congress repealed its prohibition against sending draftees outside the Western Hemisphere and extended their period of service to six months after the war's end. All men between twenty and forty-four were declared eligible for military service, although few over thirty-eight were ever drafted. More than fifteen million Americans eventually served in the armed forces: ten million in the army, four million in the navy and Coast Guard, 600,000 in the Marine Corps. The unprecedented demand for manpower affected every American institution, including higher education which put aside great books and debates and trained tens of thousands of young men on its campuses. About 275,000 women also volunteered in the war effort as WACS in the army, WAVES in the navy, and as women marines.

World War I had been a static war, usually fought from trenches and measured in yards. World War II was a mobile war, fought from tanks and aircraft carriers and measured in miles. To fight this global war, America transformed itself into what President Roosevelt called a "great arsenal of democracy." Dozens of naval bases and hundreds of airfields were built all over the world. An infantry division of eight thousand fighting men required six thousand support personnel to keep it "fed, supplied, paid, doctored, amused, transported, and its equipment repaired."[2] Of particular importance to this enormously complicated enterprise was the Merchant Marine which shipped most of the men and materiel to Europe and the South Pacific. The largest builder of tankers throughout the war was the Sun Shipbuilding & Dry Dock Company, headed by J. Howard Pew and his younger brother, Joseph N. Pew, Jr.

As extraordinary as America's effort was, it was not the total war of Great Britain, Germany, and Japan. In America women were not drafted, food rationing was not draconian, and although gasoline and tires were restricted, hundreds of thousands of cars appeared on the roads "for purposes remotely connected with the war."[3] Taxes were increased, but profits were not limited (in fact, corporate profits in 1943 exceeded those of 1929). America was never invaded, and no bombs fell on its cities.

The war lasted longer than anyone dreamed because most of the experts underestimated the toughness and stamina of the "little, bandy-legged" Japanese, who had not, in fact, lost a war since 1598. By New Year's Day 1942 the Japanese troops had landed on Guam, Hong Kong, Borneo, Wake, and the Philippines. "Tojo," wrote historian William Manchester, "was outblitzing Hitler."[4] By mid-1942 the Japanese had occupied about one-tenth of the globe. Admiral William F. Halsey, Jr., had too quickly predicted that Japan would be crushed by 1943, for it would take another two years and the atomic bomb before the Japanese reluctantly surrendered.

Nor was it a cheap war, costing approximately $350 billion, ten times that of World War I and one-and-a-half times the national debt. The government did what it always did when it needed money—it raised taxes and borrowed. The number of people who paid income tax went from seventeen million to fifty million when the base tax rate was increased from 4 to 6 percent. The graduated tax was raised from 13 percent on the first $2,000 to 82 percent on income in excess of $200,000. The corporate tax was also sharply increased. Wages and prices were controlled under the Office of Price Administration (OPA) and later the Office of Economic Stabilization, but nonetheless they continued to rise throughout the war. Although the major unions adopted a "no-strike pledge" for the duration, nearly 15,000 strikes broke out across the country.

A great war—the only "just" war of the twentieth century—was fought and won with America's indispensable participation and logistical support. But in the process the powerful central government which had emerged during the Depression became even more powerful and more centralized. Big government, it seemed, was here to stay.

The Sweet Campus Life

But before the cry of "Tora! Tora! Tora!" filled the skies above Honolulu, life was sweet for most Americans, especially the young men and women on campus. There were classes and tests and dances at which the girls wore strapless organdy dresses. "God Bless America" was number three on the Lucky Strike Hit Parade, but the younger generation preferred Benny Goodman, Tommy Dorsey, and Count Basie, agreeing with them that "It Don't Mean a Thing If You Ain't Got That Swing." Sometimes the swinging got out of control, and the older generation put its foot down.

When British philosopher Lord Bertrand Russell agreed in 1940 to become a professor at the City College of New York (CCNY) and chairman of its philosophy department, the college celebrated, but the Rt. Reverend William T. Manning, Episcopal bishop of New York, declared that his lordship was a dirty old man who had, among other reprehensible things, defended adultery. Russell's appointment wound up in court when the mother of a CCNY student filed a taxpayer's suit against hiring him. New York Supreme Court Judge John E. McGeehan declared, in a searing seventeen-page decision, that in making the appointment the New York Board of Higher Education had established a "Chair of Indecency" at CCNY.[5] When the judge revoked the college's decision, Russell quickly transferred to Harvard which offered him a full professorship.

Needless to say, Grove City College did not make a counter offer. Rather, as the war clouds moved ever closer, President Ketler and the board of trustees focused on how their small but precious institution could best survive another world conflict.

"A Great Responsibility"

In the fall of 1939, in its sixty-third year, the school had never seemed more attractive to young men and women in search of a good liberal arts education offered at a fair price in a Christian atmosphere. Nearly three hundred freshmen were admitted, forty-six percent of them in the top fifth of their high school class. Inspired by the rising number of students—the total of 922 was the largest in school history—the board approved plans for an addition to the Mary Anderson Pew dormitory, a new dormitory for men, and a dining room addition to the Ketler dormitory. Extracurriculars thrived: Grove City had six fraternities, eleven sororities, four literary clubs, three religious groups, a dozen academic clubs and honoraries, seven varsity and twelve intramural sports for men, and a like number of intramurals for women. But all the classes and clubs and games could not change the reality of the rapidly approaching conflagration.

When France fell in the summer of 1940 and America stepped up its lend-lease to Great Britain—locked in a deadly air battle with Nazi Germany—some Grove City students became openly apprehensive about the war and America's possible entry. President Ketler responded by reminding everyone what was at stake. Emulating the patriotic spirit of his father before World War I, Weir Ketler told the faculty at their fall meeting, "We have a great responsibility to our nation." Whatever the debates and the divisions of the past, he argued, it was now time to develop "a more positive position" in favor of U.S. preparedness.[6]

The college's preparations were at first rather haphazard. As early as the fall of 1939, Grove City was authorized by the Civil Aeronautics Authority to start a civilian pilot training program. But the number of students interested was so small that the program did not begin operations until the fall of 1940. Shortly thereafter Grove City became one of six schools in the region to begin teaching an engineering defense-training program that became, after the war started, the Engineering, Science, Management Defense War Training Program.

When the extension of Selective Service was approved in August 1941 and the first Grover was drafted into the army that fall, some students were shocked. One coed remarked resentfully, "Can't we just give [the Japanese] those old islands, and then they'd be happy, and none of our boys would be killed?" ' A male student was equally blunt, saying, "A college career is too important to give up for the army when the army has more men than it needs now."[7]

But the army didn't have nearly enough men to fight a global war, and *The Collegian* spoke for the majority of students when it editorialized, "Everyone, both old and young, will have to make sacrifices if democracy is to survive over goose-stepping tyranny."[8]

In June 1941 Grove City College celebrated its sixty-fifth anniversary and Weir Ketler marked his twenty-fifth year as its president. The Ketler achievements were impressive: Student enrollment had tripled, from about 300 to 934. The campus had expanded dramatically, from ten buildings on forty acres of land to sixteen buildings on nearly one hundred acres on the Upper and Lower campuses. The school still had only a small endowment, but its debt was even smaller, and it operated in the black from year to year. Grove City was known, respected, and selected by students and parents throughout the region. The board of trustees commended President Ketler and gave him a three months' vacation with pay.

Less than ninety days after his return to campus, America was at war. Addressing the entire college in chapel, Dr. Ketler urged that everyone "show a spirit of unity, of loyalty to the government and its leaders, courage in facing the difficult problems that lie ahead and a willingness to make the sacrifices that the situation requires." At its mid-December 1941 meeting the board of trustees backed him up, unanimously passing a resolution authorizing Grove City College "to participate actively and wholeheartedly in the support of the Government in the war effort."[9] And so it did. Recruitment officers from the army, navy, and marines frequently visited the school. President Ketler reported to the board in June 1942 that Grove City graduates were "in the first contingent" that landed in the Solomon Islands. Former students were soon stationed at bases in New Zealand, Australia, New Guinea, India, China, Egypt, North Africa, England, and Iceland.[10]

They were caught up in a war marked, as every war is, by the heroic and the banal, by the inspiring and the bizarre. In the South Pacific twenty-five marines were killed during the Battle of Cape Gloucester by huge falling trees. In Europe, American GIs did not shave or get their hair cut while in combat, wrote historian William Manchester, not because they wanted to become flower children, but because they lacked "razors, shaving cream, mirrors, hot water, and time."[11]

Some shipwrecked sailors survived, like Grove City's Harold Reagle who spent thirty-nine days in a small open lifeboat. His tanker had been torpedoed by a German submarine twelve days out of Cape Town, South Africa. He and eight other merchant mariners drifted in a damaged boat for 1,600 miles before coming ashore at French Guiana. Fortunately it rained thirty-two of the thirty-nine days they were at sea, and they managed to catch the rainwater in three small pieces of canvas. Reagle, who lost forty pounds during the month-and-a-half-long ordeal, would always remember his Christmas 1942 dinner: "2 ounces of water, one-half a graham cracker, and one-half ounce of chocolate."[12]

Meanwhile, at Grove City College, a faculty defense committee, in cooperation with a similar student committee, studied how to evacuate buildings in case of air raids, and also blackout procedures. Faculty members were active throughout the community, serving on the Mercer County selective service board, as observers for the Army Air Corps and as air raid wardens, serving on the county tire rationing board, and helping to run Red Cross drives.[13]

The war effort on campus began in earnest in March 1942 with the startup of a naval training school to train radio operators and technicians. Units of one hundred men were instructed in mathematics, physics, electricity, mechanical drawing, radio, and communications by a full-time staff of fourteen instructors. To accommodate them, all male students were evacuated from Memorial Hall, which was converted into a barracks with double bunk beds and other necessary military equipment. Several regular faculty members taught full- or part-time in the program. During the naval school's first six months some 1,800 men and women received instruction.

The college's commitment to the program was clearly patriotic but also pragmatic. As President Ketler admitted to the board of trustees, "It is our hope that... in the long run it will have a stabilizing effect" on the school.[14] And indeed life on campus remained relatively normal for both the students and the military visitors until the fall of 1942. The men-in-training took full and frequent advantage of what one observer called the "warm feelings" of Grove City for "the uniformed men in their midst."[15] And the Bible School met for its forty-sixth annual session in the summer of that year.

But college as usual stopped abruptly in November 1942 when the Selective Service lowered the draft age to eighteen. The following March the army placed an air corps school for preflight training at Grove City College. The program was smaller than that of the navy and more general in its curriculum, including more classes in the social sciences, English, and the sciences. But the trainees were provided with intensive instruction in navigation, Morse code, military tactics, and procedures in flying. By the time the air corps program ended in the spring of 1944, it had trained nearly one thousand pilots, navigators, and bombardiers.[16]

As an increasing number of male students were drafted in the spring of 1943, the faculty voted to give degrees to seniors called to active duty during their final semester. The yearbook listed over three hundred Grovers on an alumni honor roll, and The Collegian printed a "From the Front" column in each issue. The Pan Hellenic Council held bond drives, and the Interfraternity Council stopped holding formal dances and spring parties in order to save gasoline. Varsity football and basketball were cancelled, although athletic director Robert Thorn attempted to maintain golf, track, tennis, and soccer. Inflation persisted, and the school reluctantly increased tuition from $85 to $100 a semester.

Its experience was replicated across the country. Washington, D.C., set up specialized army and navy training programs at hundreds of educational institutions. By 1945, education historian John S. Brubacher estimated military programs accounted for as much as 50 percent of the income of some men's colleges.[17]

In May 1943 Grove City College was honored when Senator
Robert A. Taft, a once and future presidential candidate, delivered
the commencement address. After stating candidly that he had
been opposed to America's entering the war, Taft declared that
Americans now had no choice but "to carry this war through to
overwhelming victory over Germany, Italy, and Japan. Otherwise
the world won't be worth living in."[18]

The Ohio senator devoted the bulk of his talk to the task of
keeping peace after victory had been achieved. He rejected the
notion that an all-powerful America could dominate the world
strategically as Britain had during the nineteenth century, as well
as the suggestion that it could control nations "through the dis-
pensation of money and goods... in all directions, largely on
credit." In his opinion, Taft stated, "international cooperation
must be worked out along the same general lines suggested in
the League of Nations," which, he emphasized, he had favored
after World War I.[19] Any such plan, the senator insisted, "must be
based on the retention of sovereignty by every nation" and through
general covenants and bilateral treaties. The maintenance of peace,
Taft went on, should rest primarily, not on an international police
force, but on the desire of sovereign nations to carry out "the
covenants into which they have solemnly entered." But if aggression
should occur, said the man so often and erroneously described as
an isolationist, "we should be willing to take an active part in maintaining peace," and he referred specifically to the use of "our armed
forces." If these legal conditions, and certain economic ones, were
met, Senator Taft concluded, "I have no doubt that the American
people would approve a treaty obligation binding us to cooperate
with other nations to keep the peace of the world."[20]

The senator's commonsense approach to international
relations and his confident assertion that "it is only a question

of time... before our armies march to Berlin and Tokyo" received warm applause.[21]

But in the meantime, the total number of civilian students at Grove City College that fall was a mere 481. Only eighty-nine were men, prompting President Ketler to admit ruefully that it was "the fewest boys in College in 25 years." But ever the optimist, he insisted, "it seems that we have touched the bottom and are on the way up."[22]

Turning Points

The same could be said of the mammoth global conflict being fought on two widely separated fronts. In July 1943 Sicily was invaded by American and British forces led by the American with the pearl-handled revolvers, Lieutenant General George S. Patton, Jr., and the Englishman with the swagger stick, Field Marshal Bernard Montgomery. One month later the Germans and the Italians gave up their defense of the island, and a bewildered Mussolini was forced to resign. Early that same year, after months of intense fighting on Guadalcanal, the Japanese surrendered the island to American forces. One of those who fought at Guadalcanal was Marine 1st Lieutenant George Ketler, the son of President Weir Ketler.

In a letter home Lieutenant Ketler referred to the many dead Japanese "scattered about," as well as the "badly shattered" buildings everywhere on the island. But when he stopped at a heavily damaged Catholic mission, he discovered a large and untouched statue of the Virgin Mary standing in the middle of the ruined chapel. "It struck me," reflected the young marine, "that no matter how hard a despot tries to destroy religion, something always survives... and it blossoms forth stronger than ever."[23]

After Guadalcanal the United States, under General Douglas MacArthur, followed a strategy in the Pacific of leap-frogging

the most heavily defended islands and attacking more isolated
and vulnerable targets. But for all the ships and planes and tanks
and landing craft, in both the Pacific and Europe, the bulk of the
fighting was done by the American infantryman, who was the
most heavily laden foot soldier in the history of warfare, carrying an average 84.3 pounds each day. He wore or carried an
M-1 rifle, a steel chamberpot helmet and helmet liner, a knife, a
canteen, an entrenching tool (a combination pick and shovel), a
bayonet, a first-aid pouch, a web belt with cartridge magazines
in each pocket, two bandoliers of extra ammunition, hand
grenades, plus a poncho, mess kit, cigarettes, a Zippo lighter, letters from home, and assorted rations such as canned ham and
eggs from H. J. Heinz Company. He also carried part of his outfit's
communal weapons—a Browning automatic rifle, a Browning
light or heavy machine gun, or a 60- or 81-millimeter mortar.
He may have resembled a beast of burden, but he was in fact a
modern warrior.[24] He and the other Allied soldiers were winning
the war.

In the spring of 1944—even before the historic invasion of
Normandy in June—President Ketler felt encouraged enough by
the progress of the war to ask the faculty to undertake a review
of the curriculum and to suggest changes for the postwar period.
In his December report to the board of trustees, he stressed the
challenges the college would face when "a considerable number of
young men now in the armed forces will return to college."[25]
Already, about a dozen male students on campus had seen service, and several men who had been honorably discharged were
hoping to enter Grove City in the second semester.

The Great Invasion
No invasion force had crossed the English Channel for two-and-
a-half centuries until June 6, 1944, when an allied armada of

600 warships and 4,000 supporting craft began landing 176,000 men on the German-held shores of Normandy. The coastal defenses of the Nazis were formidable and well entrenched, but after six weeks of intense and costly fighting, the Battle of Normandy was over. High-ranking members of the German high command were convinced of imminent defeat and attempted to assassinate Hitler. The attempt failed and the Fuehrer continued the war, placing his trust in secret weapons like the V-1 and V-2 rockets.

But the outcome was sure. The normally unflappable J. Howard Pew shared his jubilation with Weir Ketler, describing the Normandy victory as "phenomenal." He had personal reasons to be proud of the navy's role—many of the supporting craft had been built by the Sun Shipbuilding and Dry Dock Company. The ships, he pointed out, "literally blasted out the most complicated and comprehensive barriers that had been erected to prevent landings, as well as destroyed thousands of mines that had been planted along the beach."[26]

The war in Europe ended on May 7, 1945, three weeks after President Roosevelt died of a cerebral hemorrhage while drafting a Jefferson Day address and one week after Adolph Hitler died a coward's death, committing suicide in his Berlin bunker. In September 1944 the American chiefs of staff had estimated that it would take eighteen months after the surrender of Germany to defeat Japan. In fact, the war in the Pacific ended with a nuclear bang—actually two of them—three months after V-E Day.

Many Americans have expressed deep and abiding regret about exploding the atomic bombs. But as historian Samuel Eliot Morison wrote, "It is difficult to see how the Pacific war could otherwise have been concluded, except by a long and bitter invasion of Japan."[27] And since Russia would have been a partner in such a campaign, the result would probably have been a divided

Japan, as happened to Germany. When President Truman was informed that using the bombs might save as many as one million American lives (and even more Japanese lives) and that Japan adamantly refused to surrender, he gave the order to proceed. "I... never had any doubt that [they] should be used," Truman wrote in his memoirs.[28]

As Grove City College prepared for the 1945–46 academic year, President Ketler could look back with satisfaction on the school's contributions to the winning of the war, particularly the air corps training program and the naval training school, which graduated a total of 3,759 sailors and marines in its forty-nine classes. The financial advantage to the college was a modest four percent charge for the use of its facilities. Although there is no official accounting of those who served in World War II, the alumni newspaper listed 499 Grovers who were on active duty and sixteen who died in action. In May 1945, *The Collegian* estimated that twenty-nine had been killed in action or died in service, seven were missing in action, and five were POWs.[29] In recognition of the college's efforts, the government launched in the late spring of 1945 the *SS Grove City Victory*, a 10,800-ton cargo ship.

Those who had been trained at Grove City were openly grateful. W. W. Altman, a member of the first class of the naval training school in 1942, served as chief radio technician on the *USS Renshaw*, which saw action in the Solomon Islands, Bougainville, Saipan, Guam, Leyte, and Luzon, once sinking a Japanese submarine. "In behalf of all the men of Class 1," Altman wrote the student newspaper, "we say—'Thank you.' We also send our best to Comdr. Grogan, wherever he is... one of the best 'skippers' we have ever had."[30]

The war had forced the college to make many, often major, adjustments in its curriculum and its student body (even allowing the women to wear slacks and shorts on campus and to smoke in the dorms). The peace would now bring an array of different and more subtle challenges.

A Feeling of Hope

A year before the war ended Congress passed the GI Bill of Rights (officially the Servicemen's Readjustment Act of 1944) which, among other benefits, provided full scholarships for four years at an approved institution of higher learning. The bill was a significant advance in federal support of higher education. Unlike the land-grant concept, there was no limit to the kinds of institutions that could participate—private as well as public colleges and universities were eligible for indirect aid through their students. Some 2.2 million men and women eventually took advantage of the multibillion-dollar offer. They had won a war and now they wanted to enjoy the peace. You didn't have to be a rocket scientist to see that a college education usually meant a better job, more income, and the ability to buy that house with a white picket fence sooner rather than later.

The GI Bill was quintessentially American—big, bold, and not overly concerned about long-range consequences. For the first time in American history, the program offered, and the people accepted, direct government funding of a student's attendance at a college or a university. One historian called the G.I. Bill "the most important educational and social transformation in American history."[31] Other federal programs and more money for higher education would soon follow, and the wall between government and higher education would slowly disintegrate.

Taken together, the G.I. Bill of 1944 and Public Law 550 of 1952, which similarly aided the veterans of the Korean War, "represented the largest scholarship grant ever made in the history of American higher education."[32] Another new kind of government support for colleges and universities was housing, supplies, and equipment. Shortly after the end of World War II, Washington, D.C., donated surplus military supplies and buildings (often Quonset huts) to those colleges struggling to accommodate newly arrived veterans. This assistance was formalized in 1950 with a congressional authorization of $300 million in long-term loans to colleges, private and public, for the construction of dormitories.[33] Grove City College did not apply.

The first four decades of the twentieth century saw little federally funded research in academia, but World War II produced a dramatic increase in campus budgets and projects. Following the war, federal scientist Vannevar Bush argued (in his seminal report *Science: The Endless Frontier*) that federal subsidies for peacetime research were also vital to the nation. By 1949 the Department of Defense and the Atomic Energy Commission accounted for 96 percent of all federal money spent on campus research. Between 1951 and 1953, during the Korean War, university research and development more than doubled, from $1.3 billion to $3.1 billion. In the 1960s, under the impetus of the Vietnam War, the governmental role became so entrenched that federal spending in this area soared to $15 billion a year.[34]

Wave after wave of students flowed into higher education for the next forty years. Just two years after the end of World War II, 2.3 million students were enrolled in some 1,800 four-year and two-year institutions (four times the number in prewar 1940). In 1946, 57 percent of full-time college students were veterans. Grove City College happily joined the parade: that year, the overall percentage of veterans at the college was 51 percent; in the spring semester, 240 out of 300 men were veterans.

College enrollment continued to rise during the 1950s and 1960s reaching 8.5 million students in 1970. Ten years later, the grand total was twelve million—7.5 million in four-year schools and another 4.5 million in two-year colleges. Out of an estimated 12.6 million students in higher education in 1990, 10.5 million were in public institutions, with about three million in private colleges.

Grove City College benefited handsomely from the soaring public interest in higher education that was stimulated by the federal subsidies. Male enrollment at the college, for example, jumped from just seventy-three in 1944–1945 to 334 in 1945–1946 and 864 in 1946–1947. Even the summer school blossomed with the number of males rising sharply from fifty in 1944 to 304 in 1946. Registrar Harold O. White praised the ex-servicemen's "serious attitude and desire to get the most out of their college work." But Dean Hoyt wished wryly that "it could be impressed upon the new students that study does not ruin one's social standing."[35] In another twist from prewar days, many of the veterans were married and had children. Living off campus in apartments or trailers, they did not "readily submit to college rules and regulations" which they considered "juvenile and degrading." Moreover, they often held jobs which limited their participation in the usual extracurricular activities. It is not an exaggeration to say, as professor Hans Sennholz does, that the veterans were almost "unknown" to their fellow students.[36]

Even with many veterans living off campus, housing remained a pressing problem for President Ketler and the board of trustees. Plans were thus approved for an addition to the Mary Anderson Pew dormitory, enabling the school to house 340 women on campus. When Ketler reported to the board, with some trepidation, that the addition would cost $152,000, J. Howard Pew told Ketler to "go ahead." He would work out "where the money is coming from... shortly." It was yet another of the many generous pledges the Pews had been making to Grove City College for over fifty years. As the family had been doing for decades, J. Howard Pew instructed Ketler to say nothing to anybody "about who is going to give you this money."[37]

There were now so many students that neither the chapel nor Crawford Hall could seat all of them. To accommodate the students' increasing needs, the trustees began considering the construction of a new men's dormitory, a new women's dormitory, a library, an engineering building, and an athletic and recreation building—the last strongly supported by the alumni—at an estimated cost of nearly $3 million.

An alumnus on active duty in Germany in the late spring of 1945 had even sent a money order as a contribution "to my pet project—the Student Union Building Fund. Perhaps I shall be entitled," he wrote President Ketler, "to sit in a chair in the Alumni Room and tell stories of how we 'won the war.'. . . I believe that all the alumni will agree that such a building will be one of the nicest things to which to look forward at that first homecoming after the war is over."[38]

It was not until 1949, however, that the trustees approved a $3 million fund-raising campaign with the Pew Memorial Fund, pledging $1.5 million if the college would match the amount. It did, and ground was broken in February for the two dormitories which would accommodate as many as 1,500 students. Grove City College had come a long way since 1876, when the first class of thirteen students of the Pine Grove Normal Academy had gathered in the upper room of a new school hall.

Neither the trustees nor the president would be pushed into any precipitious action. The faculty was cautiously expanded from forty-seven to sixty-two by the end of the decade and given a 10 percent salary increase along the way. Dr. Ketler's proposal for a retirement and hospitalization plan for the faculty was rejected. Tuition rose in 1949 to $250 a year with room and board expenses varying from $225 to $265 a semester. And after years of discussion, four women finally joined the board of trustees that same year: J. Howard Pew's sister, Mary Ethel Pew; H. J. Crawford's sister, Mrs. George Breene; Judge Sara Mathilde Soffel of the common pleas court of Allegheny County; and Mrs. Horace Baker.

There were also changes in administration. Following E. B. Harshaw's death, bursar J. P. Hassler took on the additional job of college treasurer. When Dr. Addison Leitch resigned as dean of men in 1945, athletic director Robert Thorn took his place. The most significant change came in 1949 when Alva John Calderwood, who had served Grove City for fifty-three years as teacher of Latin, mathematics, English, philosophy, the Bible, education, Greek, and history, and for thirty-four years as dean of the college, died at the age of seventy-six. He was, recalls a granddaughter, "a tall raw-boned man with a thatch of wavy hair, a large nose, big ears, thin neck, and smiling eyes." His remarkable memory enabled him to greet graduates years later with a cheery, "Well, hello, Joe! It's really good to see you again! How's your cousin Millie who was so sick during the flu epidemic?"[39] For the better part of three decades, according to one observer, Calderwood was "the balance wheel" between President Ketler with his strong board of trustees and the faculty on one side and the students and the community on the other.[40] Dr. Creig S. Hoyt, chairman of the chemistry department, succeeded Calderwood as dean of the college.

It was in these postwar years that Grove City College began to diverge more sharply from public and other private institutions regarding income and operations. State-supported schools now received as much as three-fourths of their income from nonstudent sources—most of it from the government. Private schools depended on an endowment or gifts for about 50 percent of their income. But Grove City, at the direction of its board of trustees and particularly board president J. Howard Pew, persisted in operating on what it received in student tuition and fees. Although the college did accept a large number of students under the GI Bill after the war, the number of veterans on campus had dipped sharply by the early and mid-1950s. Unlike many other schools, Grove City College did not turn to the government to make up the income difference but continued its practice of spending only what it received each year from its students.

Such a tuition-driven policy necessitated a no-frills administration and a heavy teaching load for the faculty, but it assured Grove City College an independence from government that fewer and fewer schools would enjoy in the years ahead. "I know I will be called a 'reactionary,'" J. Howard Pew told Grove City alumni in 1948, "for expressing my violent opposition" to federal aid for schools, "but I can see that this but marks the beginning of dictated governmental control.... Little by little this control will expand until, like a blighting cancer, it will infect our whole educational system."[41]

In 1949, on the eve of the development fund drive to raise $3 million and in his thirty-second year as president, Weir Ketler waxed philosophical about the role of the modern college. Stating that the cathedrals were the great achievements of the Middle Ages, Ketler suggested that "the cathedrals of today are the educational institutions.... To me a college is a magnificent expression of the idealism of America."[42] But that idealism was being compromised in many academic cathedrals.

The Government Cometh

When enrollment plummeted during the war, wrote historian Christopher Lucas, many colleges became "almost entirely dependent" upon government subsidies for their very survival.[43] And when student enrollment soared in the postwar years, many colleges could not kick the habit and remained dependent on government money received through a variety of programs. First, there were the more than two million students who took advantage of the GI Bill. Then there were the hundreds of millions of dollars for government research. By 1947 the federal government's overall investment in higher education had reached $2.4 billion—one-half of the income of all American colleges and universities that year. To put it simply, the government had become the "largest single source of support" for higher education.[44]

An influential document of the time was the final report, in February 1948, of a presidential commission on higher education, *Higher Education for American Democracy*. The report, prepared for President Truman, declared without reservation that every American should be "enabled and encouraged to carry his education, formal and informal, as far as his native capacities permit."[45] The primary enabler would be the government. Free public education should be extended to include two years of study beyond high school. Every state should establish a system of "community colleges." A federal program of college scholarships should be established, with at least 20 percent of them going to nonveterans. Federal aid should be provided to the states for the current operations of public colleges and universities. And a generous program of federal grants should be launched to cover the capital outlay (i.e., the physical plant) of such public institutions. The commissioners concluded that private colleges, then enrolling less than half of the college population, were no longer the most important form of higher education in America—the future lay with the public colleges and universities. *Life* magazine declared in a full-page editorial that access to college should be "a civic birthright."[46]

Although visions of federal dollars danced in the heads of many, other educators asked such questions as: "Were there really that many young people of college age competent to pursue a higher education?" "Would higher education for such large numbers lead to the elevation of national standards or to the reduction of all higher learning to a general level of mediocrity?" "What would be the place in this program of the private institution, the denominational institution...?" And finally: "Would extensive federal aid be followed by tight federal control?"[47]

This last question was what bothered the farsighted the most, but it was brushed aside by university presidents and trustees anxious to keep their schools well filled. Thus, when the impact of the original GI Bill and the Korean GI Bill faded, demands increased for implementation "of at least some aspects of the Commission's ambitious plan."[48] Cast aside was the unanimous conclusion of a commission of the liberal American Association of Lobbies: "We as a nation should call a halt at this time to the introduction of new programs of direct federal aid to colleges and universities."[49]

The Cold War's Impact

Higher education in America was also profoundly affected by the Cold War, which began almost as soon as the hot war ended. The United States rapidly demobilized—defense spending plummeted from $81.6 billion in fiscal 1945 to $13.1 billion in 1947—but the Soviet Union maintained its many armed divisions along the borders of Eastern and Central Europe. Moscow combined the threat of invasion from without, and the practice of subversion from within, to install communist governments throughout the region. Speaking at Westminster College in Fulton, Missouri, in March 1946, Winston Churchill bluntly and famously declared,

"From Stettin in the Baltic to Trieste in the Adriatic, an Iron Curtain has descended across the continent."[50]

In America communists and their sympathizers were hard at work. They tried to take over the unions in Hollywood but were repulsed by patriotic stagehands, writers, and actors, including the president of the Screen Actors Guild, Ronald Reagan. Communists campaigned openly in 1948 for "progressive" candidate Henry Wallace, who blandly commented, "If [communists] want to support me, I can't stop them."[51]

With the two trials of former State Department official Alger Hiss (tried and convicted for perjury rather than espionage because of the statute of limitations) and Moscow's continuing drive to dominate Eastern Europe, most Americans concluded that communism was a clear and present danger. In a March 1946 Gallup Poll, 60 percent responded that the United States was "too soft" in its relations with Moscow. Even civil libertarians offered little criticism when a group of prominent college presidents, led by James B. Conant of Harvard and Dwight D. Eisenhower of Columbia University, declared that communists should be excluded from employment as teachers.[52] Grove City College did not require any such guidance: the chances of the college hiring a communist teacher were as remote as that of J. Howard Pew leaving the Presbyterian church.

The Cold War significantly affected every major aspect of American higher education, including research, enrollment, and infrastructure. It was a rare university or college that could respond to the tense East-West conflict and yet retain its essential independence. Grove City College did so by the simple expedient of eschewing the educational dole. Most colleges, however, happily accepted what had once been called the king's shilling. Federal support of higher education jumped dramatically in the late 1950s

with the launching of the Soviet satellite Sputnik, which panicked
the nation, and the subsequent passage of the National Defense
Education Act (NDEA), designed to help America catch up to the
Soviet Union in science and engineering. The National Defense
Student Loans (later called National Direct Student Loans and
then Perkins Loans) were supposed to be temporary, but they were
"the first really broad national program of student aid enacted in
our history."[53] Unlike the GI Bill, which limited its aid to veterans, the NDEA offered federal monies to everyone.

The NDEA was followed in 1962 with the allocation of
$2 billion for the construction of student residence halls and
other facilities. The following year the Higher Education Facilities
Act expanded the support to build new classrooms, laboratories,
and libraries. Annual federal spending for university research
reached $750 million and kept on climbing.

While the millions and then the billions poured forth, a few
skeptics dared ask whether the federal largesse was an unalloyed
benefit. They noted that the new buildings paid for by the government had to be operated and maintained: where was that
money coming from? They wondered whether federal aid would
be followed by federal dictation or direction, with a consequent
loss of autonomy. If not, it would be the first time in human history that he who paid the piper did not call the tune. Years later,
in an editorial about the propriety of corporate-academic ties, the
New York Times commented: "Oscar Wilde could resist everything
except temptation. University presidents, it seems, can resist
everything except money."[54] The same could be said, more appro-
priately, about government-academic ties.

A few schools like Grove City College saw the inherent danger in government generosity and firmly said, "No, thank you."
Some schools acknowledged the addictive nature of federal aid
but could no more resist the proffered subsidy than an alcoholic

can pass up a vodka martini, shaken, stirred, or straight. President Charles F. Phillips of Bates College in Maine insisted that a private college "can make its greatest contribution to a free society if it does not become dependent on government for its financial support." But, he conceded sadly, "the majority of the presidents of our private colleges" do not agree—they have "bowed" to the "increased participation of the federal government."[55]

They did so even when several of their most distinguished peers—the presidents of Johns Hopkins University, Union College, the California Institute of Technology, the University of Missouri, Stanford University, Brown University, and the former president of Columbia University—jointly warned in 1952 that "it would be fatal were federal support to be substantially extended... [for] the freedom of higher education would be lost."[56] More typical were the bland reassurances of Harvard president Nathan M. Pusey a decade later that the independence of private universities was "virtually untouched by this very large flow of Federal money."[57] Such statements eased the conscience and allowed the money to flow full force.

Sometimes the discussion regarding the roles of the state and the school turned surreal. Public colleges and universities accepted government funding and then argued that their "internal" affairs should be managed by them and not by any outside agency. Some legislators and academic administrators, Christopher Lucas writes, were more realistic and collaborated to create giant multicampus institutions run by central governing boards. The rationale was that such a board, answerable to the governor and the legislature, would eliminate waste, prevent duplication of programs, and discourage academic "empire-building."[58]

But centralized governance did not produce the predicted results. Rather, it became the vehicle for academic "pork barrel" politics as academics and legislators worked hand in hand to advance

their mutual interests, which often turned out to be the creation of
what Russell Kirk called "Behemoth University." Control did vary
from state to state: Pennsylvania developed a two-tiered system
under which major state-supported schools like Pitt and Penn State
were allowed in the main to set their own policies. But inevitably
most state governing boards and legislatures set out to exercise
greater control, until by the 1990s, faculty members and administrators were forced to draw up strategic plans, mission statements,
and detailed operational analyses mandated under state law.

Public institutions were subjected to "a level and intensity of
state surveillance and supervision unlike anything" previously
experienced.[59] Their situation, as unpleasant as it was, should
really have come as no great surprise to anyone: government, like
kudzu, does one thing best—it keeps growing.

First Principles
Whether in peace or war, good times or bad, Grove City College
remained true to its mission, especially to ensuring a Christian
atmosphere for its students—who took full advantage of that
atmosphere. In the late 1940s and early 1950s, chapel was held
five mornings a week, Tuesday through Saturday, with Sunday
chapel in the evening. Denominational groups were encouraged,
resulting in the Canterbury Club (for Episcopalians), the
Wesleyan Fellowship (for Methodists), the Westminster College
Fellowship (for Presbyterians), and the Newman Club (formed by
Catholics in 1946). According to a 1949 report by President Ketler
to the board of trustees, "about half of the students [are] registered as Presbyterians." Only fifty out of more than 1,400 students
were not church members.[60]

Accordingly, no one thought it remarkable that women were
required to wear skirts when eating in the dining rooms, except
for Saturday and Sunday breakfast. For formal dances and din-

ners, according to Hans Sennholz, they wore full-length ruffled gowns and ballet slippers. Freshmen women had to be in their dormitory by 8:30 P.M.; in the spring, curfew was extended to 9 P.M. For upper-class women the hours were 10 and 11 P.M. All women, regardless of their class or age, needed written permission from their parents to leave school overnight. There were no campus-wide demonstrations against these regulations, which were, in fact, not much different from those at most private colleges during the 1950s.

What was different about Grove City students, most of whom were not studying for the ministry, was a commitment to practicing their faith. Continuing a college tradition, the interdenominational Christian Service League organized a missionary group, held retreats, sponsored Gospel Teams that held services in local churches, and taught Sunday school at the Pennsylvania George Junior Republic, a local school for underprivileged children. A Council of Religious Organizations was formed to coordinate the work of the league as well as the YMCA and the YWCA.

Seeking to promote patriotism as it had in the past, in 1951 the school established an Air Force Reserve Officers Training Corps that graduated its first twenty-five commissions in June 1954. Like his father before him, Weir Ketler was convinced that the military program was "insurance in time of peace" and a necessary "defense in war."[61]

It was a prudent act given the aggressive actions of the Soviet Union. Although revisionist historians try to justify it, throughout the late 1940s puppet communist governments were thrust upon the people of Poland, Bulgaria, Rumania, and Czechoslovakia. And the Soviets supported communist guerrillas in Greece, backed communist strikes and political agitation in France and Italy, and instituted the Berlin blockade.

Deliberate and unremitting Soviet expansionism had a strong impact on American politics and led to the election of Republican Dwight D. Eisenhower as president and a Republican Congress in 1952. Although often described as a moderate or "modern" Republican, candidate Eisenhower enthusiastically embraced the GOP's official 1952 campaign slogan—"Korea, Communism, Corruption"—and took full advantage of the public's strong anticommunist mood. At one campaign stop, for example, he asserted that a national tolerance of communism had "poisoned two whole decades of our national life" and had insinuated itself into American schools, public forums, news channels, labor unions, "and—most terrifyingly—into our government itself." Sounding more than a little like the controversial Senator Joseph R. McCarthy of Wisconsin, Eisenhower attributed the fall of China and the "surrender of whole nations" in Eastern Europe to communists in Washington, D.C.[62]

In the tense atmosphere of the Cold War and in response to the widespread public concerns about domestic communism, J. Howard Pew ordered a study of subversive activities in the colleges and churches. The study revealed that "fifty of the largest universities in the country were teaching economics" with "subversive" textbooks. Pew remarked that the country was in more danger now than "at any other time" in its history.[63] He made certain that the economics department at Grove City College had the right textbooks and teachers, including the economist Hans Sennholz, who would attract students interested in the free market for the next thirty years.

The legislatures of some thirty-three states agreed with Pew, passing laws that permitted the ouster of disloyal teachers. In twenty-six states teachers were required to sign a loyalty oath, pledging to support the state and federal constitutions and "to discharge faithfully the duties of a teacher."[64] Even so ardent an advocate of civil liberties as Norman Thomas, the leading American socialist, asserted that "the right of the Communist to teach should be denied because he has given away his freedom in the quest for truth."[65] "At a time when Stalin was still dictator of the Soviet Union," wrote education historian Diane Ravitch, and "reports of his regime's brutality were fresh, there was no more sympathy for the right of a Communist to teach than there was for the right of a Nazi to teach."[66]

Grove City at Seventy-Five

As Grove City College prepared for its seventy-fifth anniversary in 1951, President Ketler took stock of the school's resources. He believed that Grove City would function best with an enrollment of no more than 1,300 students; J. Howard Pew favored additional students if the ensuing additional income would help balance the budget. The curriculum seemed to be in need of only minimal changes: a sociology major was added in 1954. Dr. Ketler reported to the faculty that the school would be evaluated by the Middle States Association during the 1955–1956 academic year. It was the first in-depth evaluation of Grove City College since the 1920s and would create an unanticipated academic crisis.

Meanwhile, the Alumni Council began taking its responsibilities more seriously; it created an annual-giving fund in 1951–1952 (raising a modest $15,619.27) and began to keep official records of its meetings. On the occasion of the school's seventy-fifth commencement, President Ketler reported that more than 6,500 men and women had graduated from Grove City College.

It was clear that the faculty was aging and needed fresh blood and brains. But when Dr. Ketler asked the board of trustees for a retirement program so that replacements could be hired, the board balked. It was not until 1955 that a retirement fund for the faculty, administration, dormitory and maintenance staffs was established—with a personal gift of $50,000 from J. Howard Pew, who also donated stock valued at $61,000. Several outstanding scholars nevertheless joined the faculty, including professor of philosophy and religion Peter Monsma, who had studied with the famed philosopher and theologian Karl Barth in Germany, and who regularly invited students to his home for a "hymn-sing;" and William W. Swezey, with a doctorate of science from Johns Hopkins University, who taught biology and then became dean of the college, succeeding Creig Hoyt in the spring of 1957.

Then there was the remarkable quartet of teachers, all hired by President Ketler in 1956, who would have "a lasting and profound effect" on Grove City for the next several decades— economist Hans Sennholz, coach and, later, athletic director Jack Behringer, Robert H. Sisler who taught theater arts, and Fred Kring who would serve as assistant dean of men, dean of men, and finally dean of students.[67]

Meanwhile, the master plan of the Olmsted Brothers for the Upper Campus was completed in the 1950s with the building of West Hall for women and South Hall (later named Hopeman Hall) for men, the $1.15 million recreation and alumni hall, the Buhl Library, and an east transept on the Harbison Chapel. The modern Grove City gymnasium was used as a model by the National Association of College Directors of Physical Education at their annual meeting. The Gothic-style library, named for Henry Buhl who had served on the board of trustees for nearly thirty years, was built with the same sandstone and limestone as that of Crawford Hall and Harbison Chapel. Finally, during 1956, an east transept was added to the chapel—a gift from Ethel Pew—and was dedicated to Weir Ketler. At last, the entire student body of 1,200 could be seated in the chapel at the same time.

In January 1956 the man who had once said that he intended to help his father "for just a few years" quietly submitted his letter of resignation to the board of trustees after serving forty years as president of Grove City College. Weir Ketler mentioned in passing the major and minor crises through which he and the college had passed and then asserted with his customary modesty that he and the college could not have survived and prospered without "the unity, the courage and the generous support of members of this Board."[68]

The board knew very well where the credit lay and saluted Dr. Ketler for his decades-long devotion to the college and his abiding influence on the lives and character of thousands of young men and women. J. Howard Pew commended him for his singleness of purpose—to train young people "in the fundamental truths of Christianity and freedom, and their interdependence one upon the other."[69] The students praised the retiring president for the "sure, steady, constant progress" the college had enjoyed under his leadership.[70]

Weir Ketler was always quick to acknowledge that he had built on the sure foundation laid by his father. Although different in personality—Isaac, often fiery and uncompromising; Weir, usually calm and prudent—the two Ketlers never deviated from the college's mission of providing an excellent education at an affordable price in a thoroughly Christian environment. Under their direction a tiny academy in a small western Pennsylvania town became a model liberal arts college, hailed throughout the state and beyond.

The Ketler era of some eight decades ended in 1956, but the Ketler legacy, rooted in freedom and faith, would be drawn upon frequently as the quiet fifties drew to a close and a far different decade began.

CHAPTER FIVE

The Dangers of Leviathan

The decade of the sixties that began with such high promise and soaring rhetoric ("Ask not what your country can do for you," declared President John F. Kennedy at his inaugural. "Ask what you can do for your country.") ended with a nation divided over a distant war ten thousand miles away and racked by demonstrations and violence on a thousand campuses. Why were so many students rioting? Why did they rage so?

To begin with, they did not want to fight and perhaps die in Vietnam. They were also shocked and grieving over the murders of John Kennedy, Martin Luther King, Jr., and Robert F. Kennedy. But then they were also saluting anti-American heroes like Fidel Castro, Che Guevara, and Mao Zedong. In this they were rebelling, as youth always will, against the institutions of the previous generation—but in this case violently. They were rejecting "Amerika" and what some of the elite intellectuals charged it stood for—segregation, capitalism, colonialism, and all the other dead ideas of dead white males. They were advocates of an adversary culture that cried "Free Speech!" and silenced anyone who disagreed with them. One of the characteristics of the generational revolt, noted academic Lewis S. Feuer, was the "will to demonstrate, to be disobedient, to 'bring the system to a grinding halt.'"[1] Although a *Fortune* poll reported that only 12.8 percent of college students were "revolutionary" or "radically dissident," this militant minority disrupted and paralyzed institutions of higher learning from coast to coast by the late 1960s—and got away with it.

Not just the campuses were under attack—like China, America was experiencing a Great Cultural Revolution. And as in China, it was the Four Olds—old customs, old habits, old culture, old thinking—that were being challenged and often stamped on during the 1960s. Nothing seemed safe or sacred.[2] Enovid, the birth control pill, was approved by the federal government. Jane Jacobs wrote *Death and Life of Great American Cities*, which mocked the urban planners. Michael Harrington's *The Other America* dramatized poverty in America and led to massive governmental action. Tom Hayden and other members of Students for a Democratic Society championed New Left activism and became instant heroes. Betty Friedan's *The Feminine Mystique* inspired militant feminists to form the National Organization for Women. Martin Luther King, Jr., and other civil rights leaders led a march on Washington that drew 250,000 black (and white) participants. The Supreme Court ruled that New York public schools could not require students to recite a State Board of Regents prayer in the classroom. The Beatles invaded the United States. Television became a major force in American life and politics, setting the public agenda night after night. Congress enacted laws to wipe out poverty, underwrite education, and provide Medicare and Medicaid. Waves of racial riots engulfed the inner cities summer after summer. Homosexuals at the Stonewall Inn in Greenwich Village took on the cops. Hollywood turned out films like *Bonnie and Clyde* and *The Wild Bunch* that exalted killing and won awards. Hundreds of thousands of blue-jeaned, longhaired young Americans held "moratorium" demonstrations against the Vietnam War in Washington.

While the center wavered, conservatives challenged the Left and gave voice to a Silent Majority. Young Americans for Freedom proclaimed its faith in limited government and free enterprise. Senator Barry Goldwater published *The Conscience of a Conservative*, which quickly sold 3.5 million copies. Phyllis Schlafly detailed the political machinations of the Liberal Establishment in the best-selling *A Choice Not an Echo*. Ronald Reagan was elected governor of California by a landslide. Television featured such popular perennials as *The Lucy Show* and *Gunsmoke*. Viewers packed theaters to see the inspiring film *The Sound of Music*. Billy Graham's evangelical crusades drew millions in America and around the world. All three major presidential candidates in 1968 opposed American withdrawal from Vietnam.

Between the Left and the Right were millions of Americans, members of the baby-boom generation, who saw life far differently than had earlier generations. Things which their parents and grandparents had considered privileges, writes historian James T. Patterson, they perceived as entitlements: "In personal life this meant rapid gratification; in policy matters it meant deliverance from evil."[3] They truly believed that they could wage and win wars against most contemporary problems from poverty and cancer to a conflict in Vietnam. These grand expectations—fostered by the prevailing mores—led group after group in America to demand that government guarantee their rights. But such utopianism was bound to fail, defeated by the inherent flaws of government and human nature.

The Answer for All Problems

At the very center of this utopian ethos was the belief that education was "a miracle cure for society."[4] No one believed more deeply in this than President Lyndon B. Johnson, who proclaimed, "The answer for all our national problems comes in a single word... education."[5] Academics like President Clark Kerr of the University of California agreed, pointing out that knowledge was now the leading sector in the growth of the economy. "What the railways did for the second half of the last century and the automobile for the first half of this century," Kerr argued in 1963 at Harvard University, "may be done for the second half of this century by the knowledge industry."[6]

Caught up in this golden dream, higher education expanded exponentially in the 1960s and early 1970s. The number of colleges and universities rose sharply from 2,040 to 3,055. Students tripled from 3.6 million in 1960 to 9.4 million in 1975, the majority of them in public schools. The annual cost of higher education soared to $45 billion. While even the most optimistic anticipated that such rapid growth would create problems, including the critical one of quality, few predicted that educational performance would fall as sharply it did. The College Board revealed in 1975 that scores on the Scholastic Aptitude Test (SAT), taken each year by more than one million high school seniors, "had declined steadily since 1964."[7]

Too much was happening to too many too quickly. Colleges with enrollments of a few hundred were the norm in the 1930s, but by the mid-1970s, several universities had more than fifty thousand students. In 1960 around 40 percent of all high school seniors were applying to college; a decade later the percentage had jumped to 52 percent. In 1950 the student population was evenly divided between public and private colleges and universities. By 1963 public enrollment reached 64 percent of the total.

Isaac C. Ketler, Grove City College Founding President, 1876–1913

J. H. Pew in 1918 at age 36

President Alexander T. Ormond (center) with students in 1915

Students and faculty gather at Founder's Hall in the early 1890s

Football spectators at the 1910 Grove City v. Westminster game

1907 Football Team

1903 Basketball Team

1909 Baseball Team

Grove City College women's basketball, circa 1915

1915 May Day exercises near Founder's Hall

Weir C. Ketler, Grove City College President, 1916-1956

Dale Smock with the College's first radio transmitter used for scheduled broadcasts

Dr. Creig Hoyt instructing some fashionably "knickered" students in the Rockwell Hall chemistry laboratory

Weir C. Ketler and J. H. Pew with 1940 Board of Trustees

A formation of Grove City Cadets

Army Air Cadets gather in front of Memorial Hall

Registrar Dr. H. O. White served under four presidents from 1912 to 1960

Dr. "Jake" Hassler handled college finances for 40 years (1924–1964)

The West Hall Lounge in Mary Anderson Pew Dormitory in the 1950s

1932 faculty processional over Rainbow Bridge

Dean of the College Dr. William W. Swezey began his Grove City College career (1946–1973) as a professor of zoology

J. Howard Pew relaxes at the dedication of Helen Harker Hall in June 1971

Attorney David M. Lascell and President Charles S. MacKenzie address the media outside the Supreme Court in 1983

Dean Fred Kring honors retiring economics professor Hans Sennholz as President Jerry Combee and others look on

Chemistry professors Ed and Sara Naegele

At the 1996 inauguration of Dr. John H. Moore (L-R): Professor Bruce W. Ketler; President of the Board of Trustees J. Paul Sticht; Dr. Moore; Trustee;David M. Lascell: inaugural speaker Edwin J. Feufner

With 1982 commencement speaker Senator Jesse Helms (L-R): Wayne W. Allen; Myles W. MacDonald; Robert McClements, Jr.; Sen. Helms; President Charles S. MacKenzie and Board of Trustees President Albert A. Hopeman, Jr.

Albert A. Hopeman, Jr., President of the Board of Trustees, 1972–1998

Dr. Richard A. Morledge '54, Dean of the Chapel from 1984 to1999, with the new Dean of the Chapel, Dr. F. Stanley Keehlwetter

Alumni Secretary Lee Fennell (right) and President MacKenzie showing the J. Howard Pew Memorial Lecturer plaque to Dick Jewell '67

Grove City's first Alumni Secretary Jack Kennedy
holds Alumni Achievement Award Plaque in 1977
that was renamed in his honor in 1980

Professor John A. Sparks and his son, John, Senior Men of the Year in 1966
and 1995

Vice President for Student Affairs Nancy Paxton applauds the student body

President Jerry H. Combee introduces the first class of students to receive notebook computers in 1994

Grove City College students in morning chapel

The life of the university and college, wrote educator Diane Ravitch, was "transformed." The best professors insisted that they be allowed to concentrate on research and writing and to teach only a few advanced courses in their specialty, leaving scant time for undergraduates and general education. The number of administrators grew and grew, creating a complex bureaucratic structure that oversaw admissions, fund-raising, financial aid, the physical plant, faculty relations, and governmental programs. Larger schools meant larger classes and less contact between teacher and student. The school's sense of purpose became more diffuse, and the campus's sense of community was diminished. Even Clark Kerr, who hailed what he called "the multiversity... a city of infinite variety," conceded that undergraduates had been neglected and that "recent changes... have done them little good."[8] Little wonder that for this reason, too, they raged and rebelled.

The great majority of students going to college in the immediate postwar years, according to historian Christopher J. Lucas, were single, attended school full-time, lived on campus, and pursued a liberal arts degree program "bounded by extensive common course requirements."[9] But by the 1960s many college students divided their time between working and going to school, commuted to campus, and took longer than four years to finish their degrees. Many were married, and many more intended to pursue a postgraduate degree than had their earlier counterparts.

Yet, certain fundamental questions about the role and mission of the college or university persisted: Was teaching more important than research and scholarship? Were there limits to the obligations and responsibilities that academic institutions assumed? Did colleges and universities exist to provide a well-trained and intelligent work force to society or did they have a higher mission? And perhaps most important of all, Who should pay for the costs of the modern college or university?

Conservative author Russell Kirk, who may have lectured on more campuses in the 1950s, 1960s, and 1970s than any other American, had a ready answer for the mission of a college: It should furnish society "with a body of tolerably well-educated persons whose function it is to provide right reason and conscience in the commonwealth."[10]

Regarding the pressing problem of money, John A. Howard, then president of Rockford College, recalls his 1963 experience when he wrote to the president of a large university inviting him to join a group of college presidents who were challenging the ever growing federal subsidies of education. The well-known educator declined, explaining that although he was in full agreement with the group's position, "his own university was now so dependent upon funds from Washington that he could not exercise his rights as a citizen on this issue without jeopardizing the university he served."[11]

Grove City College was determined, as it had been from its founding, not to put itself in so subservient a position.

A New President

The new president of any institution—from the federal government to a Fortune 500 company to a college or university—wants to make his mark and that usually means changing the institution he now headed, sometimes at the margins, sometimes at the center.

John Stanley Harker, Grove City College's fourth president, was energetic, experienced, and exceedingly direct in his speech and opinions. He knew the college well, having graduated from it in 1925 with a B.A. and been head of the alumni association for several years. His connection with Grove City was reinforced through his marriage to Helen Calderwood, class of 1923 and the tall attractive daughter of Dr. A. J. Calderwood, the longtime dean of the college.

Helen Harker would prove to be an invaluable, if unsalaried, member of the Harker administration; like her father she memorized the name of every student so that she would be able to greet the student by his or her first name at chapel or a social event. To every freshman, she would say, "We're expecting great things of you." "He was the organizer," explained Harker's daughter Ruth Mills, "she was the people person." One alumnus called Helen Harker "a female Jim Farley" because of her faculty for names. (New Yorker James A. Farley was Franklin Delano Roosevelt's campaign manager in 1932 and famous for never forgetting a face or a name.)[12] If she was crossing the campus and noticed a student who obviously had a cold, she would invite him or her to the President's House, saying, "Do come over." And, recalls Anne Harker Dayton, "she would feed them orange juice and aspirin... and by the time they left, she knew who their parents were and what town they lived in and what their major was."[13]

Stanley Harker also brought pastoral experience to Grove City. He had earned a bachelor of divinity degree from McCormick Theological Seminary in Chicago as well as a master of arts and a Ph.D. from the University of Pittsburgh. After serving in various Presbyterian churches in New York, Pennsylvania, and Ohio, in 1951 he became president of Alma College, a small Presbyterian college in Michigan. While at Alma, he increased student enrollment and the faculty, doubled the endowment, and oversaw the construction of several buildings without increasing the school's debt. (He also indulged in a lifelong passion and went hunting every season.) Seeking a man of strong faith and an experienced college administrator, Grove City's board of trustees led by J. Howard Pew unanimously chose Stanley Harker to succeed their old friend and colleague Weir Ketler.

At his very first trustees meeting in November 1956, President Harker did not temper his words: while Grove City College was undoubtedly one of the most attractive schools in the country, its academics did not match up to its buildings. The new president called for a substantially larger budget to hire better teachers, improve the library, increase the support staff, and offer a curriculum "of which we can be proud."[14]

The blunt Harker analysis was confirmed the following spring when an evaluation team of the Middle States Association visited the campus and then declined to reaffirm accreditation, scheduling another examination in 1960. While members of the visiting team praised the impressive physical plant, the bright students, and the committed faculty, they were sharply critical of the inadequate salaries, the poor chain of command, the high student dropout rate, the large class size, and the inadequate library. They were especially disappointed in the college's self-evaluation which they characterized as "shallow, evasive or non-responsive."[15] (The self-evaluation had been overseen by a very ill Creig Hoyt, who died in May 1957 just weeks after announcing his retirement after forty-four years of service to the college.)

Every member of the college community was numbed by the Middle States Association's rejection. But President Harker's reforms produced such marked and rapid academic improvement that the visiting Middle States Association team commented in 1960 that "in virtually every field of activity the college has improved and is moving ahead" and wondered "how so much could be done in so short a time."[16]

The new dean of the college, William S. Swezey, carefully examined the curriculum, and only one year later President

Harker could report to the board of trustees that the college had been organized into departments and several majors had been eliminated. The B.S. in Commerce degree was discontinued in order "to return business preparation to the true liberal arts tradition."[17] Pennsylvania's Department of Public Instruction granted the college authority to certify young people for elementary education, starting in the fall of 1958 (Grove City had long been authorized to certify secondary school teachers). And at Dr. Harker's recommendation, student enrollment was increased to over 1,600—by the end of the decade there would be nearly two thousand students.

Change also came to the chapel: compulsory attendance was reduced from five to four times a week (with J. Howard Pew's grudging assent), and attendance was recorded through a card system rather than by the faculty. Students could sit where they wished, instead of the men on one side and women on the other. Guest preachers were also brought in for the Sunday evening Vespers to offer students more religious variety.

Parents Day was moved from the fall to May Day weekend, a student activities fee of $10 was begun (helping to pay for the campus appearances of such celebrities as musical legend Louis Armstrong and rocket scientist Wernher von Braun), new student organizations like the Future Teachers of America sprang up, and a Tour Choir went on the road. Students pressed for national Greek organizations so they could live together, but the board of trustees reiterated its long-standing policy of allowing only local sororities and fraternities and no Greek housing.

The Harkers felt they should live on campus where they could play a more active role in the life of the school and open their home to the students and faculty. Accordingly, in 1957, a handsome red brick President's Home was built at the entrance to the Upper Campus. An invitation to dinner with the president often meant the opportunity to dine on game that Stanley Harker had shot and Helen Harker had prepared. "One night we had roast venison," remembered Sara K. Naegele, who taught in the Department of Chemistry for more than twenty years. "One time we had pheasant breast. Mrs. Harker was an excellent cook."[18]

President Harker loved sports and was convinced that a strong athletic program built school spirit, attracted good students, and helped fund-raising. According to school historian David Dayton, Harker did not favor retaining athletes who did not meet the scholastic standards of the school but did encourage "sports-minded alumni and friends to give money for athletic scholarships." Financial help was provided needy members of the football and basketball teams, recalls trustee Richard Jewell, as well as some swimmers.[19] Soon the football team under Coach Jack Behringer began winning games, a rifle team was organized, and baseball was reestablished as a varsity sport. "We have one male out of every four participating in varsity sports," reported Harker to the board of trustees. "And if intramural sports are... included, virtually all young men on campus now have some sport interest."[20] The president's efforts climaxed in 1966 when the football team achieved a record of 8-0-1, the first undefeated season for the Wolverines since 1926.

More students produced a need for more classrooms, and J. Howard Pew again led the way, pledging $100,000 toward the construction of what would be named Calderwood Hall after the former dean "whose keen wit and... Christian philosophy of life will never be forgotten."[21] Two historic buildings on the Lower Campus were reluctantly razed—Recitation Hall, erected in 1879, and Ivy Chapel, built in 1893. But in keeping with the school's respect for tradition, memorial markers to the two buildings were dedicated on November 10, 1959, the seventy-fifth anniversary of Grove City's charter as a college.

A personal priority of Harker during his fifteen years as college president was the Buhl Library, designed to hold 200,000 volumes but containing barely 50,000 books when he came to campus. By constantly pleading, cajoling, and badgering for the necessary funds, President Harker succeeded in more than doubling the library's holdings to 115,000 by the year he retired in 1971.

Another Harker cause was faculty salaries which he insisted were too low if Grove City College were to compete for the services of the ablest teachers. With the help of a $200,000 grant from the Ford Foundation and other nongovernmental sources, he was able to raise the salary of a full professor from $6,600 in 1956 to $17,161 in 1970. Professor Hans Sennholz, who had his differences with President Harker over the years, noted that "GCC pay remained competitive with that of other institutions of learning throughout the country."[22] Concerned about the graying of the faculty (the average age in some departments was over sixty), Harker aggressively sought young and academically sound teachers.

The college had never had a loan fund for its students, adhering to J. Howard Pew's philosophy that the young men and women who attended the school would be better prepared for life if they paid their own way. But when trustee B. C. Hopeman died in 1958, his will provided the handsome sum of $750,000 to establish the Cornelia Warren Hopeman Memorial Fund for student loans. The Hopeman Memorial Fund explained in part why Grove City College declined to participate in a federal student loan program created by the National Defense Education Act. But the more central reason was the determination of the school not to let anyone outside the immediate Grove City family acquire the power to dictate its policies and procedures. Independence was too dear a possession to be sold at any price.

Grove City College had been culturally conservative from its founding in 1876. In the 1960s it became politically conservative.

A Young Republican Club was formed in 1960, and a Conservative Club, under the sponsorship of faculty member Hans Sennholz, soon thereafter. YRs Bard Schaack and Bob Lech attended the National Republican Convention in Chicago that summer and later persuaded prominent Republicans like West Virginia Governor Cecil B. Underwood and Kentucky Senator Thruston B. Morton to speak at Grove City. A series of lectures in the fall of 1963 by conservative intellectual William Y. Elliot of Harvard were so popular they were moved to Crawford Hall to accommodate audiences of more than six hundred students— about one-third of the school.

But even Grove City was not immune to the counterculture. Rock and roll filled the dorms, black lights appeared at dances, crew cuts and white shirts among the men almost disappeared and long hair and sandals often took their place, women took to maxi coats and hot pants, and the alcoholic consumption at fraternity parties shot up.

Grover men had long held Friday night "roundups" at which a keg or two of beer was consumed at a remote site outside the city limits. But in his memoir, the dean of men Frederick S. Kring describes the 1961 Texas-sized stag party attended by 148 male students. Alerted by the state police, Kring, President Harker, and Dean Swezey all made their way to Dougherty Road (called Whiskey Springs Road by local residents) and personally broke up the roundup. Following a lengthy meeting of the Discipline Committee the next day, two men were suspended from college and 146 men received "social probation" and/or restricted use of automobiles. The free-spirited Kring (known widely as "Red"

Fred because he invariably wore a red jacket, red shoes, and a red beret, and drove a red car) stoutly defended his forbearance. Whenever in later years, he wrote, one of the 146 "climbed an additional rung on his ladder of professional success, I uttered a prayer of thanksgiving for our leniency in salvaging his career."[23]

"Academic Freedom"

Although Grove City College is best known in the academic world for its rejection of federal funding of any sort, it attracted national attention in 1962 when it declined to renew the contract of one of its professors—and was subsequently censured by the American Association of University Professors (AAUP) for violating "academic freedom." Today, forty years later, Grove City remains on the AAUP's list of censured administrations—evidence of the college's refusal to kowtow to a leading institution of the education establishment and of its ability to attract good teachers and good students without the AAUP's imprimatur.

The administration's reasons for letting Dr. Larry Gara go included his "dismal" teaching methods, his draconian grading habits, and his poor performance as chairman of the Department of History and Political Science. Gara and his supporters on and off campus accused the college of violating his tenure "rights" (although the college has never offered tenure to any teacher), hiring two private detectives to investigate him, and penalizing the forty-year-old teacher for his pacifist and liberal views.

What are the facts?[24] Larry Gara, who received a Ph.D. in history from the University of Wisconsin, was hired by Grove City College in 1958 to fill a vacancy created when a professor of history and political science left just as the fall session was starting. Gara had limited teaching experience: one year as an instructor at tiny Bluffton College in Ohio, one year as a lecturer at Mexico City College in Mexico City, and three years as an assistant professor at Eureka College in Illinois (from which Ronald Reagan had graduated in the early 1930s).

Gara arrived at Grove City with an ideological chip on his shoulder. A member of the Society of Friends, he was sentenced to prison in 1943 for refusing to register for military service and served three years. President Harker (whose mother came from a Quaker background) knew of Gara's conscientious objector background and still offered him a position because Gara had a Ph.D. from a respected university and promised that he would not let his pacifist views color his teaching. Harker did not learn until much later that Gara had also served part of an eighteen-month sentence in 1950 for counseling a student at Bluffton College, who had refused to register under the Selective Service Act of 1948.

Gara's first two years at Grove City went "well," Harker conceded, but even then Gara was giving Ds and Fs to more than a third of his students in freshman history.[25] As the complaints from students and parents mounted, Dean Swezey began a series of meetings with Gara; one session was before the Curriculum Committee. In the spring of 1962, when the air was filled with charges and countercharges, Gara denied that any such curriculum meeting had occurred and called Swezey a "liar" to his face. That prompted Dr. Harker, also present, to respond: "Larry, stop the comedy of your conveniently short memory. I was at that meeting. Every statement that the dean has made is absolutely correct.... Do you want me to bring a dozen other men in and confront you?" According to Harker, Gara "dropped his head and made no reply."[26]

At the same time there is no denying that Larry Gara was, in the AAUP's words, "a productive scholar in his field," producing some nineteen scholarly articles and publishing four books, including the well-received *The Liberty Line: The Legend of the*

Underground Railroad. But teaching, not research and writing, comes first at Grove City College.

Students were particularly disturbed about Gara's perfunctory performance in his ancient history class and discovered one day, when he left his notes on his desk, that Gara had pasted the pages of another history text in his notebook and was sitting there "day after day reading another man's book to the class."[27] Gara was sensitive about his teaching. When a bored student—who later joined the Grove City College faculty—withdrew from Gara's class after just three days, an upset Gara vowed that the offending student "would never be permitted to graduate from GCC."[28]

Gara concedes that no one in the administration ever told him what to teach or not to teach. The ad hoc committee of the American Association of University Professors, which visited Grove City in May 1962, following the history professor's dismissal, concurred, stating in its official report that academic freedom in the classroom "was not violated by... the administration."[29]

But the AAUP could not resist bringing up such extraneous information as a "heated" 1961 debate between Gara and Hans Sennholz about American foreign policy and nuclear war in the pages of *The Collegian*, and that Sennholz had been an editorial adviser to *American Opinion*, the magazine of the ultraconservative John Birch Society.[30] Seemingly the AAUP extended the principle of academic freedom to professors of the Left but not of the Right. And in fact Sennholz had never been a member of the society.[31]

As for the two private investigators who spent several days on campus, the AAUP admitted that "no proof" of a connection between their activities and Gara's dismissal was submitted by Gara or anyone else. President Harker and Dean Kring publicly disavowed any knowledge of the investigation. What truly

aroused the AAUP about the Gara incident was not any violation of academic freedom, but the college's indifference to tenure.
By totaling Gara's five years of teaching before coming to Grove
City and his five years there, the AAUP asserted that "Professor
Gara must be regarded as having served his probationary period
and to have had tenure at the time of the decision not to renew
his contract."[32] That Grove City College did not offer tenure to
its faculty did not matter to the AAUP: for it, tenure was an academic entitlement.

Although there were some student demonstrations—one of
which lasted until 3:00 A.M. in the morning—and Jack Anderson
wrote a critical and erroneous column that J. Howard Pew had
wired President Harker to "fire" Larry Gara, the college stood
firm.[33] Dr. Harker, the most liberal of Grove City College's presidents, and Fred Kring, the most liberal of the college's deans, were
agreed that Gara's contract should not be renewed. They gave
Gara the opportunity to resign and "go elsewhere with a clean
record," but the disgruntled professor went public. Six other
teachers, most of them recent arrivals at Grove City, tendered
their resignations in protest against the college's treatment of
Gara, but the overwhelming majority of the faculty signed a
strong statement of support of the administration.[34] "Our staff
has been improved greatly," reported Harker to the board of
trustees, by the departure of Gara and the other "disgruntled"
teachers.[35]

Every year Grove City College receives the same letter from
the American Association of University Professors conveying its
"continuing interest in effecting the removal of AAUP's censure."[36] Every year the college ignores the invitation, confident it
made the right decision.

Radicalism and Rebellion

The radicalism of the sixties did not spring full-blown from the American campus, but had its roots in the deceptively quiet fifties with the publication of influential books like C. Wright Mills's *The Power Elite* and Paul Goodman's *Growing Up Absurd*. Mills, an open marxist, argued that decision-making in America was centralized in the hands of powerful elites in government, business, and the military. His conspiratorial concept of an interlocking directorate that controlled America appealed to those on the left who felt estranged by the direction of American politics. It explained their ineffectiveness. "It suggested to those out of power," wrote historian Diane Ravitch, "that they might in fact be part of the great mass of hoodwinked citizenry rather than a lonely minority."[37]

Goodman, a self-proclaimed anarchist, charged that "semi-monopolies" in business, unions, and government were so concerned about profits and jobs that they ignored personal freedom and genuine culture. They had created a society without human values. But unlike Mills who described an apparently invincible power elite, Goodman believed that "if ten thousand people in all walks of life will stand up on their two feet and insist, we shall get back our country."[38]

Rhetoric was not enough for the radicals. Students became effective political activists through their participation in the civil rights movement. In the campus protests of the 1960s white students used the moral outrage and confrontation tactics they had learned in civil rights activities throughout the South. The first major battleground was the University of California at Berkeley which, starting in September 1964, was plunged "into a crisis unprecedented in American higher education."[39]

Of Berkeley's 27,000 students, only some five hundred were committed political activists, but this small minority was on fire to change the course of America. What better place to begin than their campus? Returning Berkeley students in the fall of 1964 were greeted with copies of an incendiary "Letter to Undergraduates" that urged them to *"Organize and split this campus wide open!... DO NOTHING LESS THAN BEGIN AN OPEN, FIERCE, AND THOROUGHGOING REBELLION ON THIS CAMPUS."* The demands included the immediate abolition of grades in undergraduate courses and rules in student dormitories, and the institution of a permanent student role in the running of the university.[40]

The university administration hesitated and then responded by announcing that students could no longer use a walkway at the university entrance—as they had been doing for years—for political fund-raising and recruitment. This act of pettifoggery infuriated students across the political spectrum, and the Free Speech Movement sprang into being. Most students eventually went back to class and their studies, but the movement was taken over by radical students who presented the situation as "a classic civil rights conflict" between the university as the oppressor and the students as the oppressed. The administration, Diane Ravitch pointed out, was unable to convince anyone that the issue at hand was not free speech but the need to maintain the university "as a marketplace of ideas, not a staging ground for political action."[41]

The confrontation culminated in a giant night rally by the Free Speech Movement on December 2, 1964. An ensuing sit-in in Sproul Hall so alarmed the university chancellor that he called in police to clear the building—773 people were arrested. Half the student body was immediately radicalized and declared their sympathy with the strike urged by the FSM. More than eight hundred professors urged the administration to drop all charges against FSM leaders and cancel the regents' ban on off-campus activities by students.

University authorities caved in, and the chancellor was replaced, but the radicals were not interested in resolving differences but in revolution. The Free Speech Movement was succeeded by the Filthy Speech Movement, and "a loose alliance of radical students, hippies, and 'street people' kept alive the spirit of protest" at Berkeley and beyond.[42] The ineptness and inarticulateness of the Berkeley administration would be duplicated by that of many other colleges and universities. The radical rhetoric and confrontational tactics of the Free Speech Movement became a model for the Students for a Democratic Society (SDS) and other leftist groups.

The radicals acquired an important issue in the spring of 1965 when President Johnson committed American ground troops to the war in Vietnam, and his administration began using the draft for its manpower needs. Campus protests against the war spread—although a majority of students continued to support the war until 1968. The summer of 1967 marked the birth of the "counterculture" which rejected middle-class values such as family, work, religion, and authority. The counterculture championed sexual experience and immediate gratification; its symbol was the "hippie"—bearded, beaded, blue-jeaned, and usually high on one illegal substance or another. Because the Christian core of the American university had long since disappeared, the counterculture—hedonistic and anarchic—quickly spread coast to coast.

The Campus Explosion
The American campus, long simmering, exploded in the spring of 1968. A focal point was Columbia University, located in the nation's media center, New York City. The SDS chapter at Columbia had been urgently seeking an issue to create a Berkeley-like confrontation with the administration. It found one in the

proposed construction of a new university gymnasium in Morningside Park, an area that lay between the school and Harlem. SDS protested and was joined by the Students Afro-American Society (SAS), which called the gym "racist" because it would occupy public land that "belonged" to the people of Harlem.

While the administration deliberated about its response, some one thousand black and white students occupied five university buildings in late April. Red flags flew from the tops of two buildings, and the offices and classrooms inside were filled with posters of Marx, Malcolm X, and Che Guevara, and revolutionary slogans like "Power to the People!" The radicals smoothly shifted the issue at hand from the Morningside gymnasium to the Vietnam War, racism, and oppressive authority at Columbia and in Washington, D.C. An ad hoc group of the faculty intervened, repudiating the university's leadership, especially President Grayson Kirk, a distant figure "who commanded neither respect nor loyalty."[43] In a deliberate act of contempt the radical occupiers urinated on the carpet in Kirk's office.

Once again a university administration was caught between an uncompromising board of trustees and a flexible faculty—and confronted by a disciplined band of intransigent students. On the seventh day of occupation President Kirk reluctantly sent for the police and more than seven hundred students, of whom 524 were Columbia students, were arrested. As at Berkeley, the police action created mass support for the radicals among Columbia students and faculty. A broken Kirk resigned as president that summer after a second occupation of a university building in May. On that occasion students smashed their way into the office of a professor who had opposed the demonstrations and burned his carefully accumulated research on French history. SDS founder Tom Hayden praised the militant tactics and predicted more revolutionary acts in the future. The object, he wrote, was not to reform but to transform the university into a new institution "standing against the mainstream of American society."[44]

The movement that had begun with the demand for free speech at Berkeley had become, in Diane Ravitch's words, "an effort to politicize the university and coerce those who disagreed."[45] Faculty who did not support students were humiliated and intimidated. Administrators who resisted were branded racists and traitors.

The radicals seemed to be everywhere. San Francisco State University was closed for three weeks. A student-faculty rally forced the resignation of Rice University's president. At the University of Wisconsin the Black People's Alliance called a strike. When blows were exchanged, the governor called out 1,900 National Guardsmen, and tear gas covered the campus. At Harvard, undergraduates invaded University Hall, evicted the deans, and began rifling confidential files. Black militants occupied the Student Union building at Cornell, and after being granted full amnesty by an accommodating administration, left the building triumphantly brandishing shotguns and rifles.

Among the lessons learned, once again according to Diane Ravitch, was that administration capitulation to the student radicals invariably proved "disastrous." Another was that confrontational tactics were inherently self-limiting and rarely worked twice on the same campus. A third was that the great majority of students were only temporarily radicalized and, while sympathetic with such goals as racial equality and an end to the war in Vietnam, wanted to get on with their education and their lives.[46]

"Moratoriums" (student demands for an end to the Vietnam War) in Washington and elsewhere angered members of the "Silent Majority," who resented the young protestors ridiculing American institutions and avoiding military service. "They are telling you your son died in vain," said a construction worker bitterly. "It makes you feel your whole life is s—t, just nothing."[47] And then there was the contradictory message of the radicals' gurus who preached harmony, love, and toleration but encouraged confrontation, hatred, and intolerance. "They profess to the love of all mankind," remarked President Edward J. Bloustein of Rutgers, "but many of them steal and cheat from each other and from us. They seek universal peace, but often undertake or applaud violence in the service of their ends. . . . They cherish the freedom to express themselves, but would often deny that right to those they violently oppose."[48]

Through all the storms of the sixties, wrote historian James T. Patterson, America "remained one of the most religious cultures in the Western World."[49] Billy Graham and other evangelical preachers drew multitudes to their meetings. An estimated 43 percent of Americans regularly attended church services in 1968, compared to 10 to 15 percent in England and France. And fundamentalist leaders began speaking out about current issues after decades of ceding the political debate to the liberal National Council of Churches and similar organizations.

As the polarization and fragmentation persisted—most shockingly at the violence-laden Democratic National Convention in Chicago in the summer of 1968—old and neoconservatives began coming together and building the foundation for the remarkable political victories of Ronald Reagan and Newt Gingrich in the 1980s and 1990s.

The Grove City Way

While students across the country were taking over buildings and even blowing them up, Grovers formed Students Against Violence. While radicals were shouting down those who opposed them, Grove City students were holding seminars, debating on the lawn, and even inviting the commander of the ROTC unit on campus to talk to them. The first teach-in on Vietnam was held in November 1965 and attracted nearly four hundred students, about one-fifth of the school. Sponsored by the Young Republicans Club, the teach-in featured presentations by Dr. Robert Neff of the history department, who basically supported the war; Warner D. Mendenhall of the political science department, who argued that the United States was fighting against Vietnamese nationalism and not communism in Vietnam; and Dr. Roy Kauffmann of the English department, who outlined three possible courses of action by the United States—withdrawal, staying the course in the hope of bringing all sides to the bargaining table, and military escalation. Declining to take a position personally, Kauffmann stated that demonstrations against the war were an exercise of free speech and therefore "far more important than the alleged lowering of morale" they might generate.[50] Grove City students preferred to exercise their free speech on campus; only four Grovers traveled to Washington in October 1968 to participate in the mammoth demonstration there against the Vietnam War. In contrast to the rioting at many schools following the Kent State deaths in March 1970, Grove City College remained peaceful. "If you should have trouble," commented a proud parent at the Parents' Day that spring, "do not call in the National Guard. Just call the Parents Association back to campus!"[51]

Grove City College was an island of calm in a troubled sea because ordered liberty prevailed there. Everyone knew how the school worked and abided by the rules. The board of trustees set school policy in consultation with the president. The administration was firm but not authoritarian in the implementation of that policy. The primary responsibilities of the faculty were academic, not administrative. The students were intent on obtaining an education that would help them to do well after graduation and, when possible, to do good. The school's Christian atmosphere and commitment obviated widespread experimentation in sex and drugs and discouraged rampant hostility to authority.

No better example of the different road traveled at Grove City can be found than the campus's reaction to the Carpenters Union's attempt to organize the school's nonteaching staff in the turbulent May of 1968. While other students were destroying private files, closing down schools, and urinating on presidential rugs, Grove City students—and faculty—refused to join a union picket line. Instead, for seven days, they took over the duties of the maintenance staff and mowed grass, weeded gardens, hauled garbage, delivered clean laundry, cooked and served food, and mocked the union organizers. The union leader alienated the community when he distributed a leaflet that threatened, "If we do not win our demands, you will not graduate."[52]

As a result of the unstinting efforts of student and faculty in the face of the employees' strike, the campus never looked better to arriving mothers and fathers on Parents Day 1968.

The Harker years from 1956 through 1971 were marked by a number of impressive accomplishments, including the construction of eight new buildings with an investment value of over $7.5 million. Pew generosity ensured their debt-free status. The Pew family gave at least $50 million to Grove City College over the decades, an act of exceptional philanthropy toward a small liberal arts college.

Grove City's insistence on raising the money for its buildings from private rather than governmental sources caught the attention of certain people in Washington, D.C., who could not understand such strange behavior. In the middle of the campaign to raise funds for Hoyt Hall, J. Howard Pew recounted, "a dapper young bureaucrat" from Washington came calling on President Harker. He explained that it was unnecessary to devote so much time and energy to fundraising because the government "would welcome the opportunity to furnish the college with all of the money it needed." Harker looked at his visitor in amazement and replied, "If I accepted your offer, I would lose my job." Pew admitted that he had "never expected to see the day when the government actually solicited the opportunity to give the taxpayer's money away."[53] He was being ironic: such solicitation was the logical result of the Great Society's philosophy that there is no problem that cannot be solved by the wisdom and generosity of the federal government.

The size of the faculty and their salaries doubled under Harker while the student body increased from 1,250 to 2,050. The school's academic level steadily rose. All full-time teachers had at least a master's degree, and thirty-four of them had Ph.D.'s. In 1970, 20 percent of the freshman men and 72 percent of the women were in the top tenth of their high school. Health and retirement programs for the staff and faculty were started, and the Zerbe Health Center, named after a generous alumnus, was opened. Tuition rose to $990 a year by 1970 but was still one of the lowest in the state and the region.

It is likely that Grove City College did not explode as many colleges and universities did during the turbulent sixties because of the flexible disciplinary policy of the Harker administration. "It could be," reflected longtime trustee R. Heath Larry years later, "that when President Harker and Dean Kring kind of winked at things, they were doing us a service, in the sense that they were letting the steam off just a little, enough to keep from having an uproar." Trustee Richard G. Jewell, a student at Grove City during the '60s, says that Fred Kring understood that "running a college campus was like boiling potatoes—you had to leave the lid on but let some of the steam off."[54] President Harker agreed, arguing that "if a college treats its students as partners in a great educational adventure, no Reds or Parlor Pinks are going to take it over." Remarked one thoughtful alumnus, "You were never a number at Grove City."[55]

The good feelings that prevailed between the administration and student body were also due in no small measure, to the generous hospitality of Fred and Hilda ("Hurricane") Kring, who held "humongous" gatherings at their home, and to the unstinting socializing of Helen Harker, who personally greeted every incoming freshman and new faculty member. Mrs. Harker also entertained annually and generously the members of every fraternity and sorority in the President's Home. "I was there helping," remembered retired chemistry teacher Sara Naegele, when the Harkers were moving out, "and she still had stacks of aluminum pie pans she had saved, just stacks of them, from all those pies she had served over the years to the kids."[56]

Encouraged by the open attitude, the student "partners" pressed their strong dissatisfaction with two Grove City traditions—compulsory chapel and intervisitation rights. Because of the steadily increasing number of students, separate chapel services were held for the freshmen in Crawford Hall and for upperclassmen in Harbison Chapel. At last the trustees decided to combine the services and then in June 1970 agreed to reduce required attendance at chapel from four to two times a week. The same year, President Harker along with Dr. Kring, now dean of students, suddenly instituted an intervisitation program in women's dorms on Friday evenings and men's dorms on Saturday evening, without consulting with the board of trustees. Until then, Grove City College had reportedly been the only college in western Pennsylvania that officially barred intervisitation in the evenings.

Controversial speakers also appeared. The student government in 1971 invited Bill Baird, the most famous abortionist in America, to speak on campus. Although abortion was then illegal in Pennsylvania—the Supreme Court would not hand down its *Roe v. Wade* decision until two years later—Baird discussed the abortion option and the services of his New York clinic. Some students, including the editor of *The Collegian*, were mesmerized by his presentation. An editorial called abortion "a necessary fact of life" and urged the student government to begin a "fund-raising drive for Baird's clinic."[57] But faculty members and trustees were disturbed by Baird's appearance, as well as that of black activist Dick Gregory and radical feminist Ti-Grace Atkinson, going so far as to wonder whether Grove City was joining the counterculture revolution.

An evaluation team of the Commission on Higher Education of the Middle States Association meanwhile visited Grove City College in November 1970 and generally lauded the college for its low-cost quality education. It attributed the lack of student and faculty unrest at Grove City to the fact that everyone seemed to know what was expected of them: "The picture that emerges ... is that of a college that has a clear sense of purpose and a program of studies consistent with that purpose." The visiting educators described the academic program as "adequate but dull" and noted disapprovingly that there was no tenure for the faculty.[58] President Harker accentuated the positive findings and ignored the negative. His spirits were raised the following May when a team from the Pennsylvania Department of Public Instruction visited the college, and its chairman declared that with the exception of two teachers colleges, Grove City College was "the best college in the State for preparing teachers."[59]

The many duties of a college president can wear down the most resilient of men—Weir Ketler proving the exception—and

Stanley Harker had been telling the board of trustees for a couple of years that he wanted to resign as president. As was his
methodical wont, J. Howard Pew had been giving careful thought
to Harker's successor. While acknowledging the significant physical improvements at Grove City College, the eighty-eight-year-
old Pew was worried about the soul of the college, telling friends
that he wanted "a revived emphasis on Christian values and character."[60] The school's number one benefactor had been shocked
on a visit to the campus to find outside the Ketler men's dormitory a pile of beer cans.[61]

Following an intense search, J. Howard Pew believed that
he had found the right man to lead Grove City College: Charles
Sherrard MacKenzie. At forty-six Dr. MacKenzie was an impres-
sively well-rounded educator and Presbyterian minister. He had
studied at Gordon College, Boston University, and several universities in England and Germany, and had received a doctorate
in theology from Princeton University. He had been an Air Force
chaplain, a social worker, and a teacher at Columbia University
and Stanford University, as well as a pastor at prominent
Presbyterian churches in New York City, New Jersey, and California that had blossomed under his evangelistic preaching. New
York papers described him as a "church repair man."[62]

The Drafting of a President

Sherry Mackenzie and his wife Florence were having breakfast
one sunny morning in the late summer of 1970 in their San
Mateo, California, home when the telephone rang. A deep gruff
voice announced that it was J. Howard Pew, calling from
Philadelphia. Dr. MacKenzie had met the businessman and his
wife years before when he had been the chaplain on a cruise
through the Mediterranean, and the Pews had faithfully attended
services. When Mrs. Pew contracted pneumonia, the young chap-

lain and Mr. Pew had prayed together constantly for her recovery. One evening, Pew confided to Dr. MacKenzie that "all he had was dedicated to bringing America, which he loved passionately, to Jesus Christ."[63] A close friendship developed based on a common love for the Lord and an equal concern about the leftward theological drift of the Presbyterian Church.

Separated by a continent, the two men had not talked to each other for years, but now Pew revealed that Grove City College was seeking a new president and asked whether MacKenzie would consider accepting the position. "My first impulse," recalled MacKenzie, "was to respond, 'No, we're happy with our work here in California.'" Yet some power seemed to hold him back, and he answered, "Well, send us information about the college. We will pray about the situation and get back to you." Later, he said, after he had received and studied the material that had been sent, "I felt there was something different about Grove City College. Its immense potential was intriguing."[64]

Pew made clear to Dr. MacKenzie that he wanted the college to be a high-quality, low-cost alternative for families of modest means; to stand for constitutional freedoms and to stress that "those freedoms derive from biblical Christianity;" to continue its practice of maintaining a small administrative staff that would faithfully implement the policies of the board of trustees; and to lift its academic standards, "though this was not his first priority."[65]

Even with Pew's staunch support, Sherry MacKenzie was not immediately confirmed. He attended a board meeting in November 1970 where he received a "somewhat cool" reception, caused, he later learned, by some board members who wanted to assert their independence from the often autocratic Pew. He then met with the nomination committee at Pew's Philadelphia office where he was interviewed along with another finalist, the dean of a graduate school of theology. Despite Grove City's reputation as a "conservative" school, MacKenzie was not asked about his political views, attesting to the school's inherent respect for academic freedom. Finally, in April 1971, the board of trustees accepted the search committee's unanimous recommendation and extended an invitation to Charles S. MacKenzie to become the fifth president of Grove City College.

"We accepted the offer," recalled MacKenzie, "and for the first time in months felt at peace," although, he later admitted, the American college was going through exceedingly difficult days.[66] The confrontational sixties had left higher education troubled and uncertain. Administrators had grown timid, fearful they would alienate their faculty and students. Students and faculty, having tasted power in the '60s, wanted more. The more perceptive members of the academy realized they had lost much of the public's respect and support. And demographers were predicting that declining college enrollment and retrenchment were on the way. The MacKenzie era began when "anxiety, suspicion, and alienation pervaded the whole culture."[67]

Before President MacKenzie formally took up his duties at Grove City, he spent a long weekend with Albert A. Hopeman, Jr., the vice president of the board of trustees and a highly successful businessman, at his summer home on New York's Canandaigua Lake. Board president Pew was ill and asked his longtime friend and business associate Hopeman to brief the incoming chief executive about "his" college.

The evangelical educator and the conservative businessman, who would work closely and effectively at Grove City College for the next twenty years, agreed to maintain the mission and policies established by the Ketlers, the Pews, and the generations of trustees and faculty over almost a century. Grove City College would remain a small liberal arts and science college of some

2,100 students. Courses would not proliferate "simply to follow the academic fads of the day," but a core curriculum would be adopted. No endowment would underwrite annual operating costs so as to strengthen the school's philosophy of fiscal responsibility. And no federal government money would be accepted. The faculty would concentrate on teaching, the students on learning, and the administration on implementing the policies set by the trustees in concert with the president. Over all, a biblical worldview and Judeo-Christian ethic would be reinforced.[68]

And indeed the MacKenzie-Hopeman years were remarkably successful. Over the next two decades the school received accolades from *U.S. News & World Report*, *Money* magazine, *National Review* magazine, the Templeton Foundation, and several professional college guides. The great majority of Grove City seniors received excellent job offers or were accepted at leading graduate schools. The SAT scores of Grove City freshmen increased annually, averaging an impressive 1,113 by the early 1990s. The number of Ph.D.'s on the faculty steadily rose. Tuition, room, and board still totaled only $7,300 in 1991, which made Grove City one of the nation's top academic bargains. Over $38 million was expended on the physical plant now valued at more than $80 million. Some $20 million was poured into financial aid funds for students. In all but one year, the school operated in the black, the exception coming when $1 million was spent improving the Technological Learning Center. Christian moral standards were revived along with evangelical teaching.[69]

Through it all, especially in the face of the inevitable criticism, President MacKenzie remembered J. Howard Pew's counsel, "Never try to be liked, try to be respected." How often he wished that "Mr. Pew" could have been there to see his college become

increasingly honored, often under the most challenging of circumstances, including a memorable legal struggle with the federal government. But in the late fall of 1971, J. Howard Pew, who
had provided so much of the school's moral and financial leadership for nearly six decades, died at the age of eighty-nine. At
his funeral, the famed evangelist Billy Graham, who had known
and worked and prayed with the Pennsylvania philanthropist and
business leader for many years, remarked, "A giant of a man has
fallen."[70]

CHAPTER SIX

The Master Builder

It was 1901, the beginning of a new century, and America was on the move. Charismatic Theodore Roosevelt was busily expanding the presidency, financier J. P. Morgan was forming the first billion-dollar corporation, U.S. Steel, ex-farm boy Henry Ford was designing a safe, reliable, and cheap car, General Electric was establishing the first research laboratory, and two Ohio mechanics named Wright were trying to launch the first powered flight. In January of that year, on a mound called Spindletop near Beaumont, Texas, the largest oil strike in history occurred.

Joseph N. Pew immediately sent his young nephews Robert and J. Edgar to appraise the field (first instructing them to purchase a gun) and upon receiving a favorable report started buying oil rights. "You just had to put a hole down anywere," J. Edgar later commented, "to find [oil]."[1] Pew senior began making arrangements for the crude oil to be shipped east by tanker—bypassing the railroads controlled by Standard Oil—then processed near Philadelphia. To handle the new venture, he incorporated the Sun Company of New Jersey on May 2, 1901, and began constructing a new refinery on the Delaware River at

Marcus Hook, Pennsylvania. He asked his nineteen-year-old, six-foot-two son John Howard to leave Boston Tech (now the renowned Massachusetts Institute of Technology), where he was doing graduate work, and help the company find ways to make the Texas crude oil more profitable.

"Those were just about the happiest days of my life," John Howard later reminisced about Marcus Hook. Every morning the plant whistle blew at 7:30 A.M., the start of a work day that often lasted until nine or ten in the evening. Indeed there were many nights, remembered Pew, who wore overalls like everyone else, "when we worked all night." He and the other Sun employees—there were only about fifty of them—knew little about operating an oil refinery. On top of that they were trying to process Texas crude, which was different "from any oil that had ever been produced in this country—thick and sulfurous with an asphaltic base.[2]

Like Edison, Ford, and the other inventors of the late nineteenth and early twentieth centuries, the Sun team started from scratch and developed its own processes. One unpleasant result was an emission of dark sulfurous smoke that turned the town black overnight. The company unhesitatingly cleaned up and repainted every dirty building. "The good people of Marcus Hook were mighty nice about it," Pew recalled, "and let us keep our plant running."[3]

At Pew's insistence, the company took more direct action to reduce the loss of petroleum vapor into the atmosphere through the installation of floating-roof tanks. This was, of course, many years before any talk of air pollution. The other oil companies, according to a retired Sun engineer, knew about such tanks but were reluctant to proceed because of the cost. "So back then," he recalled, "we might have had 50 or 60 floating roofs, when the others had maybe one or two. But Mr. Pew was willing to spend the money because he knew the proper thing was not to turn those vapors loose in the air."[4]

Howard spent the next eleven years of his professional life at Marcus Hook where he and his engineering crew developed a highly successful and profitable lubricating oil, Sun Red, and then the first high quality asphalt—hydrolene—that could be used for paving highways and driveways. By 1910 more than one hundred products carried the Sun name. For much of that period, Howard lived and worked in Lindenthorpe, the cottage across the railroad from the Number One Boiler House. He learned how to refine, package, and ship crude oil, and how to evaluate and motivate men—even when they had had one drink too many. Many of the workers had emigrated from Ireland and southern Europe, and John Howard asked the local priest for help when they didn't show up. Thereafter he had only to mention the priest to get "his men back to work."[5]

The Pew family, meanwhile, moved from Pittsburgh to Philadelphia in 1904, and the next year Joseph Newton bought a large house in Bryn Mawr outside the city, naming it "Glenmede" in honor of his mother Nancy Glenn. At one of the frequent parties at Glenmede, John Howard met his future wife, the lovely, vivacious Helen Thompson of Pittsburgh. After a two-year courtship, they married in 1907. Helen later revealed, laughing, that her father had been relieved to learn that his new son-in-law could drive—enabling him to earn a living as a truck driver in case the oil business failed. When the young couple discovered they could not have children, they quickly adopted three— Roberta, George, and Frances. John Howard was a generous and devoted father—albeit "austere," Frances recalled—who took time to be with his children not just on special occasions but whenever they wanted to talk things over.[6]

It was a full and rewarding life for the young husband, father, and oil executive. And then on October 10, 1912, his father suddenly died of a heart attack in his office. Joseph N. Pew, the decisive, hardworking entrepreneur who had made the Sun Company one of the most profitable oil companies in America, was gone at the age of sixty-four. Who could succeed so formidable a founder? In less than two weeks, thirty-year-old J. Howard Pew, disciplined and yet decisive, prudent and yet creative, was elected president of the Sun Company by the family. For the next thirty-five years, he would lead the company to new heights of success and influence, always motivated by the principles of freedom and faith set forth by his father.

At the same time, regardless of the neverending demands of his business life, J. Howard Pew helped direct the affairs of the small college which had come to mean so much to him and his father—Grove City College. He joined Grove City's board of trustees (at Joseph Newton's suggestion) in 1912 and served as a member and then as president until 1971, nearly sixty years. He looked forward to visiting the campus, talking with students and faculty, and giving an annual progress report to the visiting parents and alumni. He never failed to emphasize the mission of the college. "At Grove City College," Pew said in 1949, "we stress the value of religious, political and economic liberty. Our priceless liberty is recognized as the very cornerstone of American civilization. It is our most precious heritage."[7]

An American Family
The first Pews emigrated from England to the New World colony of Virginia in the 1630s and, despite disease, weather, Indians, and royal laws, multiplied and prospered. But the call of the West was irresistible. When West Virginia opened up during the American Revolution, members of the Pew family were among the early set-

tlers of that untamed land, and at the turn of the century a young Pew helped to found "the village of Pittsburgh" in western Pennsylvania. Another Pew settled a little farther north in what was still a wilderness.

John Pew, the grandfather of Joseph Newton Pew, came to Mercer, Pennsylvania—some sixty miles north of Pittsburgh— in 1797. He was one of the first eleven settlers in the region and secured a tract of 150 acres. "Life at the frontier," wrote Pew biographer Mary Sennholz, "hinged around a large family."[8] John and his wife Elizabeth Vaughn, who probably grew up in Washington County on the West Virginia border, arrived in Mercer with four children. Eleven more would be born there.

John and Elizabeth Pew were devout Presbyterians who took their faith seriously and dispensed charity generously, even befriending Indians. The wife of the local Indian chief frequently visited Mrs. Pew to learn English. The Pews were also patriots. During the War of 1812 the two oldest boys, Samuel and Abraham, saw active duty in the Mercer Light Infantry and Mercer Blues. The volunteer army, according to Abraham Pew, "did good service against the British and Indians."[9]

Their brother John, born in 1800, and too young to march against the British in 1812, started his own farm in 1823, just two miles south of Mercer. He soon married Nancy Glenn, and they raised ten children, including their youngest son, Joseph Newton, born on July 25, 1848. It was in this home of "serious Christian almost Puritan ideals," wrote Grove City College president Isaac Ketler years later, that the future founder of the Sun Company spent his early childhood and young manhood. It was a home with "no lack of moral purpose and decision," even on controversial issues like slavery.[10]

When the General Assembly of the Old School Presbyterian Church met in Cincinnati in May 1845, and declared that slavery was "no bar to Christian Communion," John Pew and other like-minded Presbyterians repudiated the declaration and the practice of slavery that they called a "crime against society." They formed the Synod of the Free Presbyterian Church. Until January 1863 when President Lincoln issued the Emancipation Proclamation, these Free Presbyterians "unremittingly kept up their protest against the institution of slavery" and bore witness against any church that acquiesced in what they called the "open sore of the world."[11]

John Pew was a vocal leader of the antislavery Presbyterians of Mercer County, as was his older sister, Sarah Pew, who, following the Emancipation Proclamation, was among the first to give a Christian education to former slaves in Virginia. It was from his father, mother, and family members like Aunt Sarah that Joseph Pew acquired the Christian ideals that molded his life and career.

Like most pioneers and almost all Presbyterians, the Pew family regarded education as essential both for the development of the intellect and the proper sense of duty to the community and the country. All of the Pew children, including Joseph Newton, attended private schools before entering the Mercer Academy. Newton was so good in school that at age eighteen he was asked to teach in a one-room public school in the small community of London, Pennsylvania, a few miles south of Mercer.

One of his star pupils during three years of teaching in London was a young man named Isaac Ketler, who later recalled that the two young Pennsylvanians, Newton and he, "were country boys having little of this world's goods, but blessed with good parentage and abounding health, and ambitious ideals. The friendship formed under these circumstances and in the district school was never broken and was never marred."[12]

Joseph Newton Pew attended Edinboro Normal School for one year to advance his education but then eagerly entered the world of business, opening a real estate office in Mercer. Undoubt-edly he was inspired by his father who had long traded in real estate but with limited success. Young Pew soon moved to bustling, booming Titusville, where oil had been discovered in 1859.

Joseph Newton Pew was an entrepreneurial whirlwind—selling real estate and insurance, making loans, getting into the oil business—and he quickly accumulated a small fortune of $40,000. But he lost it and another $20,000 even more quickly through an investment in what turned out to be worthless oil cer-tificates. He then tried his hand in the Parker's Landing and Bullion oil fields before moving to Bradford, Pennsylvania, in 1876 where he attracted the attention of banker Edward Octavius Emerson, who was impressed by the twenty-eight-year-old Pew's energy and resourcefulness. The two men formed the Keystone Gas Company, which piped natural gas to drilling sites in the Bradford oil fields. Soon the company was also supplying gas for heat and light to residents of Bradford and then Olean, New York, thirty miles to the north. It was one of the first uses of natural gas for domestic purposes in America.

Emboldened by their success, Pew and Emerson formed a new company, the Penn Fuel Company, and took on a new and far greater market, Pittsburgh. In 1882 Pittsburgh was "alive with new industry and commerce and gaining rapidly in industrial importance."[13] A young and hardworking population with a high percentage of immigrants was ready to lead the city to promi-nence in industries like steel, electric power, and aluminum.

But for all their modern ways few Pittsburghers used nat-ural gas. The Penn Fuel Company proceeded to build gas pipe lines to the city and tout the many advantages of natural gas. In a short while Pittsburgh became the first major city in America to use natural gas at home and in the factory. A key customer was the Carnegie Steel Mills. Pew was so eager to sign up the influential

Andrew Carnegie that he offered to supply gas to the steel maker's mills "free of charge." Convinced at last of the economic advantages of natural gas, the independent Carnegie told the jubiliant Pew that he had a new customer, but added, "I'll pay for it."[14]

By the mid-1880s, the Sun Company's official history points out, Pew and Emerson had successfully exploited a cheap by-product of the oil boom to create "a small but profitable industry" in a sector of the petroleum industry—and this was crucial—not controlled by the Standard Oil Trust.[15]

Life was not all work for Joseph Newton Pew. He had married Mary Catherine Anderson—whose ancestors included an aide to General George Washington—in December 1874 and had begun raising a family. As in most frontier towns of the time, "the social life in Bradford centered around the church." The Pews conducted daily morning worship in their home and attended the Presbyterian church every Sunday.[16] It was on January 27, 1882, in their Bradford home that Mary Pew gave birth to her second child, John Howard.

America in the 1880s was flexing its muscles. The population was 50.1 million and increasing rapidly because of a high birthrate and mass emigration—mainly Italians, Russians, and eastern Europeans during the 1880s. In New York, Thomas Edison's company began supplying electricity, casting an incandescent glow over the nation's largest city. John D. Rockefeller and his associates organized the Standard Oil Trust, with Rockefeller holding one-fourth of the shares. Within a decade, about five thousand companies consolidated into three hundred trusts or corporations. (Preferring independence, Pew and Emerson did not join the ranks of the cartels.) Chester A. Arthur, goodlooking and genial, succeeded to the presidency when a deranged civil servant killed James A. Garfield. Franklin Delano Roosevelt was born, and Charles Darwin died—both men would cast long shadows over America in the decades ahead.

Growing Up Good

After two years of constant commuting between Bradford and downtown Pittsburgh, Joseph N. Pew moved his family in 1884 from the frontier to the city. The Pews enjoyed the plays, shops, and parties of Pittsburgh, but Joseph Newton always remembered his roots. With his wife and children, he often visited his boyhood home in Mercer and in 1885 bought it from his brother. The Pew children recalled spending happy summers "in the country."[17]

Life did not vary much for the Pews regardless of where they lived. A tight-knit family, they worked, played, and prayed together. They were members of the East Liberty Presbyterian Church, and Howard later said, "My father saw to it that I never missed attending Sunday School and church."[18] School was almost as important: the Pew children attended top private schools in Pittsburgh and later Philadelphia; Howard attended the prestigious Shady Side Academy to prepare for college.

While the Pew children were training their minds and building their faith, their father continued to expand his gas business. When Pittsburgh investors offered to buy the Penn Fuel Company, Pew and Emerson agreed to sell and then immediately formed a new company, the Peoples Natural Gas Company which serves Pittsburgh and western Pennsylvania to this day.

When oil and gas were discovered near Lima, Ohio, in 1896, the two partners dispatched nephew Robert C. Pew to look things over; he recommended obtaining leases for oil exploration, drilling, and production. In short order, the Lima operation outgrew the western Pennsylvania business, becoming one of Ohio's leading suppliers of crude oil. Pew and Emerson first formed the

Sun Oil Line Company and then in 1890 the Sun Oil Company (Ohio) to handle all aspects of the oil business—production, transporation, storage, refining, shipping, and marketing. Four years later the partners, along with a Cleveland company, organized the Diamond Oil Company which bought what became the company's Toledo refinery. They subsequently formed the Bay Terminal Railroad Company to create a spur line for moving tank cars between the railroad and the refinery. They were well on their way to creating a fully integrated and profitable petroleum company. Then in 1899 Pew bought out Emerson and took full control of the company.

By 1900, Joseph N. Pew was thinking seriously about devoting himself exclusively to petroleum operations. "My father taught me," J. Howard later explained, "not to diversify my efforts, but to put all my eggs in one basket and take a firm grip on the handle."[19] Which is exactly what his father did by selling People's Gas to Standard Oil. From then to his death in 1912, Joseph N. Pew ran an ever expanding petroleum company whose many parts were managed, and quite efficiently, by his nephews and children.

At Home in Grove City

"I hardly remember a time," said J. Howard Pew, "when I did not know Grove City College."[20] He often visited the campus as a boy and recalled climbing over the beams and rafters of a building under construction—one of Isaac Ketler's projects. When he decided the Shady Side Academy in Pittsburgh had done all it could to prepare him, he enrolled at the college in 1897 at age fifteen.

The three pillars on which J. Howard Pew built his life—faith, freedom, and patriotism—were present in abundance at Grove City College. The serious, intellectually curious young man received solid instruction in a wide variety of natural science courses ranging from chemistry and astronomy to geography and geology; he also studied English, Latin, German, history, philosophy, and other liberal arts subjects. In his junior year he took a course in the Bible and like every other male student at Grove City, he was part of what became the school's Reserve Officer Training Corps (ROTC). In recognition of his military "proficiency," he was made corporal. Howard roomed and boarded in town—for about $3 a week—but usually spent the weekends at the Pew homestead in Mercer or sometimes at the family home in Pittsburgh. Although he owned a horse and buggy, he occasionally rode his bicycle all the way to Pittsburgh.

J. Howard graduated from Grove City College in 1900 at the age of eighteen—after only three years of study—but always brushed aside any allusion to his academic abilities. He would point to the several summer schools he had attended and add, with a smile, "I didn't like school, after all."[21] Still, he must have been a good student: his swift passage through Grove City and his ready acceptance by the future MIT corroborate his high intelligence. One classmate—Angeline Stewart—remembered him as "a rather shy and quiet boy" who did not play sports or engage in extracurriculars.[22] Nor did he have a girl friend, which, considering his youth and Presbyterian upbringing, is not surprising.

Although he appreciated the importance of studying thermodynamics and structural design at Boston Tech (he always referred to it as "Boston Tech," even when everyone else spoke of "MIT"), J. Howard found himself wondering what was happening in his father's company, especially after the amazing oil discovery in Texas. And so he was ready for Joseph Newton's call when it came in 1901 and grateful to be able to test himself in the field. He passed the test so well that the family chose him to become the new head of Sun Oil following his father's death in

1912. Under his leadership the company grew into a billion-dollar global enterprise with 27,000 employees and forty thousand stockholders. It expanded, in fact, more than twentyfold—"in peace or wartime, economic boom or depression, deflation and inflation."[23]

The secret of Sun Oil's success was described by Pew as the ability to offer "the public what it wants at prices which it is both willing and able to pay." The company never expected nor asked for guarantees from anyone. It never assumed it had "a divine right" to a share and a place in the oil industry. "If someone else," said Pew flatly, "could serve the public better in quality or price, he was entitled to the business."[24]

In several ways, *Fortune* magazine once suggested, the company resembled a nineteenth-century partnership more than a twentieth-century corporation. Everywhere you turned in its Philadelphia headquarters in the 1930s there were Pews—salty, pipe-smoking J. Edgar, smiling, outgoing Joseph N., Jr., and in the president's office, a rather stern-faced J. Howard, looking, a friend remarked, "like an affidavit all over."[25] Family owned and operated, Sun Oil enjoyed one distinct advantage over its competitors: it could make quick decisions when necessary. While one giant oil corporation debated for weeks whether to adopt a new refining process, the Pews took exactly thirty minutes to give the go-ahead.[26]

A Natural Entrepreneur

Emblematic of the Pew style was the series of events that led to Sun's entry into shipbuilding. In 1915 J. Howard Pew visited England on an inspection tour—the biggest part of Sun's business was the shipping of lubricants to Europe—and made a side trip to Germany. Shown German submarines under construction, Pew became convinced that his company should build its own tankers rather than depend on others to handle the overseas distribution of its products. The sinking of the British ship *Lusitania* in May 1915 confirmed his thinking. Sun plunged ahead and completed the construction of its shipyard in Chester, Pennsylvania, in record time. With Joseph Pew (J. Howard's younger brother) in charge of the shipyard, the Sun Shipbuilding Company was started in May 1916, and its first ship, the S. S. *Chester Sun*, was launched in October 1917. By the next year some ten thousand men were building 10,000-ton tankers at the rate of one a month. Sun Shipbuilding would become one of the company's most successful divisions.

In peacetime as in wartime, the Sun company acted quickly and decisively. On June 28, 1919, the very day a peace treaty was signed between the Allies and Germany formally ending World War I, Sun tankers entered the German ports of Hamburg and Bremen and unloaded their valuable oil cargo—six weeks ahead of the competition. Pew later described how he waited for a telegram from Washington confirming the signing of the treaty and then immediately ordered the Sun fleet, ready and waiting, to steam into the German harbors. Later asked how much the company had earned by his initiative, Pew shrugged his shoulders. He was, he explained, more interested in rendering a "vital service" to people in need than in a quick profit.[27]

The company's most important move in the 1920s was to enter the fast-growing gasoline business, as usual in its own way. Sun opened its first service station in 1920 selling a single "premium" gasoline at a regular price. With only one grade rather than the three different grades of other producers, the Sun company required less storage space and equipment, less labor, fewer bookkeepers, fewer marketing trucks, and fewer pumps for the station operators. The advertisers of three grades of gasoline were, moreover, often in a quandary about which brand to promote, but never Sunoco advertisers. "Blue Sunoco" covered the gasoline market at a price always set several cents below premium.

The Sun company also demonstrated its innovative spirit by building a series of gasoline pipe lines *from* rather than *into* its Marcus Hook refinery. Sun thus became the first American company to transport refined products by pipeline into marketing areas—beginning in Cleveland, then Syracuse, and eventually into New Jersey. It was "a revolutionary idea," pushed hard by Joseph Pew, who took on the herculean job of obtaining over one thousand permits to cross highways, 183 to cross railroads, and thirty-four to cross rivers and canals. More than one thousand landholders had to be persuaded to grant easements; the most difficult to obtain was for a piece of land that had once belonged to William Penn.[28]

The Sun Oil Company—the name was adopted in 1922— prospered during the laissez-faire twenties and declined to kowtow to the federal government during the New Deal thirties. When the National Recovery Administration (NRA), in 1933–1934, tried to regulate prices, including gas and oil prices, the Pews refused to comply—on principle. They made it clear they would resist any attempt at government price-fixing until the Supreme Court either ordered them to do so or, as happened, declared the NRA unconstitutional.

J. Howard Pew articulated the company's uncompromising commitment to a philosophy of free enterprise in a 1938 address at Princeton University: "When I speak of the free enterprise system at its best, I mean when it is entirely free—free from monopoly, private or governmental; free from government control or intimidation; free from trade agreements which result in price and production control after the manner of the cartel system of Europe."[29]

For Pew, free enterprise was far more than a way of doing business. At its best, he said in the same Princeton talk, it comprehends good sportsmanship, gives fair play to the laws of supply and demand and of competition, develops discipline, character, and initiative, raises the standard of living, and improves the morale of the people.[30]

Pew was a wise manager as well as a remarkable entrepreneur. He regarded himself as a trustee responsible for the interests of employees, investors, and consumers. If Sun's management failed to treat any group fairly, he felt, the interests of everyone would be jeopardized. "Fairness and justice for all," he declared, "must be our motto," particularly toward the employees of Sun Oil.[31]

The company, with few exceptions, maintained its full force of employees even when the New Deal was trying to regulate its affairs. And wages and fringe benefits were not reduced even during the depths of the Great Depression. To the contrary, employees were invited, beginning in 1926, to participate in stock purchase plans that made them partners in Sun Oil. Had an employee entered the plan at its start and received just ten shares at each distribution over the years, he would have owned, at the time of Pew's death in 1971, 410 shares with a value of $145,281.50 (over $600,000 in 2000 dollars). As a consequence the company never experienced a single strike through war, depression, recession, and other economic downturns.

The Pew policy of fairness and justice was, in short, a practical application of the Golden Rule. Most businesses fail, he once told a group of workers, because "they do not have the proper human relations." And without the proper human relations, Pew added, "there does not exist the proper spirit and will to produce." And only the companies that produce the most goods per worker, he concluded, "eventually succeed."[32] Because Sun Oil always sought the proper human relations, it knew success early on, and stayed successful.

The president of the company privately practiced what he publicly preached. When an explosion at the Marcus Hook Refinery injured and hospitalized several men, Pew visted them each morning for six weeks, bringing them newspapers and magazines. When they needed skin grafts, he arranged for a top surgeon to do the operations. As the years passed, he faithfully attended the funerals of those he always considered fellow workers—especially those whom he had known at Marcus Hook in the early 1900s—and he cared for the needs of their families. With a strict admonition not to publicize his assistance, he personally enabled dozens of their children to attend Grove City College.

The early 1930s—the Depression years—were a critical testing time for the company and its management philosophy. Gross operating revenue dipped from $98 million in 1930 to $69 million in 1931 and $67 million in 1932. Net income dropped from $7.75 million to $3.1 million in the same period. But President Pew remained imperturbable and insisted in the company's 1931 annual report that this was "an opportune time" to complete the building and improvement program (just like Grove City College, which moved ahead with the construction of the Harbison Chapel and the new Hall of Science and a new dormitory, at the same time).

Sun built a multimillion-dollar pipeline from the Marcus Hook Refinery to Cleveland, modernized its tanker fleet at a cost of $9.5 million, and laid a crude oil pipeline in Texas. While other companies, large and small, were laying off workers and cutting back operations, Sun Oil prudently expanded its activities. After reviewing the financial reports for the first quarter of 1931, J. Howard Pew ordered that the following message, reassuring and exhortatory, be sent to all company offices: "There will be no reduction in salaries nor rates of pay throughout the company—please impress upon everyone to help make the second half better than the first half."[33] Inspired by such confidence in the future and in them, the people of Sun Oil responded with redoubled effort and efficiency. By 1934 profits were back up to almost $7 million.

His striking ability to anticipate the future was confirmed at about the same time when, according to biographer Mary Sennholz, he concluded that "Hitler was going to ruin Germany either by internal strife or foreign war." Whereupon Pew sold Sun's interests in a German firm that was marketing its lubricating oils and greases. When he was prevented by the German government from withdrawing the cash proceeds of the sale, Pew bought six-inch steel pipes in Germany and had them shipped to Philadelphia. The value of the pipes—to be used for the company's pipelines in America—matched the money generated by the sale of its German interests.[34]

Even with the Depression and the gathering clouds over Europe, Pew did not neglect Grove City College, seeing in it—and similar institutions—an instrument with which to build a better world for men to live in. In a 1932 talk to Grove City College alumni, he expressed his satisfaction that their college was equipping its students "for success in business," not by teaching specific rules and methods, "for these necessarily change," but by inculcating "broad principles and sound fundamentals, for these will persist, and will gain in value." The most important of those fundamentals, he said, were "good morals" and "high character." It was on this occasion, apparently, that Pew first recited publicly the poem "The Bridge Builder," which reflected his own belief that the older generation must build bridges for the generations that follow.[35]

Champion of Freedom

Articulate and determined, J. Howard Pew became a leading
spokesman for the oil industry and the free enterprise system.
He staunchly opposed artificial economic restraints whether they
proceeded from the government or a private monopoly. In 1933,
for example, he opposed the railroad lobby's attempt to force
commercial vehicles off the road through increased taxes and regulations. For him, as for the Founders of the Republic, freedom
was indivisible: a diminution of economic freedom would
inevitably lead to a curtailing of freedom in every other aspect of
life. Thus, while other business leaders temporized or fulminated
privately against FDR and his economic planners, Pew went public. He helped to form the American Liberty League, a bipartisan
coalition of conservative Republican and Democratic businessmen, that charged the Roosevelt administration with having
"traveled a long sector of the road to socialization."[36]

In his talks across America in the 1930s, J. Howard Pew was
part Paul Revere, part Billy Graham, and part Edward Gibbon.
During an address at the University of Virginia in July 1935, for
example, he argued that three thousand years of history had
demonstrated conclusively that planned economies do not work.
The pharaohs of Egypt, he pointed out, had seized all the land,
parceled it out to the masses, and then exacted one-fifth of what
was produced. When the economy inevitably declined, they had
doled out grain to the starving people. "The tombs of the
Pharaohs," Pew said, "became the burial place of Egyptian civilization... a perfect type of a Planned Economy."[37]

Later that year he detailed the New Deal's continuing campaign, despite the Supreme Court decision declaring the NRA
unconstitutional, to foment a "social and economic revolution."
He compared the American business community to Rip Van
Winkle and warned his fellow businessmen that unless they woke

up, and soon, they would find themselves regimented from top to bottom with "the politicians and their bureaucratic underlings as our bosses."[38]

"The big idea which Christianity brought into the world," Pew told a group of ministers at the Princeton Theological Seminary in 1939, "was the conception of the fundamental equality of men." Under the Constitution, that principle of equality has been carried farther in America than any other country. But recently, he warned, there has arisen a school of thought that promotes "the old idea of running everything from the top and of having our thinking done for us by a selected few." He urged the rejection of the planners who, he said sarcastically, "know so many things that simply aren't true."[39] Instead of serfdom, Pew offered a hymn to freedom:

> Nobody must be barred, no invention rejected, no idea untried; everybody must have his chance; and under our American system of free enterprise and equal opportunity everybody gets just that chance.
>
> It is our freedom that has brought us to this high estate—intellectual freedom, religious freedom, political freedom, industrial freedom; freedom to dream, to think, to imagine, to experiment, to invest, to match wits in friendly competition. This is our great American heritage.[40]

Just three months after Hitler invaded Poland and started World War II, J. Howard Pew was asked by the National Association of Manufacturers (NAM) to address the theme, "What the future holds for the American system of free enterprise." The future was bright, Pew stated, if everyone agreed that government must be the servant and not the master of the people. The best, the only, safeguard against a tyrannical government, he insisted, was freedom—"the freedom to think, to speculate, to experiment, to inquire, to question everything and anything."[41]

Rejecting the pessimism of the modern Malthusians, Pew asserted that it was not difficult to foresee the day "when we shall tap the riches we know are in and under the sea, and harness the rays of a benignant sun to the wheels of a thousand new industries"—if the dreamers and the builders were given the opportunity to do so. Like Thomas Jefferson who famously swore that he would "oppose every form of tyranny over the mind of man," Pew declared that all history had demonstrated "how dangerous it is to put restrictions on the freedom of the human mind." And yet, he warned, the economic planners in America wanted to "set up a government robot to do our thinking for us."[42]

Pew urged his audience to declare forthrightly their opposition to economic planning whatever its form—communist, fascist, socialist. As he had for years, he called Hitler a "dictator" and grouped him with Mussolini and Stalin because all three were apostles of a planned economy. And then he disposed of the canard that he was some radical laissez-faire advocate by setting forth (in the tradition of classical liberals Adam Smith and F. A. Hayek) the true role of government: to safeguard the common man's right "to be himself—all of himself." Government will have served its proper purpose, Pew said, when it prevents "monopoly, tyranny, extortion, and every infringement of human rights." Man, he concluded, needs more not less freedom to "work out his own destiny."[43]

And yet in the midst of all the weighty speeches and the constant traveling and the heavy demands of running an enormous, complex company, Pew made time for Grove City College. He described his annual visit to the campus at commencement time as "one of the most inspiring duties as well as one of the greatest pleasures that the passing years have brought to me." Although he often referred to Grove City as "his" college, he did not dictate to its president or other school officials. Former director of admissions John Moser recalls that in twelve years, "I never had a call from Mr. Pew or his assistant about admitting anyone."[44] If Pew's recommendation was usually adopted, it was because he had studied the problem carefully, considered the options, and then offered what he believed was the best solution. It helped, of course, that he was the college's number one benefactor and had what one associate called a "formidable personality."[45]

What a College Ought to Be

Shortly after J. Howard Pew became president of Grove City's board of trustees in 1932, he offered his idea of a college education at an alumni meeting. "Education," he said, "must include the teaching of good morals, the discipline necessary to produce character, and the teaching of knowledge—but knowledge without good morals and high character is without value."[46] On his visits to the college for the next forty years, he would reiterate the integral importance of morals, character, and knowledge within a Christian framework.

When the Mary Anderson Pew Dormitory was dedicated to his mother in June 1937, J. Howard revealed at the ceremony that both his mother and father were interested in supporting Grove City because they were convinced that "here would rise a true college of Christian citizenship."[47]

Whether at a congressional hearing in Washington, D.C., at a NAM conference, or on the campus of his favorite college, Pew declaimed about the many dangers of the New Deal. Will the state destroy American enterprise? He asked rhetorically at the dedication of the new dormitory. If so, he reasoned, then

"there will be no need for this institution or for others like it."
If the state does not destroy American enterprise, he argued, it
will be because the graduates of this and similar institutions of
higher learning will so strengthen and improve "our enterprise
system as to make it invulnerable."[48] For Pew, the mission of
Grove City and other true Christian colleges was indispensable.
For him, education founded on faith and freedom was the best
cure for the moral and social pathologies that the modern world
has produced.

But there was no such thing as a free cure. He insisted that
Grove City College operate, not as an eleemosynary institution,
but as a business. "[The school] was to be operated frugally,"
explained longtime trustee Heath Larry, "so that the average candidate for college could afford it." Pew was therefore opposed to
the use of the endowment for operating expenses, including student aid. He wrote Weir Ketler in 1940: "If I had any idea that
the Board wanted to create a big endowment for Grove City
College, I would not only feel that my interest, time and money
had been wasted, but I would of course want to resign from the
Board."[49] He sought to inculcate into everyone at Grove City,
stated Larry, that they were "partners in a business enterprise that
must live on the income it takes in each year."[50]

In his annual talk to the alumni as president of the board
of trustees, Pew always took considerable satisfaction in pointing
out that Grove City College had again operated in the black. He
reported in 1947 that over the last thirty-one years, the college
had received in student tuition, room, and board "some $300,000
in excess of all operating expenses, which was plowed back into
the construction of new buildings. This is a record which, I submit, is unique and one of which we all may well be proud."[51]

The Pew philosophy of running a college like a business
was warmly endorsed by Weir Ketler, who could wield as sharp a

blue pencil as any Sun Oil accountant. He did not object to—
indeed he welcomed—J. Howard Pew's businesslike approach to
the affairs of Grove City College. When Pew suggested that an
analysis of grounds and buildings expenses that he had received
was "not as complete as perhaps it should be," Ketler quickly provided a more detailed accounting. On another occasion, when
Pew urged the college president to increase the size of the student body to help pay for new buildings and additions, Ketler
stepped up recruiting, although he did not favor an ever increasing student enrollment.[52]

Winning Through Initiative

J. Howard Pew and the companies he headed made two vital contributions to winning World War II: fueling more than half of all
American army and navy airplanes, and building over one-third
of America's tankers. The former accomplishment was all the
more remarkable because Sun Oil ranked only fifteenth among
American oil companies just before the war. Both wartime contributions were the result of Pew's farsightedness. Sun's aviation
fuel was the military's fuel of choice because of its higher
octane—produced through a new catalytic process developed by
the French engineer and inventor Eugene Houdry and the Sun
company in the 1930s. When no other American company would
take a chance on Houdry's new and untested process, Sun Oil did.
As a result, when the air battles began in the skies over Europe
and the South Pacific, fourteen Houdry catalytic cracking plants
in America were producing quality gasoline.

Hundreds of tankers sailed from the docks of the Sun
Shipbuilding Company in the 1940s because J. Howard and
Joseph Pew decided to start building their own ships just prior
to World War I. It is almost impossible to overstate the import of
the Sun shipbuilding effort which was carried out without regard

for profit: Sun comptroller Robert Dunlop estimated that the return to the company was no more than 2 percent.[53]

In 1942, German submarines in the North Atlantic stalked and sank American and Allied ships almost at will. In that one year, over three million tons of shipping, loaded with oil and gasoline for planes, tanks, and ships, were destroyed by U-boats. But for every ton sunk, a new ton was built and sent to sea by America's shipbuilders. The Sun Shipbuilding Company led the way, building 250 major vessels and repairing 1,200 ships during the war. In 1942—the war's darkest year—Sun Shipbuilding built two-thirds of all the new tankers, the following year, one-half. Sun built, in total, 40 percent of America's tankers during World War II.

Because of Sun Shipbuilding and the other American builders, the fuel kept flowing to Europe, and the German attempt to rule the North Atlantic failed. Although Hitler more than doubled the number of submarines in 1943, the Allies countered with more convoys and escorts, new antisubmarine devices, better training, and the inventive research of scientists and technicians. Germany built 198 U-boats between May and December 1943 and lost 186 of them. By the end of the year, wrote Samuel Eliot Morison, the Allies had won the Battle of the Atlantic.[54]

Pew was always confident that America would lead the Allies to victory so long as American industry and agriculture were allowed to do what they did better than any other country in the world—exercise initiative. American industrial and agricultural wheels turned faster than those in Europe, he insisted, not because Americans were smarter or had greater natural resources or were better at mass production, but because of that intangible thing called initiative.

"It cannot be bought in stores," he said at the War Congress of American Industry in December 1942, "nor can it be acquired from books. Initiative is an attribute of the spirit.... [It] finds its expression in competition; and competition is possible only where there is freedom of choice and action."[55] "Free men," he said emphatically, "always will outproduce slave labor."[56] It would be the height of folly, he declared, to imitate Hitler and his socialist methods.

Instead, he urged the American government to keep restrictive policies to the absolute minimum, cut away bureaucratic red tape, and open "the door of opportunity" to management and labor. "Do these things," Pew predicted confidently, "and the output of war materials will soar to heights that even today would be called fantastic."[57] And so it was: In the five years between France's collapse in May 1940 and V-J day in August 1945, America produced nearly 300,000 warplanes, over 102,000 tanks, more than 372,000 artillery pieces, 2.5 million trucks, over 87,000 warships, 5,425 cargo ships, almost 6 million tons of aircraft bombs, 20 million small arms, and about 40 billion rounds of ammunition. The nation had come a long way from the early 1930s, when the army had doled out streetcar tokens for transportation to the chief aide of its commanding general—a major named Dwight D. Eisenhower.[58]

With the war's successful conclusion, Pew immediately began insisting that wage and price controls be removed. He warned against politicians who were everywhere "reaching out for more and more power." He took the occasion of his annual talk to Grove City College alumni in June 1946 to declare that the nation was approaching a danger point. He quoted the *Wall Street Journal* that "no people ever entered a compulsory state through a door on which the price of admission was plainly posted." The faculty, trustees, and alumni of Grove City College and other institutions of higher learning had a responsibility "to help keep that door plainly and clearly posted." If we are not willing to do this, he declared, "then we do not deserve to live in a free society."[59]

The following year, again speaking to the college's alumni, Pew urged them to defend the "American system of enterprise." He scornfully dismissed the collectivists, saying that "no economic planning authority could ever have foreseen, planned, plotted and organized the amazing spectacle of human progress that the world has witnessed in this country during the last 100 years." Such a miracle, he stated, could have occurred only where there was "a wide-open invitation to all the genius, inventive ability, organizing capacity and managerial skill of a great people."[60]

That same year, 1947, after having guided the Sun Oil Company through two global conflicts, a wrenching depression, and the emergence of communism, fascism, and the modern welfare state, J. Howard Pew handed over the presidency to the company's thirty-seven-year-old comptroller, Robert G. Dunlop. At age sixty-five and after three-and-a-half decades as president, Pew said that the company deserved new energetic leadership. But much more was involved than a change of CEOs.

John Howard Pew and his father Joseph Newton Pew before him were entrepreneurs who had built the Sun Oil Company into an international enterprise by taking risks, using their imaginations, and daring to do what other oil companies dared not do—for example, developing a high octane gasoline in the 1930s through the controversial Houdry process. A no less daring venture several years later was the construction of a plant in the north of Canada to convert a tar-like substance found in Canadian sand into synthetic crude oil. The plant necessitated the commitment of 25 percent of the net worth of the company. When others began saying nervously, "Give it up. It's never going to pay off," Pew did not give up, and his steadfastness produced the first large-scale extraction of oil from the tar sands of

Alberta—and provided at least a partial answer to America's overdependence on Middle East oil.[61]

Robert Dunlop had been personally trained by J. Howard Pew and agreed totally with his philosophy that the freedom to think and act was the key to success in business and life. But Dunlop had not worked in the rough-and-ready oil fields and boom towns of western Pennsylvania and Texas; he had not steered the company through the economic storms created by war and depression. He was a corporate manager, highly skilled to be sure, and a model of rectitude like his predecessor, but he was a manager nonetheless, not an entrepreneur. With Dunlop's succession Sun Oil signaled it was no longer a nineteenth-century partnership but a modern twentieth-century corporation. Still, some things remained the same. J. Howard Pew continued to serve Sun Oil as a member of the board until 1963 when he assumed the board chairmanship with the death of his brother Joseph and then became chairman of the executive committee in 1970 when the company merged with Sunray DX Oil Company.

Faith, Freedom, and Philanthropy

From his office on the nineteenth floor of the Sun Oil Building in Philadelphia, Pew persevered in promoting the tenets of faith and freedom that had been at the core of his life and career. In 1948, with his brothers and sisters, J. Howard organized the Pew Memorial Trust, which became the family's principal philanthropic vehicle. The original gift of 800,000 shares of Sun Oil stock grew to more than six million shares and a value of over $600 million at his death. He also established the J. Howard Pew Freedom Trust "to acquaint the American people with the. . . vital need to maintain and preserve a limited form of government in the United States" and "to promote recognition of the interdependence of Christianity and freedom."[62]

He devoted more time to helping Weir Ketler manage the affairs, large and small, of Grove City College. Reviewing the copy of a promotional brochure in 1948, he deleted a long passage that described the Pew generosity over the years, explaining he thought it was "a mistake to stress the Pew family. . . we don't want the prospective contributors to feel that they should let the Pews do it all."[63] He continued to have the general auditor of the Sun Oil Company review the books and records of the college. He arranged in 1953 for Albert A. Hopeman, Jr., to join the board of trustees. He persuaded Weir Ketler to delay his retirement—Ketler had hoped to step down as president that same year. He delivered the 1955 commencement address, telling the departing students, "Faith in God is the great heritage of our generation," and asking, "What will be the heritage of the generations to come?"[64] And he served as chairman of the nominating committee which unanimously selected John Stanley Harker as the next president of Grove City College. In an emotional letter to his old and departing friend Weir Ketler, Pew wrote, "No one knows better than I do how much we are all indebted to you for carrying on the work of the College for 40 years."[65]

As hard as J. Howard and the other Pews tried, they could not conceal their far-ranging and open-ended generosity. It has been estimated that the Pews gave more than 90 percent of their income to philanthropic causes.[66] There were substantial gifts to hospitals and charities in the Philadelphia area as well as to national groups like the Boy Scouts, the Girl Scouts, the YMCA, and the Cancer Fund. There were grants to independent colleges—not state universities—especially black colleges. Long before the 1954 Supreme Court decision of *Brown v. the Board of Education,* J. Howard Pew and his father before him had supported education for students of all colors. Grove City College itself had been integrated from its founding in 1876 (although few blacks came to the isolated rural campus miles from any city). And the Pew Memorial Trust made sizable grants to the United Negro College Fund and black colleges like Hampton, Bishop, and St. Augustine's.

Then, of course, significant foundation support went to many Christian and evangelical institutions, including the Billy Graham Evangelistic Association, the National Association of Evangelicals, the Moody Bible Institute, and Youth for Christ, as well as to publications like *Christianity Today* and the *Presbyterian Layman*. Pew personally helped found the Christian Freedom Foundation because "a free market can exist only in a community where the people generally accept honesty, truthfulness and fairness"—all qualities to be found in a Christian community. And he started *Christian Economics* in 1950 to encourage entrepreneurs to confine their activities to the making and the distribution of goods and services that "will not harm, but on the contrary will benefit their fellows."[67]

He enthusiastically supported the work of Leonard Reed and the Foundation for Economic Education (FEE), both financially and personally, joining FEE's board in 1950. Pew was impressed by FEE's emphasis on the moral and spiritual antecedents of individual freedom. He underwrote the distribution of works like Reed's *Accent on the Right* and *Students of Liberty* and contributed an occasional article to the foundation's monthly publication *The Freeman*.

Since 1940, J. Howard Pew had been president of the board of trustees of the General Assembly of the Presbyterian Church, raising funds for the national church and overseeing its assets. As one of the most influential lay Protestants in America, it was not surprising that in 1950 he was named chairman of the National Lay Committee of the National Council of Churches. It was a powerful post: The council claimed to represent thirty-four million Protestants.

Conflict between the liberal clergy and the conservative laymen of the National Council was inevitable. The clergy were eager to promote a radical socio-economic agenda aimed at restructuring American society, but they were conspicuously silent when the Soviets seized control of Eastern and Central Europe. The laymen, led by J. Howard Pew, firmly opposed the clergy's domestic activities, pointing out that they had no biblical mandate for such political action. The Lay Committee argued that the church should devote its energies to evangelism, Christian education, and developing spiritual and moral character rather than "issuing calls for expanding government intervention and welfarism."[68] The resulting impasse led, in 1955, to the dissolution of the Lay Committee of the National Council of Churches and the formation of the Presbyterian Lay Committee, which committed itself to winning people to Jesus Christ and proclaiming the word of God. At about the same time Pew helped to establish, along with Billy Graham, *Christianity Today*, which became one of the most influential religious publications in the world.

The year 1963 was filled with sorrow and grief for J. Howard Pew. First, his younger brother Joseph, who had been his partner and colleague for fifty-five years, died. They had guided the company's fortunes for decades, frequently visiting each other in their offices on the nineteenth floor of the Sun Oil building and lunching daily in the nearby Racquet Club. And then not long after, his wife Helen passed away. Their daughter Frances Pew Hayes later said she was surprised that her father had the strength to live on without the woman who had been close by his side for more than fifty years.[69]

"Mrs. Pew and I," J. Howard once wrote in a simple but eloquent tribute, "had fifty-seven years together, for which I am most grateful. But I realize that her time had come, and it was best for her to pass on; but with me it leaves a void which can never be filled. It may be presumptuous on my part, but I must tell you that she was a truly remarkable woman. I never knew her to say an unkind word about anyone; and I am sure she never entertained an unworthy or mean thought."[70]

Despite the personal losses, Pew continued his widespread charitable and educational commitments, especially to his favorite school, Grove City College. Usually described by his critics as inflexible, Pew could accept change if there was no possible alternative, as when he approved the enrollment of the college's faculty in the Social Security program—a move he had long opposed. He also arranged for a generous $500,000 grant from the Pew Memorial Trust to expand Grove City's retirement program for its staff and faculty. In a letter to President Harker, he asked as usual that the grant "not be given publicity."[71]

Governed by God

At eighty-one, still healthy of body and keen of mind, Pew kept fighting the good fight, often quoting William Penn: "Men will either be governed by God or ruled by tyrants." In the mid-1960s he undertook one more mission for his beloved Presbyterian Church. Until then, Charles S. MacKenzie points out, Presbyterians had professed that the seventeenth-century Westminster Confession of Faith was a "reliable interpretation of Biblical teaching." But many modern clergy considered the Westminister Confession anachronistic because it presented the Bible as the "true, infallible word of God." The modernists drafted a "new" confession which along with the older creeds was to be a "guide" to the Church's beliefs and members.[72]

The 1967 confession left out biblical words that resonated with professing Christians—like sanctification, providence, Holy

Scripture, repentance, redemption, judgment, trinity, and atone-
ment. Instead, there were twenty-three references to "reconciliation"—but a reconciliation of man to man rather than man to
God. Pew and other members of the Presbyterian Lay Committee
were adamant in opposing the new confession which they charged
would dilute the Christian faith, weaken the authority of the Bible,
and encourage the church to become a secular organization more
concerned with the social and political than the spiritual and
moral. Their determination to stand firm for the old confession
was strengthened by the accelerating unrest on college campuses,
in the inner cities, and in the nation at large. They were moved
when they received hundreds of letters from fellow Christians who
asked, along the lines of one Illinois layman, "When I joined the
Church, I stated my faith in Jesus Christ as my personal savior. I
wasn't asked to subscribe to any economic, social, or political
issue. Is this now about to be changed?"[73]

A resolute Pew toured the nation, telling dozens of audi-
ences that "the Confession of 1967 confronts the Presbyterian
Church with a challenge regarding her faith in the Holy Scripture.
It denies clearly the position held by Christendom for almost
20 centuries and affirmed by the Westminster Confession that the
Bible is the true Word of God."[74]

Professional lecturers of any age would have been impressed
by Pew's appearances. He would get up in front of a large audience and talk for nearly an hour, without a note, on the separa-
tion of church and state. His command of the complex material
was based on many hours of personal research. Convinced that he
was a more effective speaker without a text, he memorized each
speech by reading it perhaps a dozen times and then reciting it
to himself.[75] His stamina was remarkable: On one five-day trip,
when he was in his mideighties, Pew spoke in Seattle, Portland,
San Francisco, Los Angeles, Denver, and Dallas.[76] But despite the

concerted efforts of Pew and others, the Presbyterian Church adopted the new confession and, as predicted, lost many thousands of members.

At the same time, J. Howard Pew was not a denominational antediluvian but a warm admirer of leaders of different faiths including John Cardinal Kroll of Philadelphia and President Ernest Wilkinson of Brigham Young University. A particular favorite of Pew was Billy Graham, whom he began supporting in 1948 when the evangelist was a young, unknown Baptist preacher from the hills of North Carolina. The two men became close friends and confidants.

"When I think of J. Howard Pew," remarked Graham after the philanthropist's passing, "I think of total integrity."[77] Those who knew Pew agree that he would rather have died than compromise his principles—especially on a matter of faith. For example, although nominated many times, he would not accept the position of elder in the Presbyterian church until the age of seventy-six, and then only after the most thorough preparation and meditation.

Nor was Pew all stern visage and dark business suit. He enjoyed jokes, puns, poems, and limericks. At Halloween he relished having the children of friends and associates come to the house and try to scare him with their colorful masks. As a hobby he raised orchids in a small arboretum behind the house and encouraged women guests to pick out an orchid for themselves. His speeches were lightened with numerous analogies and humorous stories. He was fond of comparing economic planners with the lightning bug which, he noted, "is brilliant but it hasn't any mind; it travels through existence with its headlight on behind."

And he invariably ended his talks with an uplifting poem by John Greenleaf Whittier, Rudyard Kipling, or Angela Morgan.

His favorite was "The Bridge Builder" by Will Allen Dromgoole, which ends:

> "Old man!" cried a fellow pilgrim near,
> "Why waste your strength with your building here;
> Your journey will end with the ending day,
> And you never again will pass this way;
> You have crossed the chasm deep and wide,
> Why build a bridge at eventide?"
>
> The builder raised his old gray head,
> "Good friend, on the path I have come," he said,
> "There followeth after me today
> A youth whose feet will pass this way.
> This stream which has meant naught to me,
> To that fair-haired boy may a pitfall be;
> He, too, must cross in the twilight dim.
> Good friend, I am building this bridge for him."[78]

Pew was a man of simple pleasures. He played bridge almost every night at home and golf every Wednesday afternoon and Saturday morning—but never on Sunday. No matter who wanted to see him on a Wednesday afternoon, he would courteously decline, adding with a smile, "You wouldn't want to deny an old man like me one afternoon of recreation a week, would you?"[79] He loved to read, and one of his most treasured books was an original edition of the King James Bible, which lay on a table next to his favorite reading chair in his Ardmore home. He also delved deeply into philosophy and economics—particularly Friedrich A. Hayek, the classical liberal, and Ludwig von Mises, the Austrian economist. He commissioned a number of scholars, young and old, to do research for him in theology and church history, including the eminent British writer, Philip Edgecomb Hughes.

Most of all, J. Howard Pew was a man of genuine Christian charity who believed he should share generously what God had given him, especially with those in serious need. When a gardener on the Pew estate in Ardmore incurred crushing medical expenses, Pew paid all the bills not covered by insurance with a personal check. And he proferred the gardener some shrewd advice: "Don't pay the doctor all at once. Pay him a little at a time. It will help to keep his bill lower next time." Pew shunned any publicity about his gifts. When a hospital suffered a serious fire and its administrator came to Pew for help, he give the hospital $250,000, directing as usual that his assistance not be publicized. But the hospital openly boasted about the Pew gift, and it never again received a donation from the Pews.[80]

For all his wealth Pew spent little on himself. He enjoyed "plain but tasty food"—no tea, coffee, or vanilla, but rather orange juice, milk, and chocolate. His usual luncheon at the Racquet Club across the street from his office was a slice of roast beef on a piece of bread. Although he himself liked to smoke about three good Havana cigars a day, he did not permit cigarette smoking in his presence. Once asked why, he launched into "a long and lucid lecture on the chemistry of smoke and how its benzine qualities could cause cancer."[81] He drove a large, but not expensive, American car—in the late sixties, it was a five-year-old Oldsmobile—and his hand-tailored suits were worn until they were nearly threadbare. His raincoat was so old and frayed it looked as though it belonged in a homeless shelter.

In the fall of 1971, following a heart attack while vacationing in the Canadian Rockies, eighty-nine-year-old J. Howard Pew was still weak but seeing a few friends, including Charles MacKenzie, the new president of his beloved alma mater. "We rode through the hills of Valley Forge," recalled MacKenzie, and "he talked only of his dreams for Grove City College. He said how he longed to see the College be an instrument in God's hands." And then Pew said, wistfully, "But I'm afraid I may never see my college again.'" Two months later, on November 27, he died.[82]

    J. Howard died confident that he had found the right man to lead "his" college in the years ahead, one who would stress the priceless American heritage of religious, political, and economic liberty. Just how demanding those years would be—including a historic legal battle against the federal government—neither Pew, MacKenzie, nor anyone else at Grove City College could have imagined.

CHAPTER SEVEN

Not for Sale

At first glance it looked like one of those form letters a college president is always getting from the federal government. As president of Grove City College, which fiercely guarded its independence, Charles MacKenzie usually put such correspondence at the bottom of the pile. But this letter was different. Dated July 1976, it was from the Office for Civil Rights of the Department of Health, Education, and Welfare (HEW), and advised him that Grove City would have to sign an "assurance of compliance" with Title IX of the Education Amendments Act of 1972 forbidding schools to discriminate against women. In effect, the agency was asserting that it would tell Grove City (and almost every other college in America) how many students of each sex it could admit. If it did not comply, warned HEW, the college would lose its federal funding.

President MacKenzie sat at his desk in Crawford Hall pondering his response. To begin with, Grove City had never discriminated against women: it had been coeducational since its founding in 1876. Of its two thousand students at present, about 50 percent were men and the other 50 percent women. The college had no objection to women's rights, or the rights of any other minority for that matter. MacKenzie himself believed in equal opportunity and had worked hard to integrate the Broadway Presbyterian Church in New York City when he had been its pastor, and he had later served on a human relations commission in California. For more than a century Grove City College had itself voluntarily followed a policy of nondiscrimination.

The inherent danger here, it seemed to MacKenzie, was that if he signed Form 639 (later succeeded by Form 639A), the college would be agreeing not only to abide by Title IX but all future amendments and bureaucratic interpretations of that title. HEW was seeking in effect to govern almost every aspect of college life, from admissions policy to housing. That, MacKenzie concluded, "would be tantamount to turning over control of the college's future to the federal government."[1] And that he would not do— nor would the college's board of trustees allow him to do so. At issue was, not compliance or noncompliance with Title IX, but the question: "Who runs a private educational institution like Grove City College—the federal government or its trustees and officers?" Grove City College was private, independent, and Christian, and intended to stay that way. MacKenzie dismissed the HEW threat to cut off federal funds because the school did not receive any.

There was good reason for the college's concern about government encroachment in higher education. As witness the experience of Reed College, a small private college in Portland, Oregon. When the college set out to hire new faculty members, it was informed by HEW that it had to advertise nationally instead of through the usual academic media. Reed, which normally received about five hundred faculty applications a year, was flooded with more than six thousand. Unsated, HEW required Reed to keep records on the thousands of applicants who were not hired and to make detailed reports on the leading rejected candidates, including their race, sex, job qualifications, prior experience, and why Reed did not hire them. The HEW mandate cost Reed an extra $40,000—"with no provable benefit for the college."[2]

Schools large and small were feeling the heavy regulatory hand of government. Harvard President Derek Bok estimated that in 1975 complying with government regulations cost Harvard $8.3 million and took up 60,000 hours of faculty time. Washington's increasing involvement in academe over the past decade was reflected in the tenfold increase of pages devoted to higher education in the *Federal Register*, the official index of government regulations. The following story, probably apocryphal, was often told at education meetings: When a college administration asked a government granting agency for permission to destroy some dead files, the agency, after months of delay, finally replied: Permission granted but be sure to keep one copy of everything.[3]

HEW admitted later to Grove City (and to Hillsdale College, which also refused to sign the federal agency's compliance form) that colleges that accepted federal funds or students that received federal assistance would have to maintain "detailed records of all student and employee applications, enrollments, academic records, personnel files, suspensions, hirings, firings, promotions, denial of promotions, etc.—all broken down by race, age, sex, and ethnic origin—and submit them upon demand to federal authorities."[4] The prospect of maintaining such byzantine record-keeping reinforced Grove City College's determination to resist the governmental edict.

When Grove City College president MacKenzie, with the firm support of the trustees and the faculty, declined to sign, he began to receive a series of increasingly threatening phone calls

from HEW officials. "The callers kept telling me that we had better sign," the president recalled, "that they had ways of making us
sign." MacKenzie challenged the bureaucrats to put their statements, especially the threatening ones, in writing, but they
declined.[5] He learned that several hundred other colleges that
had not signed the form were also being pressured to comply.
Most of them eventually buckled and signed, some with a statement of protest. Simply put, they dared not say no because they
needed the federal money to stay in business. But Grove City
College steadfastly refused—and would soon pay a high price for
its principles.

According to HEW's interpretation of Title IX, advised the
college's legal counsel, if a college had even *one* student who
received any kind of federal assistance—a guaranteed student
loan, for example, or a Pell Grant—that school was as much a
"recipient institution" as a university receiving millions of dollars in federal grants. It was illogical and arbitrary, but it was the
law as laid down by the Department of Health, Education, and
Welfare under President Jimmy Carter. Commented one college
president, "as if the government were to nationalize a supermarket because someone had bought groceries there with a Social
Security check." Grove City's legal counsel (Nixon, Hargrave,
Devans & Doyle of Rochester, New York) suggested that HEW
had two options—cut off federal assistance to Grove City students or bring suit against the college "to compel compliance with
its regulations."[6]

And so, unable to bend the will of the institution, the government made good on its threats by going after, not the college,
but its students. At the time about one-fourth of Grove City's
2,200 students were getting loans secured by the federal government or federal grants—at their own not the college's initiative.
Three hundred forty-two students had obtained Guaranteed

Student Loans (GSLs) totaling $618,500 from a private lending institution with the government guaranteeing full payment; 140 had received Basic Educational Opportunity Grants (BEOGs or Pell Grants) totaling $109,674, which were paid directly to the student by the Office of Education. Now, HEW threatened to stop the loans and grants unless Grove City College—and thirteen other schools—complied formally and in writing with its regulations. Grove City and Hillsdale were the only four-year, liberal arts colleges targeted by the government. When Grove City refused to accept the government's claims of jurisdiction, HEW summoned the college to an administrative law court in Philadelphia where it was ordered (by a judge who was a HEW employee) to show why the student grants and loans should not be terminated.

Grove City College restated its position that it did not receive federal assistance. The loans and grants, it said, were agreements made between the students and the government and therefore did not constitute federal aid to the school. The money was sent directly to the students and not to Grove City. The college wasn't even sure which students received federal funds until it certified they were enrolled in school. The question seemed to be, MacKenzie later reported, "whether a school or a church or a supermarket which receives money from customers, or contributors who have received funds from the government is to be classified as federally funded and therefore subject to government control."[7] The HEW attorneys took several hours to present their case, but Grove City's attorney, John B. McCrory, had gone on for only half an hour when the judge announced he had to catch a plane to Atlanta and abruptly ended the hearing.

Although common sense and simple justice seemed to be on Grove City's side, Judge Albert Feldman ruled that since the students paid the money they received from the government to the college for their tuition, Grove City was in fact a recipient of federal funds. He authorized HEW to cut off the loans and grants to the students. The judge, however, criticized the "total and unbridled discretion" of the Office for Civil Rights to require almost any compliance it wanted.

Feldman stressed that although the case had been brought to prevent discrimination, there was no sign that Grove City College had ever failed to comply with the law, except for its refusal to sign the form. Grove City had not been accused of discrimination against women or anyone else. "This refusal," the judge stated, "is obviously a matter of conscience and belief."[8]

The college could have capitulated. Indeed, most of the nation's 2,734 colleges and universities had given in by now and signed the HEW form. But Grove City College was truly a private, independent, and Christian school. It was convinced, in Sherry MacKenzie's words, that compliance would bring control by a secular government leading to a "secularization" of the college, a "forced abandonment" of its Christian orientation, a "diminution" in the quality of its academic program, and "greatly increased costs" to its students.[9] And so the college decided to take the offensive.

Knowing that it would be a protracted and expensive legal battle going perhaps all the way to the Supreme Court, Grove City and four of its students—Marianne Sickafuse, Jenifer Smith, Kenneth Hockenberry, and Victor Vouga—took HEW to the federal district court in Pittsburgh. The school requested that the HEW secretary and the department be prevented from penalizing the students and further harassing Grove City. The school also claimed that the regulations of HEW's Office for Civil Rights were illegal and unconstitutional because they exceeded the scope of the law and violated such constitutional rights as a student's right to the due process of law. "I believe very strongly," commented

President MacKenzie, "as many educators do, that the government's gross interference has diminished quality and innovation and promoted a homogeneous, state-controlled higher-education system."[10] HEW responded that Judge Feldman's decision was correct, and the court should simply affirm it without consideration of any other matter such as constitutionality. Many educators did not agree with HEW. "This is an extremely important case," commented President Dallin H. Oakes of Brigham Young University, "because it tests the proposition that the federal government can regulate the activities of independent institutions solely on the basis of financial aid extended to students."[11]

Why was the federal government intent on regulating the internal affairs of a small liberal arts college in western Pennsylvania whose only flaw, it seemed, was its sturdy adherence to principle and independence? Why had the overwhelming majority of American colleges and universities docilely signed Form 639A? The answer, according to Vanderbilt University historian Hugh David Graham, lay in the changing nature of federal aid to higher education and "in the civil rights legislation of the 1960s and the social revolution it spawned."[12]

The Janus Face of Federal Aid

Although there had been a cascade of federal programs benefiting American higher education in the post-World War II period, starting with the GI Bill and culminating in college tuition grants to low- and moderate-income students in 1972, few federal strings had ever been attached. These had been bountiful years for higher education: by 1968 direct federal financial assistance reached 92 percent of the nation's colleges and universities. Federal agencies provided liberal funding for campus research, construction, and training programs, asking little in return beyond the standard accounting and reporting procedures. And it was clear, wrote Hugh David Graham, that Congress did not intend that the grant-in-aid programs of the 1950s and 1960s should be "bait for a subsequent regulatory hook."[13]

Such hands-off beneficence began disappearing with the civil rights revolution of the 1960s. Title VI of the Civil Rights Act of 1964 authorized the termination of funds to federally assisted programs that did not comply with government regulations. When other groups noted the gains won by blacks through affirmative-action programs based on Title VI, they began to lobby for similar benefits for their members. Congress responded by expanding the standard "race, color, or national origin" formula of the 1964 law. First came women (Title IX of the Education Amendments of 1972), followed by the handicapped, minority language speakers, and the aged. In each case Congress left the task of spelling out the specifics of "Washington's new system of social regulation" to the bureaucrats who were quite willing to accept the responsibility.[14]

The new regulatory model was in some ways a throwback to the progressive era of the early twentieth century with its emphasis on efficient government. But unlike past legislation, and against the intent of the Founders, the primary purpose of the new regulations was not to punish past behavior but to prevent future harm—in the workplace, in the schools, in the rivers, in the streams, and in the skies—everywhere. A hundred new federal agencies sprang up to interpret and enforce a thousand new regulations. The Age of Regulatory Government had arrived.

One of the most controversial regulations was the U.S. Department of Labor's "Revised Order No. 4" of 1971 that forced businesses and organizations with federal contracts to set up hiring "goals," often on the basis of sex or race. Compliance with the order—establishing, in effect, a policy of affirmative action—in the area of higher education was given to HEW. Bureaucrats began using this authority to dictate admissions, hiring, and administration of scholarships. The agency insisted it was only giving women and minorities an "equal chance" at academic jobs, but, wrote investigative journalist Ralph Kinney Bennett, by not clearly defining "acceptable compliance" and threatening to withhold federal funds, HEW forced colleges and universities into bizarre situations.[15]

The University of California at Berkeley, for example, came up with the following "affirmative" guidelines: it needed .19 more women in its civil engineering department; 1.38 more blacks in the social welfare department; and 14.56 more women professors in the English department. The paperwork and staff time required to comply with the new guidelines cost the university an estimated $400,000 in just the first academic year. "Academic freedom is now a thing of the past," remarked President John A. Howard of Rockford College, "and federal subsidy has been the bludgeon employed to demolish it."[16]

The government was everywhere in higher education. When Brown University explained that there were no minority graduate students in its religious studies program because none who applied had met the requirements for ancient languages, a HEW bureaucrat peremptorily replied, "Then end these old-fashioned programs that require irrelevant languages." The university later received an apology from the agency for the remark, but not a reprieve from affirmative action.[17]

Even the original author of Title IX—Congresswomen Edith Green, a liberal Democrat from Oregon—believed that HEW had gone too far. "If I or others in the House had argued that this legislation was designed to do some of the things which HEW now says it was designed to do," Green said, "I believe the legislation would have been defeated. I myself would not have voted for it, even though I feel very strongly about ending discrimination on the basis of sex."[18] There was "no such thing as a little bureaucratic control," Albert Hopeman, Grove City's trustee president, wrote bluntly to David Lascell, who had taken over the legal defense of the college at Nixon, Hargrave. "It may take longer than 9 months but once control is established, complete domination will follow."[19]

An Unexpected Decision

The federal judge in Pittsburgh assigned to the *Grove City College v. HEW* suit was not a garden-variety jurist. Paul A. Simmons was the grandson of a slave and a former railroad mechanic who had taught law at a southern black university and written the briefs in several important civil rights victories. He did not seem likely, on the surface, to be receptive to Grove City's constitutional arguments.

But in November 1979, after both sides had filed lengthy briefs, Judge Simmons began hearing their oral arguments and quickly surprised the government side. Why, he asked HEW lawyer Mark Rutzick, didn't the agency pursue the obvious violators of women's rights instead of hounding colleges that supported such rights? "Why do you want them to fill in blanks on forms if it is not in any way to prevent discrimination?" Rutzick answered that the purpose of the Philadelphia hearing before Judge Feldman was not to look for discrimination, but to establish that the college had refused to sign the compliance form.

"Don't you think," Judge Simmons retorted, "that there has to be a limit to bureaucratic pressures and meddling with the rights of people?" "In this day and age," he added, "when most institutions have their hands out trying to get money from the government, an institution is saying, 'We don't want the government to give us anything.'" "The government is discouraging," Simmons concluded, "what some might believe a laudable position."[20] The HEW lawyer was rendered nearly speechless while Grove City College counsel David Lascell barely suppressed a cheer. The judge had clearly been impressed by the college's argument that it had "undertaken to do what is morally right without government persuasion" and that under the banner of sex discrimination, HEW was attempting to "control Grove City College."[21]

In March 1980, Judge Simmons handed down an eighteen-page decision that was, in the words of one national magazine, a "sweeping victory" for Grove City. The college did not have to sign HEW's compliance form. Form 639A was declared "invalid, void and of no effect whatsoever." The agency did not have the power to cut off Guaranteed Student Loans (GSLs) because, although they constituted "federal financial assistance," the loans were provided under "a contract of guaranty" and therefore not subject to Title IX. And although the Basic Educational Opportunity Grants (BEOG's) had to be considered financial aid to the college, HEW could not cut off any student's grant unless it first proved that the college was guilty of sex discrimination at "a full administrative hearing."[22]

"Because the college failed to file a form as a matter of conscience," Judge Simmons wrote, "both male and female students—although totally innocent of any wrongdoing—will be irreparably harmed by losing their financial aid, and in a case where there is absolutely no evidence of sex discrimination. Certainly, Congress never intended such an absurd result." HEW's zealousness, the judge added, reminded him of Alexis de Toqueville's warning in his classic work *Democracy in America* about "the inherent potential tyranny of the executive power." All three divisions of our policy system, Judge Simmons remarked, "should remember constantly that the price of freedom is eternal vigilance."[23]

That night Grove City College celebrated Judge Simmons's decision with what *Time* magazine satirically called a "sinful" celebration: an ice cream social in the Mary Anderson Pew west dining hall.[24] A jazz band played, and students danced in the aisles between the tables. The ability of every private college in America to resist arbitrary executive power had been successfully defended. But President MacKenzie and the other Grove City officials knew that the battle (costing $165,000 so far) was not over— an appeal by HEW was virtually certain. And after all, even so sympathetic a judge as Simmons had ruled that both the loans and the grants were "federal financial assistance."

In December 1980, David Lascell and Robb Jones, attorneys for Grove City College and its four students, submitted legal briefs in response to the government's appeal to the U.S. Court of Appeals for the Third Circuit in Philadelphia—the next legal step in the school's fight against government control. "We are trying," explained President MacKenzie, "to reaffirm the principles on which private education in this country was founded, and that is to maintain an academic community free of government intrusion."[25] Those principles were endorsed by high-ranking members of the new Reagan administration, which took office in January 1981. While campaigning for president the previous fall, Ronald Reagan himself had declared: "We must not allow the noble concept of equal opportunity to be distorted into federal guidelines or quotas which require race, ethnicity, or sex—rather than ability and qualifications—to be the principal factor in hiring or education."[26]

It even seemed for a time that the government might drop its action against Grove City College. In late March the Justice Department asked that the case be put on hold because the Education Department (which had succeeded HEW in the suit) was considering a revision of its definition of federal aid. The new language, according to the *Pittsburgh Press*, would have declared federally guaranteed student loans and certain types of federal grants to be "indirect" rather than direct assistance to colleges. That would have left Grove City College and approximately three hundred other colleges that received no other federal money "free to comply or not to comply with U.S. civil rights laws."[27]

But in mid-January 1982, after months of rumor and speculation, the Justice Department suddenly announced there would be no change in the rules—after reportedly rejecting a draft submitted by the Department of Education—and asked the Third U.S. Circuit Court of Appeals to resume the four-year-old battle with Grove City College. Through no fault of its own, the college had been caught in the middle of an imbroglio between the Reagan administration and the civil rights community. Just the week before, the Treasury and Justice Departments had decided to nullify a long-standing IRS practice that had never been approved by Congress and to grant tax-exemption status to certain religious schools, like Bob Jones University in South Carolina, that discriminated against racial minorities. The administration, satisfied with its interpretation of the law, had paid scant attention to the politics of its decision. The White House realized its error when the Associated Press reported: "The Internal Revenue Service plans to allow tax exempt status to private schools that discriminate against blacks."[28]

The uproar from civil rights leaders and blacks in the Reagan administration was instantaneous and vociferous. NAACP President Benjamin Hooks said the decision was "nothing short of criminal." Americans for Democratic Action called it "obscene."[29] Some black Reagan appointees threatened to resign. All of the White House's efforts at damage control failed, and President Reagan was forced to call a news conference at which he reiterated his opposition to racial discrimination of any kind and rescinded the change in policy. It was clearly no time to waver in the area of civil rights, and dropping the case against Grove City College would have left just that impression.

Ironically, the college had an ally in Secretary of Education Terrel H. Bell, who had proposed changing the definition of "federal financial assistance" to exclude student aid. Bell, a former Utah commissioner of higher education, felt that "aid to students that is not campus-based does not constitute aid to the institution." In response to the complaints of civil rights groups that his proposal would have excluded many schools from coverage of antidiscrimination laws, the education secretary declared that "any institution should comply with the civil rights laws." But, he insisted, HEW's compliance form was "more than compliance." It brought an entire institution "under the surveillance" of the federal government.[30] Bell was echoing Grove City College's very arguments.

The Justice Department objected that the proposed change could not be defended in court, but civil rights politics as much as the law determined the decision to proceed against Grove City College. The department, however, made an important concession—it would not contest Judge Simmons's ruling that federally guaranteed student loans (GSLs) were not covered by Title IX. Justice argued that if students received federal grants (the so-called Pell Grants), that in itself would be sufficient to bring their college under Title IX coverage. Secretary Bell endorsed the deletion of loans, telling a congressional committee that colleges should be free from the zealous reach of bureaucratic "tyrants."[31]

Senator Orrin Hatch, chairman of the Senate Labor and Human Resources Committee and a conservative Republican from Utah, also applauded the Justice Department's action. "I don't see why," said Hatch, private schools like Grove City "have to come under the federal aegis and meet all the paperwork burden and other requirements... just because they take students who may have access to government student loans." Carefully pointing out that Grove City, Hillsdale, and the other colleges targeted did not discriminate, Hatch argued that if they ever were to discriminate, "Title VI of the Civil Rights Act can take care of it."[32]

In their brief for Grove City College before the United States Third Circuit Court of Appeals, David Lascell, Robb M. Jones, and David A. Stern concluded by quoting two eminent education authorities—Yale president Kingman Brewster and former HEW secretary Joseph Califano. "My fear," remarked Brewster, "is that there is a growing tendency for the central government to use the spending power to prescribe educational policies." Califano called "diversity" the greatest contribution of private colleges and universities to "the American educational landscape" and insisted that it was this very diversity that "your national government is pledged to nourish and safeguard."[33]

HEW's interpretation of Title IX, declared Grove City College's counsel, had saddled the college with a no-win choice—"compromise its autonomy or forbid students from receiving any kind of Federal financial support." If the agency's interpretation were allowed to stand, the freedom to attend the school of one's choice—the very thing that student aid programs had been designed to secure—would be "needlessly sacrificed." The college asked the court to rule the HEW regulations invalid and unconstitutional.[34]

After hearing arguments on June 21, 1982, the U.S. Third Circuit Court of Appeals took just six weeks to rule unanimously that because some Grove City College students received government assistance through Pell Grants, the entire college was subject to government jurisdiction, and specifically to Title IX, the federal law prohibiting sexual bias on campuses. It also held that HEW could terminate assistance to students solely on the grounds that Grove City refused to sign an "Assurance of Compliance"— despite any evidence of discrimination. And, not finished, it stated that no hearings were necessary before cutting off the student aid. Calling the ruling "frightening," President MacKenzie said it meant that "any private institution can be brought under government jurisdiction solely because some of its students may benefit in some way from its largess."[35]

John R. Dellenback, president of the Christian College Consortium, an education foundation based in Washington, D.C., that represented over seventy private colleges, including Grove City, said that Title IX's intent had been distorted by the Third Circuit's decision. Dellenback, a former Democratic congressman and director of the Peace Corps, argued that when Congress set up student aid programs, its intent was to aid individual students rather than the colleges.[36]

In a little-noted section of the opinion, the three-judge panel pointed to an alternative: "Both Grove City and the students are free to avoid the conditions imposed by Title IX by ending their participation in the [Pell Grant] program."[37] Rejecting federal assistance in all its many forms was too difficult and too expensive for most American colleges. But saying no and retaining institutional independence were matters of principle for Grove City College, which was prepared—although not just yet— to refuse Pell Grants and the attached federal strings. The college truly believed that government grants constituted indirect assistance, and it hoped that the U.S. Supreme Court would agree. But if the higher court failed to overturn the lower court's ruling, MacKenzie had already begun discussing an alternative—the establishment of a fund that would provide private grants to students to help pay Grove City's modest $4,200 a year for room, board, and tuition.

Before the Highest Court

"In no country in the world," political scientist James Q. Wilson writes, "do the courts play as large a role in making public policy as they do in the United States."[38] A crucial aspect of their power is "judicial review"—the right to void laws of Congress and acts of the executive branch if they are deemed unconstitutional. About sixty nations have something like judicial review, but the power is rarely if ever exercised. In the American political system the courts are the great equalizer. You don't have to be rich, powerful, or well connected to use the courts to settle a legal question or even alter the prevailing interpretation of the Constitution. But appearing in court, especially the highest court, is not easy.

In 1983, the Supreme Court received almost five thousand petitions for a hearing but accepted only some 120 of them (the number of petitions had climbed to nearly eight thousand by 1999).[39] Most cases come to the court on a writ of certiorari (Latin for "made more certain"). At least four of the nine justices must agree that the case should be reviewed. Once the case is accepted, lawyers for each side file briefs that set forth the facts, summarize the lower court decisions, present their side of the case, and discuss the decisions of the Supreme Court that deal with the issue. The lawyers are then permitted to offer oral arguments in open court but are strictly limited in time—usually no more than a half-hour each. And thirty minutes is not a very long time in which to summarize the often complicated arguments of a constitutional issue often stretching back years and sometimes decades.

The courtroom of the Supreme Court is surprisingly small, almost intimate. The lawyer for each side speaks from a lectern less than ten feet from where the chief justice is seated. The lectern has two lights: When the white light goes on, the attorney has five minutes remaining. When the red light flashes, he must stop—instantly.[40] The oral arguments afford the justices the opportunity to do what any lawyer likes to do—ask pointed and searching questions.

Since the federal government is a party, as plaintiff or defendant, in about half the cases before the Supreme Court, the solicitor general of the United States often appears before the Court. The solicitor general is the third-ranking officer of the Department of Justice, right after the attorney general and the deputy attorney general, and personally approves or disapproves every case the government presents to the Supreme Court. He is often selected from among the leading law school professors in America. He is a formidable opponent for anyone coming before the Court for the first time. David Lascell, Grove City College's counsel, was, at age forty-four, a seasoned trial lawyer who had successfully defended the interests of major corporations like Eastman Kodak and Corning, but this would be his first appearance before the highest court in the land.

In the fall of 1983, the Supreme Court accepted *Grove City College v. Terrel H. Bell, Secretary of Education* for review. The *New York Times* saw the case as "a clash of values"—the American tradition of diversity and autonomy, especially in colleges where academic freedom could be stifled by government regulation, versus Washington's commitment to bar the use of federal funds to subsidize discrimination.[41]

In its brief, prepared by Lascell and Grove City graduate Robb Jones (who would later become chief of staff to Chief Justice William J. Rehnquist), Grove City argued that discrimination on the basis of race or sex was "morally repugnant" to its principles and pointed out that it had not been accused by anyone of any kind of discrimination. The central issue before the Court, therefore, was not discrimination but regulation. The college had always refused federal assistance because of "the expensive and burdensome regulation which invariably follows Government funding."[42] So when HEW cut off benefits to Grove City students because the college refused to sign a pledge of compliance regarding Title IX, Grove City sued the government for what it saw as an illegal assault on its independence.

The Court had to balance two constitutional values, maintained Grove City: the need to preserve "a pluralistic system of higher education" and the commitment of the government to combat "invidious discrimination" without the imposition of the "heavy hand of government regulation." If every educational institution, stated the college's brief, that benefited from federal money automatically became subject to government regulations, the private/public distinction in higher education would be "obliterated."[43]

In its brief the Justice Department changed its earlier position regarding Title IX compliance. The department now termed the Third Circuit Court's opinion an overly "expansive interpretation." It noted (as Grove City had) that under that interpretation, a federal grant of one dollar to one student could make "the entire school automatically subject to Title IX." Accordingly, while its forty-nine-page brief argued that Grove City must sign the compliance form, the Justice Department stated that the only "program or activity" helped by the federal student grants and therefore subject to federal regulation was the college's financial aid program. Sports, curriculum, dormitory rules, and all other activities should be exempt from Title IX's requirements.[44]

It was a significant concession by Justice, one that had already aroused feminist groups and led to the introduction of a congressional resolution stating that Title IX covered *all* programs of an affected institution. But the department's concession did not satisfy Grove City College, which regarded federal oversight of even one college program as the nose of the camel under the flap of the tent. Inevitably, Trustee President Albert Hopeman liked to say, the nose would be followed by the entire animal.[45]

Friends of the Court

In addition to the arguments by lawyers on both sides of the case, written briefs may be offered by "friends of the court," or amicus curiae. An amicus brief comes from an interested party not directly involved in the suit and must be accepted by both parties or allowed by the Court. Such briefs, according to James Q. Wilson, are "a kind of polite lobbying of the Court," sometimes offering new arguments but more generally declaring the key interests on each side.[46]

Speaking on behalf of Grove City College, Wabash College's brief stressed the sensitivity of the Constitution to any "government intrusion upon the academic environment." It quoted Justices Felix Frankfurter and John Marshall Harlan in *Sweezy v. State of New Hampshire* (1957) about "the dependence of a free society on free universities," which meant "the exclusion of governmental intervention in the intellectual life of a country." Such constitutional sensitivity, Wabash College argued, required that the Department of Education act "only with caution and explicit Congressional sanction."[47]

In its brief Hillsdale College asserted that independent private educational institutions like Grove City College provided "important diversity and balance to what would otherwise be an exclusively state-run system." The brief approvingly quoted Joseph Califano, the former secretary of Health, Education, and Welfare, who called private colleges and universities "guardians of independent thinking and academic freedom, enjoying a bit more insulation from the whims and pressures of politics than their tax-supported sisters."[48]

On the other side, in support of the federal government, the brief of the Mexican American Legal Defense and Educational Fund and several other minority organizations termed Grove City College's objection to federal jurisdiction under Title IX "a serious threat to federal civil rights enforcement in education and other fields." It noted that according to the U.S. Commission on Civil Rights, "nearly 30 Federal agencies have Title IX enforcement responsibilities."[49] Here was the powerful voice of the civil rights community stating that far more than the rights of a small Pennsylvania college and its students were at stake—women, blacks, Hispanics, and other minorities regarded Grove City College, however unfairly, as the representative of discriminatory forces in America.

On the morning of November 29, 1983, David Lascell, dressed in a dark blue pinstripe suit and muted rep tie, stood before a wooden lectern in the crowded courtroom of the U.S. Supreme Court. That morning, a long line of people had been in front of the Supreme Court building waiting for public admission tickets. Four smiling Grove City College students had greeted them and the Washington press corps with a large banner reading "Preserve Private Education." Inside, Charles MacKenzie and Albert Hopeman sat in the first row just behind Lascell, Robb Jones, and the other Nixon, Hargrave attorneys. Several members of Congress were present and attentive, including Representative Pat Schroeder of Colorado, a militant defender of Title IX. In a rare departure from custom, marshals brought in extra chairs for the Grove City students who had come down from the college that morning.

More than 160 years earlier, the *Los Angeles Times's* legal correspondent Jim Mann wrote, in one of the most famous Supreme Court arguments ever made, Daniel Webster had pleaded for the independence of Dartmouth College, saying, "It is a small college, and yet there are those who love it." Mann equated Lascell with the famed Webster because he too was urging the high court to permit a small private school to "remain independent" of the tide of government regulation.[50] In the Dartmouth College case, Daniel Webster had succeeded in keeping the New Hampshire legislature from altering the private school's charter. In the Grove City dispute, befitting the twentieth century, it was the authority of the federal government that was at issue.

As he stood waiting, Lascell couldn't help noticing odd things, like how large Justice William Rehnquist's hands were and the beautiful, old-fashioned quill pen on the lectern before him. How perfect, he thought, it would look on the tiger maple stand-up desk in his office. He was nervous but confident of his arguments—he had spent a good part of the last two days being tested by Robb Jones and other lawyers in a moot "Supreme Court." Such a precourt rehearsal is standard in major cases today but was unusual in the early 1980s. Lascell and his colleagues, however, did not want to leave anything to chance. And then Chief Justice Warren Burger said, "Mr. Lascell, you may proceed when you're ready."[51]

The issue before the Court, Lascell began, was whether Grove City College, seeking to avoid "government entanglement," remain independent, and operate efficiently, "must either expel students who receive federal scholarships or must agree that it is subject to government regulation." He said that the college had never sought nor received federal aid and grants and did not want to participate in any student aid program "sponsored by state or federal governments."[52]

That was as far as David Lascell got before the questions came flying at him. But that assumes, interrupted Justice Byron White, that the college has never received federal funds. That is the college's position, yes, responded Lascell. Don't the students, White pressed, use the BEOG grants to pay their tuition? Perhaps, answered Lascell, but it seemed to him that the BEOG statute considered the students and not the college to be the "ultimate beneficiaries."[53]

Title IX, continued Lascell, talked about an institution "receiving" federal financial assistance and "operating" a program or activity with that assistance. "Receive," he said, has "a plain meaning. It is not a word which any one of us would have difficulty in understanding were we not lawyers arguing a case." Receive, Lascall argued, meant "to consciously participate, and to receive, to obtain funds. Grove City does not do that." Rather, he said, "it consciously has chosen not to participate in any federal aid program of any kind."[54]

Is there "any breakdown," asked another justice, of which students received federal aid at Grove City? Lascell replied that there was very little in the college's records because it was the government and not the college that chose the students—"Grove City simply... allows them to attend once they have received those awards."[55] Questions followed about the legislative record and what Senators Hubert Humphrey and Birch Bayh, authors of the legislation, had intended ("the legislative history is very confusing," Lascell stated) and the effect of the case on women's colleges ("no effect, your honor").[56]

Turning to the question of the government terminating student assistance, Lascell said that it was the college's position that such an action would be "fundamentally unfair" because there had never been a claim of discrimination against Grove City. Funds termination had been contemplated by Congress "only as a last resort."[57] Then suddenly the red light flashed, and it was the turn of the acting solicitor general, Paul M. Bator, addressed familiarly as "professor" by several of the justices.

Justice Lewis F. Powell noted that the denial of federal aid could force some students to leave the college of their choice. "Does that deprivation of liberty seem unfair to the government of the United States?" he asked rhetorically. Chief Justice Warren E. Burger and Justices White and Rehnquist pressed whether Title IX would apply to a college whose students used some welfare money to help pay for their education. When Bator replied that the government "cannot go that far," Burger shot back, "The federal government is pretty close to it right here."[58] "We do respect [the college's] sincerity," Bator remarked, "in saying they want to stay out of the clutches of the federal government." Grove City could do just that, he suggested, by simply telling its 2,200 students not to accept any federal aid and itself subsidizing the students.[59]

Applause is not permitted in the Supreme Court, but every friend and supporter of Grove City College agreed that David Lascell had done himself and the college proud. "He charmed the Court," remarked colleague Robb Jones. Even Congresswoman Schroeder later told Lascell, "I don't agree with your conclusion, but I admire the way you said it."[60] All the college could do now was to wait for the Court's ruling, which would probably be issued the following spring.

Writing in the *Wall Street Journal* two weeks later, President MacKenzie summed up the college's position: "Private institutions like Grove City College should not be penalized or discouraged for maintaining their independence. Students attending these institutions should not be used as tools for government intervention."[61] But educators like Mary H. Purcell, president of the American Association of University Women, viewed *Grove City College v. Bell* in a far different light. Purcell insisted that if the Reagan administration's restricted viewpoint regarding Title IX were accepted, "more than a decade of progress towards educational equity in American schools will be reversed."[62] Many leaders of the education establishment felt just as strongly about the Grove City case.

A Disappointing Decision

In late February 1984, the Supreme Court handed down its decision, significantly restricting the rights of small independent colleges but nevertheless stirring up women's rights organizations and liberal members of Congress. The Court unanimously said that the federal scholarship grants (BEOGs) given to Grove City's students were direct aid sufficient to trigger the provisions of Title IX; and the Education Department could terminate the grants if the college failed to comply with Title IX and its regulations. But by a split vote of 6-3, the justices rejected the appellate court's view that the entire college was the "education program or activity" receiving the federal assistance. The majority ruled that the bar against sex discrimination extended no further than the school's financial aid office. This ruling was described as a "victory" for the Reagan administration and its narrow reading of Title IX, which previous administrations had said covered an entire institution once any of its programs received federal funds.[63]

Writing for the Court, Justice White stated that Grove City's attempt to analogize BEOGs to food stamps, Social Security benefits, welfare payments, and other forms of general-purpose governmental assistance to low-income families was "unavailing." Among other points, White said that an individual's eligibility for general assistance was "not tied to attendance at an educational institution." BEOGs, he wrote, "clearly augment the resources that the College itself devotes to financial aid."[64] But, White went on, the Court concluded that the receipt of BEOGs by some of Grove City's students "does not trigger institution-wide coverage under Title IX."[65]

The decision was somewhat softened by Justice Powell's concurring opinion (joined by Chief Justice Burger and Justice O'Connor) in which he described the case as "an unedifying example of overzealousness on the part of the Federal Government." He noted Grove City's "unbending policy" of remaining independent of government assistance, recognizing—"as this case well illustrates"—that with acceptance of such assistance "one surrenders a certain measure of the freedom that Americans always have cherished." He emphasized that the case had "nothing whatever to do with discrimination past or present."[66]

Echoing the language of Federal Judge Paul Simmons, Justice Powell lamented that one would have thought that the Department of Education, "confronted as it is with cases of national importance that involve actual discrimination," would have respected the "independence and admirable record of this college. But common sense and good judgment failed to prevail." Instead, the department insisted on pursuing the case and was able to prevail on the "narrow theory" that Title IX applied only to Grove City's financial aid office. In so doing, said Powell, the department took "this small independent college, which it acknowledges has engaged in no discrimination whatever, through six years of litigation with the full weight of the federal government opposing it. I cannot believe that the Department will rejoice in its 'victory.'"[67]

Justice William Brennan, with Justice Thurgood Marshall concurring in part and dissenting in part, rejected the Court's ruling limiting the application of Title IX to a program and not the entire institution. He charged the Court with "ignoring" the primary purposes for which Congress enacted Title IX. In fact, he called the Court's decision "absurd" and declared that the "institution as a whole should be covered." Any other interpretation, Brennan charged, "severely weakens the anti-discrimination provisions included in Title IX."[68] Brennan's opinion was frequently cited by the civil rights community in the following months and years.

Regardless of the limitation, historian Hugh Davis Graham points out, the *Grove City* ruling "expanded the reach of contract compliance regulations to virtually every school and college in the country."[69] To resist such regulatory "reach" had been Grove City College's motivation from the very beginning of its protracted battle (costing almost $500,000) against enforced compliance with Title IX. President MacKenzie's response was immediate. He said that he would recommend to the board of trustees that Grove City refuse to sign any federal form: "We will not turn over one inch of the campus to government control." He also pledged that the school would replace any federal student grant aid that might be lost with private funds.[70]

MacKenzie and the board were strengthened in their resolve by the substantial support of Grove City alumni and even non-alumni. When a legal defense fund was formed, the alumni association in 1981 contributed $25,000. A resident of Washington state who had not attended the college contributed a portion of her monthly Social Security check to the fund. Robert Smith, then director of public relations and now the school's registrar, remembers one alumnus who apologized that his check was for only $1,000.[71]

Grovers everywhere were proud of their college's unwavering commitment to remain independent. "This is going to make the college stand out nationally," said senior Charlene Finnegan, "and could benefit it in the long run. It will be the only college to be completely free of government aid in every way."[72] Finnegan was incorrect about Grove City being the "only" college to spurn all government aid, but she was right about the enduring impact of the Supreme Court decision. Grove City College was now in the legal history books, along with Dartmouth, as a school that had challenged the intrusive arm of the state.

Reminded that the Supreme Court's decision had been interpreted by some groups as a "setback" for women's rights, President MacKenzie said, "I hope it isn't and I don't believe it should be because nondiscrimination is the law of the land— any institution that discriminates can be called before the law."[73] It was a commonsense response, but not one shared by the civil rights coalition, which attacked *Grove City* as a radical reversal of the Civil Rights Act of 1964. The Leadership Conference on Civil Rights, representing 165 organizations, began coordinating a bipartisan legislative effort to overturn the decision.

Just four months later the Democrat-controlled House of Representatives overwhelmingly passed a bill declaring that one dollar of federal assistance to any program brought the entire institution under federal regulatory control. But the Republican-controlled Senate, deferring to the Republican in the White House, did not approve the House bill then or for the next two years. Senator Edward M. Kennedy (D-Mass.) was furious, chastising his colleagues: "Shame on this body.... If we table this civil rights amendment, we are saying we will tuck discrimination under the mattress."[74]

In 1985, President MacKenzie was invited to testify before the House Judiciary Committee on the subject and suggested several sensible amendments that allowed for both educational freedom and strong nondiscrimination laws. Colleges "which do not accept government funds and which do not discriminate," he said, "should remain free of government control."[75] The congressmen thanked Dr. MacKenzie for his suggestions which, however, they did not adopt. The determined college head nevertheless pressed his case wherever he could. When MacKenzie testified before the Senate Judiciary subcommittee, liberal Democratic senator

Claiborne Pell of Rhode Island remarked, "I am glad to meet the president of one of the best known and most principled colleges in America."[76]

Following the 1987 election of a Democratic majority in the Senate, a liberal-moderate congressional coalition formed and passed the Civil Rights Restoration Act the following year. President Reagan vetoed the bill, but the Democratic Congress easily overrode the president's veto by margins of 73-24 in the Senate and 292-133 in the House. The legislation's chief effect was to overturn the Grove City restrictions, making entire institutions and not just specific programs liable to Title IX and every other antidiscrimination act since 1964.[77]

Legacies of *Grove City College v. Bell*

When Grove City College sued the Department of Health, Education and Welfare in 1978 to block the cutting off of federal aid to its students, most American colleges and universities were already willing participants in a wide variety of federal programs. Direct federal aid totaled almost $9 billion that year and carried with it federal regulations regarding equal employment and educational opportunity, handicapped access, and workplace safety. Research universities received another $3.9 billion in federal support. "What the [federal] regulators undertook," wrote historian Roger Geiger, "was no less than a feat of social engineering" that established "a clear pattern of federal disregard for university autonomy in the 1970s."[78]

Not satisfied with regulating the major universities and most two-year colleges, federal bureaucrats in 1977 went after the small liberal arts colleges (about five hundred of them) that wanted only to be left alone to run their own affairs. But that was not to be, for like all large bureaucracies, federal agencies "manifested a

Weberian impulse to maximize their jurisdiction, rationalize their authority, and expand their domain."[79]

Grove City College's brave stand against HEW regulators was admired by other colleges but with very few exceptions was not imitated. College administrators, however they resented federal interference, could not envision a future without federal money. Where Grove City was fiercely independent, other colleges were agreeably dependent. Where Grove City had always rejected government assistance, other schools increasingly sought it. Where Grove City ran its affairs like a business, other campuses sailed along with scant concern for the bottom line. Where Grove City ensured a Christian atmosphere that united faith and learning, other colleges abandoned the former and distorted the latter through educational fads like deconstructionism and political correctness.

The outcome of *Grove City College v. Bell* and the passage of the Civil Rights Restoration Act of 1988 confirmed the defeatist conclusion of most American colleges: The regulatory role of government in higher education was irreversible. And then in the 1990s, historian Hugh Davis Graham states, Congress "expanded the range of federal oversight."[80] Income restrictions on Stafford loans were eased, and the federal government rather than private lenders began making direct loans to students. Colleges were now also required to collect and report campus crime statistics and initiate plans to reduce sexual assault. Education Department officials in the Clinton administration in 1996 directed colleges in the Stafford loan program to submit audited financial statements.

Grove City's board of trustees had shrewdly anticipated such governmental expansion and had already begun organizing its own student loan program in addition to the student grant plan begun in 1984 after *Grove City College v. Bell*. In October

1996, the college announced (dropping the other shoe with relief) that it would withdraw from the federal student loan programs because the Department of Education had become "much more intrusive."[81] About eight hundred of Grove City's 2,300 students, then getting federal financial aid, would now be covered by a campus loan program financed by the PNC Bank Corporation. Once again, Grove City had demonstrated that whatever the price for independence, it was willing to pay it.

In the end, what had been achieved by the six-year, half-a-million-dollar legal battle between Grove City College and the federal government—beyond a footnote in the history books? Had anything of significance occurred because there had been a *Grove City* case? To begin, it is no small thing to be a footnote in history because of a firm commitment to the principle of academic independence. In a real sense Grove City had no alternative but to challenge HEW and its successor, the Department of Education, if it wished to remain true to its founding, its founders, and itself.

Second, the college raised a standard for others to repair to, but only a few responded—most college administrators simply could not imagine life without federal assistance. The chasm from where they were to where Grove City was seemed as wide and unbridgeable as the Grand Canyon.

Third, Grove City used the years of legal struggle with the government to create its own student grant program, based in large part on the $1 million received from the B. C. Hopeman estate in the 1950s and 1960s. Grove City would not have been able to offer several hundred students comparable grants to the government's BEOGs if it had withdrawn from the federal program in 1977 or 1978.

Fourth, Grove City's legal struggle produced the Justice Department statement that it would not contest Judge Paul

Simmons's ruling that federally guaranteed loans were not covered by Title IX; Pell grants to students, Justice argued, were sufficient to bring Grove City under Title IX coverage. It was a crucial concession because in 1982 the college did not have and would not have for several years afterward the financial means to offer students both a private loan and a private grant program. But by 1996, when it withdrew from the Stafford loan plan, Grove City was ready and able to take care of the eight hundred or so students dependent on federally guaranteed loans.

Finally, the case unified the Grove City College community as never before in its history. The administration, trustees, students, faculty, and alumni readily accepted the Old Testament analogy and saw the school as David confronting Goliath—the federal government. Turning to the New Testament, President MacKenzie commented that "leaders of Christian institutions must think long and hard before accepting federal money. With money inevitably comes control. Caesar must not be allowed to seize that which belongs to God."[82]

Grove City College v. Bell was not pyrrhic but a very real victory in the school's century-long struggle to defend faith and freedom, regardless of the cost.

CHAPTER EIGHT

Illiberal Education

Although the chaotic 1960s did not physically destroy any college or university, they brought to full life ruinous trends that had taken seed on many campuses. Course requirements were eliminated, and electives multiplied exponentially. Marxist scholars openly dominated departments and professional associations. With egalitarian fervor, entrance standards were lowered in accord with affirmative action, and grades were inflated with the approval of faculty, administration, and student body. One national survey, reported historian Diane Ravitch, found that the number of institutions requiring English, a foreign language, and mathematics as part of everyone's general education declined sharply from 1967 to 1974—from 90 percent to 72 percent for English, from 72 percent to 53 percent for a foreign language, and from 33 percent to 20 percent for mathematics. At Harvard, in the 1920s, only one student in five made the dean's list; by 1976, over three-quarters did so. Some dispirited educators referred to "the collapse of general education."[1]

A reaction, however, began to build in the 1970s, even among establishment academics. Historian Page Smith, founding provost of the University of California, Santa Cruz, called the curriculum changes "a species of mindless reductionism" where all ideas were considered equal. The result, he said, was a profound impoverishment of the human spirit within the academy and an aggregation of specialists "scarcely able to communicate with one another," much less the outside public.[2] Harvard President Derek Bok laid at least part of the blame on government involvement in academic matters. "Government rules," Bok charged, "are likely to impress uniformity and rigidity on a field of activity that needs diversity, experimentation, and change."[3]

While most college presidents agreed in principle with Bok's critique, they lacked Harvard's enormous endowment and thus did not seek an end to government involvement or money. These were, after all, bountiful years for colleges and universities—budgets soared from a modest $7 billion in 1960, to an incredible $172 billion in the early 1990s. Several universities had annual budgets in excess of $1 billion, rivaling those of major corporations. Certainly no one liked the thousands of federal rules now encumbering higher education, but how could one manage all the students, teachers, staff, and buildings, as well as the administrative, marketing, and fund-raising demands of a modern school, except with federal assistance?

If these were the best of times for the postmodernist educators who scorned America, ridiculed Western civilization, and promoted a multicultural, politically correct curriculum, they were the worst of times for those traditionalists who still read Plato, Locke, and Jefferson, believed in the advantages of a classical liberal arts education, and were increasingly disturbed by the decline of the American academy.

Some schools began discussing the need for a "core curriculum" (adopted by Grove City College in the early 1970s, several years before Harvard and other Ivy League schools). But most opted for a supermarket approach to higher education, convinced that a greater variety of "brands" (courses) would entice more "customers" (students) to their "store" (campus). William D. Schaefer, a former vice chancellor of the University of California at Los Angeles, reacted strongly, saying that institutions had "mindlessly mixed vocational and academic courses without continuity or coherence or anything approaching a consensus as to what really should constitute an education." In such an atmosphere, said Dean Herbert I. London of New York University, one department voted for another's course proposal in exchange for support of its own course selection. "Of what value," London asked, "is debate about academic issues in this climate of academic backscratching?"[4]

Clearly, the debate had to be expanded to a far larger world than the one bounded by the ivory towers and green quadrangles of colleges and universities. American higher education was too important to the future of America to be left to the educators.

A Nation at Risk, issued in 1983 by the Reagan-appointed National Commission on Excellence in Education, caught the attention of the public and the education establishment alike; it had an impact, wrote educators John D. Pulliam and James J. Van Patten, "similar to that of Sputnik in 1957."[5] The report showed that on nineteen academic tests American students were never first or second but often last when ranked with other industrial nations. About 13 percent of the nation's seventeen-year-olds and 40 percent of minority youth were functionally illiterate. Some 23 million adults could not pass simple tests of reading, writing, and comprehension. SAT scores had declined steadily for seventeen years. And the average achievement scores of college graduates had fallen between 1975 and 1980. Public dismay and demands for changes in the prevailing system were widespread.

Challenging the Zeitgeist

In the succeeding years, two books led the sharp reaction against the radical zeitgeist—*The Closing of the American Mind* by Allan Bloom, a distinguished University of Chicago classics professor, and *Illiberal Education: The Politics of Race and Sex on Campus* by Dinesh D'Souza, a precocious young author and scholar at the American Enterprise Institute in Washington, D.C. The professorate, Bloom claimed, had abandoned "liberal learning" (by which he meant classical liberal arts learning) and had adopted either the latest intellectual fads or retreated to their specialties. Bloom did not equivocate but stated bluntly that a profound "crisis" confronted American higher education. His solution was disarmingly simple—provide "a good program of liberal education" and feed thereby "the student's love of truth and passion to live a good life."[6]

The Closing of the American Mind wound up at the top of the *New York Times'* bestseller list in 1989 and was described by one reviewer as possibly "the most important work of its kind by an American since World War II" (although it is doubtful that everyone read the sixty-nine-page section entitled "From Socrates' *Apology* to Heidegger's *Rektoratsrede*"). That an academic whose specialty was Plato and whose works had never sold more than a few thousand copies should wind up with a bestseller suggested how ready the general public was for a reaffirmation of classical learning. Education historian Christopher Lucas points out that Bloom was continuing an argument begun earlier in the decade by E. D. Hirsch, Jr., professor of English at the University of Virginia. In an essay in the *American Scholar* entitled "Cultural Literacy," Hirsch charged that America was drifting dangerously close to losing "its coherence as a culture" and that "we need to connect more of our students to our history, our culture, and those ideas which hold us together."[7]

It is a sign of the divided times that so sensible a suggestion was peremptorily dismissed by academic ideologues as "cultural imperialism" and "ethnic elitism." Despite the attacks, Hirsch's subsequent book, also titled *Cultural Literacy*, became a national bestseller in 1987. Endorsing Hirsch's concept and his list of geographical names, historical events, famous people, and patriotic lore, Harvard historian Orlando Patterson insisted that all of America—not just White Anglo-Saxon Protestants—required "a deep understanding of mainstream culture."[8]

The debate intensified in 1988 with a public battle between Education Secretary William J. Bennett and his opponents over Stanford University's decision to replace a required freshman course, "Western Culture," with something called "Cultures, Ideas, and Values." The new course downgraded classic works in favor of writings by women, minorities, and people of color. Bennett charged that the Stanford faculty's action would "trivialize" the university's curriculum.[9]

But it was D'Souza's *Illiberal Education*—and his unflagging promotion of the book on television and radio and his defense of it in debate on dozens of campuses—that made "political correctness" a major issue in the first half of the 1990s. D'Souza charged that American universities had deliberately filled "a sizable portion of their freshman class" with minority students, no matter their qualifications; diluted or displaced their core curricula to make room for new courses stressing non-Western cultures, Afro-American Studies, and Women's Studies; and set up and funded separate institutions for minority groups in the name of "pluralism" and "diversity." The result, he said, quoting the University of Wisconsin chancellor and future HEW secretary Donna Shalala, was a "basic transformation of American higher education."[10]

Based upon his study of conditions at the University of California, Berkeley, Stanford University, Howard University, the

University of Michigan, Duke University, and Harvard University, D'Souza concluded that affirmative action plans had only exacerbated racial and gender tensions. Because affirmative action depended on unjust means to achieve its goal, it made authentic racial pluralism and harmony all the more unlikely. D'Souza warned that if this "university model is replicated in society at large. . . it will reproduce and magnify the lurid bigotry, intolerance, and balkanization of campus life in the broader culture."[11]

The young author, born in India and himself a person of color, offered a different model based on the idea of the ninteenth-century scholar John Henry Newman that the goal of liberal learning is "that true enlargement of mind which is the power of viewing many things at once as one whole, of referring them severally to their true place in the universal system, of understanding their respective values, and determining their mutual dependence."[12] D'Souza argued that minority students and indeed all students would best learn about themselves and the universe around them, not through the narrow prism of minority and gender studies, but through the broad spectrum of true liberal education.[13]

Curriculum reformers protested that their only wish was to add multiculturalism to the existing canon, not to eliminate Western culture, but D'Souza and other critics remained skeptical. Multicultural courses, D'Souza charged, had "degenerated into a kind of ethnic cheerleading, a primitive romanticism about the Third World, combined with the systematic denunciation of the West."[14] Conservative intellectual Roger Kimball, author of the widely read *Tenured Radicals: How Politics Has Corrupted Our Higher Education*, lamented the "ideologically motivated assaults on the intellectual and moral substance of our culture." Muckraker Charles Sykes, for his part, blamed professors for most of the academy's ills in *Profscam: Professors and the Demise of Higher Edu-*

cation and *The Hollow Men: Politics and Corruption in Higher Education.* Professors, Sykes asserted, were overpaid, underworked, and guilty of inflicting thousands of useless, unreadable articles and books upon the world. "The impact of the new academic culture," he wrote, "is not merely its success in corrupting the American mind, but in stultifying it."[15]

In *Imposters in the Temple: American Intellectuals Are Destroying Our Universities and Cheating Our Students of Their Future,* senior fellow Martin Anderson, of the Hoover Institution, suggested that those most responsible for the "sorry state" of American higher education were the governing boards of autonomous universities and colleges—"the trustees, the overseers, the regents." Although conceding that professors, administrators, and students all shared in the blame, Anderson insisted that because the trustees made the rules, they were most culpable for such depredations as for example, Stanford, casting out of its curriculum the canons of Western civilization and cheating the taxpayer with phony research charges; Harvard, violating antitrust laws by price-rigging tuition fees and financial aid; Dartmouth, infringing on the academic freedom of a student newspaper; and the University of California, substituting students for professors to teach its freshmen and sophomores.[16]

As befits someone who had served in presidential campaigns and advised presidents, Anderson offered several practical suggestions: prohibit student teaching, stop rewarding "spurious research and writing," end faculty tenure, ban political discrimination, stop athletic corruption, and crack down on "institutional corruption." (All of these reforms had been standard practice at Grove City College since its founding.) These changes, he said, would enable colleges and universities to "become the temples of integrity and learning they should be. It is time to clean academic house in America; it is time to drive the imposters from the temple."[17] "Accountability," insisted author Thomas Sowell in *Inside American Education: The Decline, the Deception, the Dogmas*, "is the most important strategic objective to be achieved in colleges and universities."[18]

An articulate and trenchant challenge to the education establishment materialized in 1989 with the founding of the National Association of Scholars (NAS), a network of conservative and liberal scholars committed to the Western heritage of intellectual inquiry and freedom. Within four years NAS had thirty-three state affiliates and several thousand members. The association's steadily expanding membership and influence under President Stephen H. Balch signaled that many academics had had enough of postmodernism and were eager to defend Western civilization courses and resist the imposition of politically correct, multicultural studies.

Of special concern to NAS, revealed executive director Bradford Wilson, was the existence on most campuses of "a bureaucracy of residence life advisors, multicultural affairs offices, women's centers (for feminists only), ethnic dormitories and social centers, and special services for gay, lesbian, and transgender students." In the name of "diversity," Wilson charged, this bureaucracy was dividing and segregating students.[19] Confirmation of the divisive trend came from *When Hope and Fear Collide: A Portrait of Today's College*, written by Arthur Levine, the president of Teachers College at Columbia University, who reported that while students in the late 1970s described themselves in terms of what they had in common, the students of the early 1990s emphasized what made them different.[20] The nation's motto *E Pluribus Unum* was being turned upside down: Many were being made out of one.

Critics like the National Association of Scholars were taking on one of the most powerful institutions in America. By the end of the twentieth century, American higher education had become a leviathan of 14.5 million students, nearly 4,000 institutions, more than 900,000 faculty members and staff, and annual expenditures of some $175 billion. And yet the National Endowment for the Humanities revealed that one could graduate from 77 percent of the nation's colleges without studying a foreign language; from 45 percent of all institutions without completing a single course in American or English literature; from 41 percent without studying mathematics; and from 38 percent without having taken one history course.[21] This distressing information was greeted with almost universal silence by the education establishment. Not so conservative critics who did not hesitate to say, "We told you so!" and redoubled their resolve to save the academy.

Some began looking around for possible models. They need have looked no farther than western Pennsylvania where Grove City College was drawing high marks from national journals for its academic excellence and startlingly low tuition.

National Acclaim
Despite the heavy administrative and financial demands of the six-year legal battle with the federal government, the leaders of Grove City College intensified their efforts to make Grove City an ever better school. Because a thorough curriculum study had not been conducted for several years, President MacKenzie appointed in 1972 a faculty committee of Thaddeus Penar, William Swezey, James Paton III, Philip N. Carpenter, and Helen Dawes to consider possible curricular reforms. The president soon discovered that some courses repeated material covered in high school and failed to provide students "with a common Grove City experience." At one meeting, Dr. MacKenzie proposed a "core" curriculum, which became a "keystone" curriculum of eighteen hours

of interdisciplinary courses—twelve in the humanities, three in the social sciences, and three in the natural sciences. These core courses would be taught by the college's "best teachers" using a team approach.[22]

After narrow approval by the faculty and a go-ahead from the board of trustees on a trial basis, the first phase of the Keystone curriculum went into effect in 1973. It has since been refined and revised several times, but the idea of a core curriculum is now a permanent part of Grove City College. The college, MacKenzie pointed out, was in "the vanguard" of a movement which became within a decade the norm in American higher education.[23] The Keystone curriculum was also the college's response to the students' "intense preoccupation" with courses that would help them get a job when they graduated. Grove City underscored the relevance of a liberal arts education to the "real" world, arguing that since the average American changed careers three times in his lifetime, "the liberal arts tradition with its emphasis on values can enhance a person's capability for change and decision-making."[24]

Students—and some faculty members—had long complained about Saturday morning classes. Most universities and colleges had abandoned the tradition by the 1970s, and many Grovers wanted their school to follow suit. But at that time the elimination of Saturday classes would have forced the college to hold classes in the evenings (which the college had never done) and limit the extracurricular programs which were so much part of the Grove City experience. It was thought that the move would have also enticed students from Pennsylvania, Ohio, and New York to take off Friday night and turn Grove City into what MacKenzie called a "suitcase college" on the weekends.[25] Meanwhile, students from other parts of the country would have been stranded on campus—a condition that would, it was believed, affect admissions negatively. The board of trustees approved the status quo, and Saturday morning classes continued for the rest of the century.

Grove City and Grove City College have enjoyed good relations from the beginning. Indeed, there would have been no college without the city's express desire for the institution and without its initial financial support. Prominent citizens served on the board of trustees, while local companies provided part-time employment to students. Complaints (when they were made) usually centered around male students living in off-campus housing who had flagrantly violated the community's no-drinking laws. By the 1960s the off-campus houses had become de facto fraternity houses, among other things a violation of college policy. President MacKenzie and other officials were often called late at night regarding student drunkenness and excessive noise. The administration acted firmly in 1974 and sharply reduced the number of men living in town from 210 to 120. Late-night complaints to the president and the dean of students declined but did not cease altogether.

Fraternity antics were not limited to off-campus. During a Greek Sing one Parents' Day, some of the fraternity men were so tipsy they could barely stand, and their bawdy lyrics offended many parents. Two fraternities were suspended at MacKenzie's insistence, although at least one dean tried to dismiss the incident as an example of "boys will be boys." But President MacKenzie felt that "the time had come to draw a line as to what would be considered acceptable behavior on campus." New and stronger guidelines for future Greek Sings were issued, and the fraternity suspensions, despite a protest march by fraternity members in front of the president's house, were enforced.[26]

Through it all, the college strove successfully to keep costs down: for the 1976–77 academic year, for example, tuition, room, and board totaled $2,820, compared with a national average at four-year private colleges of $4,568.

As important as curriculum reform, college-city relations, campus discipline, and the cost of education were, the overriding issue for the MacKenzie administration was the spiritual environment of Grove City College. In his first report to the board of trustees in November 1971, MacKenzie stated his conviction, based on an intensive study of every aspect of the college, that Grove City stood at a crossroads. Humanistic and Christian forces were contending with each other for control of the school, he said, and secular humanism had made "deep inroads into the college's life." If allowed to continue, he warned, it "could soon alter the philosophy and historic position of the college." But, MacKenzie added, "strong Christian forces [were] struggling to hold the college on course." In this struggle, the president declared, a "committed and determined" board of trustees would be the deciding factor as to which side prevailed.[27] The board quickly and unanimously pledged its support, endorsing "A Statement of Identity" which restated Grove City's calling as a college "thoroughly Christian and evangelical in character."[28] And they approved the hiring of new faculty with "deep Christian convictions." MacKenzie later said that the contest at Grove City between Christian and secular forces reflected the struggle that was going on "for the soul and identity of the nation."[29]

The administration's emphasis on evangelical Christianity and the need for moral conduct on and off campus triggered a strong reaction among some students, faculty, and staff. One political science teacher stormed into the president's office, threw his contract on the desk, and shouted, "I can't stand any more of this God-damned God talk any longer. I quit!"[30] Sherry MacKenzie, seeking support and counsel, turned to former president Weir Ketler. Ketler recounted how students had at one time threatened to go on strike because of a certain disciplinary action. At a special meeting in Harbison Chapel, President Ketler had informed the assembled student body in a quiet but firm voice: "My father started this school with thirteen students. If necessary, I will start over again with thirteen students." There was no student strike. "Dr. Ketler's moral courage," MacKenzie recalled, "and his stand on principle inspired me."[31]

Someone else who kept him going was his wife Florence, described by one faculty member as "a gem."[32] An uplifting experience in the tense early years was a weekly Bible group which met in the President's Home. As many as one hundred students would gather to talk, study the Bible, and pray. "Florence was magnificent," recalled Sherry MacKenzie, "in her devotion to them," including baking for the young visitors.[33] Although Florence MacKenzie kept up a more than full schedule on campus and in town, she never stopped grieving over the premature death of her only son Robert in the fall of 1976 and died from a brain tumor in December 1981.

The often-beleaguered college president identified with a university head who said that his life was full of tension because he was "caught between five constituencies with differing expectations... trustees, students, faculty, alumni, and townspeople." But by the end of his fourth year, Sherry MacKenzie could tell the board of trustees that in the 1974–1975 academic year, "students, faculty and administration seem to have functioned with a high degree of harmony."[34] In his 1978 President's Report, MacKenzie reported that "a great many of the young people choosing Grove City are basing their decision on the school's Christian emphasis." And in his 1979 President's Report, MacKenzie quoted educator John L. Childs's dictum that "education is never morally neutral. A definite expression of preference for certain human ends, or values, is inherent in all efforts to guide the experience of the young." MacKenzie said confidently that Grove City was well positioned for the "burning issue" of the 1980s in higher education—"*what* values will be taught and *who* will determine those values."[35]

A key figure in the MacKenzie administration was Ross Foster, a young professor of philosophy who succeeded Fred Kring and served as dean of students for seventeen years. "We had the idea in 1973," recalled Foster, "that we could turn the school around in five years, but it took us about ten."[36] To enhance the school's Christian orientation, the board of trustees led by Albert Hopeman decided that allowing even 10 percent of the men students to live in town was too many, and in the fall of 1982 it did away with off-campus housing except for commuters and certain older students who lived in rooms rented by the college. The decision carried a cost because enrollment—and therefore revenue—was temporarily reduced by over one hundred men, but the trustees, recalled MacKenzie, "were more interested in doing what was right than they were in income."[37]

Responding to the inflation and other economic problems created by the Carter administration in Washington, D.C., Grove City improved the compensation and benefits package for the college's staff, significantly increased faculty salaries, and installed a tuition remission program for staff children who qualified academically. By the early 1980s the salaries of Grove City's best professors were competitive with those of the most prestigious schools. "Mr. Hopeman and I," MacKenzie explained, "sought within the parameters of the college's fiscal capability, to treat the staff as fairly and as well as possible."[38]

This did not mean giving in to the demands of three professors who had refused to retire when asked to do so by President MacKenzie. They claimed de facto tenure, argued they should be kept on the payroll until the age of seventy, and filed suit against the college. The case went to Mercer County court which found that Grove City did not have tenure and invalidated the claims of the three unwilling retirees. The decision was appealed to the Pennsylvania Supreme Court, which ruled that the college did not have and never had had tenure of any kind. Under the skillful hand of Timothy Bonner, the college's legal counsel, "the college's no-tenure policy was confirmed in concrete."[39]

Going to the Chapel

The administration also dealt with another perennial issue—compulsory attendance at chapel. Though there was no question that they loved the Lord, students chafed at what *The Collegian* called "forced worship." Emphasizing there would be no compromise with a fundamental practice of the college, President MacKenzie obtained permission from the board of trustees to modify the chapel regulation. Grove City henceforth awarded one academic point each year to a student who met the chapel requirement. The daily morning program laid a greater stress on "the Judeo-Christian values which helped to shape Western culture." The Sunday Vesper service and at least some of the weekday programs were given more of an educational cast. An outstanding dean of the chapel was engaged—first Dr. Bruce Thielemann, a physically imposing, spell-binding preacher, and then Dr. Richard Morledge, his soft-spoken, quietly charismatic successor, who liked to say, "The heart of education is the education of the heart." To the delight of the student body, the chapel requirement could be met by attending any sixteen chapel programs per semester.[40] Since these reforms a quarter of a century ago, "forced worship" has ceased to be a contentious issue among the students of Grove City College. Another important factor, points out Dr. Dale R. Bowne, the longtime chairman of the Department of Religion and Philosophy, is that particularly under Dr. Morledge, the students became deeply "involved" in the planning and presentation of the chapel programs.[41] That practice has continued under the Rev. Dr. F. Stanley Keehlwetter, who succeeded Richard Morledge as Dean of the Chapel in 1999.

The college had always been proud of its handsome neoclassical buildings and carefully maintained grounds. Following a top-to-bottom survey of the physical plant, President MacKenzie recommended that Memorial Hall, the school's oldest dormitory, undergo thorough renovation, at a cost of about $1 million. Careful thought was also given to a suitable commemoration of the college's single greatest benefactor, J. Howard Pew. The construction of the J. Howard Pew Fine Arts Center was approved, but only after the board had been assured that the facility would be used "to enrich the experience of students from existing disciplines" and not to attract "flower children" indifferent to the traditional values of the college.[42]

The final cost of the Pew Center—dedicated in the fall of 1976, the centennial year of Grove City College—was $6.5 million, about one-third of what it would cost today. As had been the practice during Pew's lifetime, the Pew Charitable Trusts contributed about one-half of the funds for the Pew Center, the refurbishing of Memorial Hall, and the new Mary Ethel Pew dormitory for women, which cost about $3 million. With the completion of the women's dormitory, all resident students were housed on the Upper Campus for the first time in the college's history. Maintenance remained a top priority of the Hopeman board. In the late 1970s Grove City installed the first tri-fuel heating system in American higher education (at a cost of $2.5 million), enabling the college to heat with coal, gas, or oil depending upon the price and availability of each energy source. And then in 1986 the Isaac Ketler dormitory was renovated at a cost of about

$4 million; three years later the B. C. Hopeman dormitory was modernized and refurnished for approximately $2 million.

While never seeking to become an athletic power, Grove City always recognized the importance of the body, as well as the mind and the spirit, in the making of a student. In 1980 the administration razed the rapidly deteriorating field house, rebuilt the track and football field, and repaired the grandstand—at a cost of over $1 million. Athletic director Jack Behringer described the new Phillips Field House and other athletic facilities as "among the finest of any small college in the nation."[43] Under Behringer, who coached the football, basketball, and track teams, and his female counterpart, Cynthia Walters, the college eventually fielded eighteen men and women's varsity teams. Behringer was proudest of Grove City's undefeated 1966 football team, Walters, of directing the annual water show during Parents' Weekend. Accorded many local and state honors, Walters helped found and served as president of the Women's Keystone Conference, the first women's athletic conference for private colleges in western Pennsylvania.

Later in the 1980s, the school added 40,000 square feet to the old recreation building and renamed it the Physical Learning Center, providing students with the latest fitness equipment. Also included in the center was a new bookstore and an expanded Student Union that eliminated the Fountain Room— the redoubtable "Gedunk" where students had been gathering to snack and talk since the early 1950s. (Explanations for the derivation of "Gedunk" range from its being a military word for ice cream and then a place that serves ice cream, to a contraction of "G.I. Dunk." Korean War veterans apparently spent a lot of time in the Fountain Room drinking coffee and dunking doughnuts.)[44] The total cost of the center was nearly $7 million—an unexpected expense of about $1 million occurred when engineers discovered a huge network of abandoned mine shafts under the recreation building. Although there was no immediate danger of a cave-in, the shafts were prudently filled with a slurry of concrete and fly ash to form a solid base for the new learning center.

The Commission on Higher Education of the Middle States Association of Colleges and Schools sent an evaluation team to Grove City in April 1980 as part of its reaccreditation process and wrote a generally favorable report about the school's academics, student-faculty relations, physical infrastructure, and its "sound and secure" financial position. It also noted the "numerous complaints" of students about the strict intervisitation policy, the lack of a sabbatical program for teachers, and a "shifting emphasis" from liberal arts to professional programs.[45]

The evaluation team, moreover, did not like the board of trustees' policy of financial confidentiality. While there was no suggestion whatsoever of fiscal impropriety or mismanagement, MacKenzie remembers that the team and the commission interpreted the confidentiality as "a lack of cooperation." It demanded a special meeting with the faculty's steering committee and the board of trustees, which took place at Baltimore-Washington International Airport. The trustees assured the commission of the college's readiness to cooperate and supply necessary financial information, provided that the commission treat the information as the college did—in strict confidence. Satisfied, the Commission on Higher Education of the Middle States Association reaffirmed Grove City's accreditation.[46]

Throughout its history the college had sought to integrate faith and reason in its approach to education. Science and technology were not spurned, but welcomed. Therefore, after consulting with educators and computer experts and visiting other schools, Grove City College built in 1983 and 1984 the Weir C.

Ketler Technological Learning Center, equipping it with the latest computer technology, including interactive video. Within two years the center was so popular with students that a second mainframe was added. Subsequently, an "Apple orchard" was installed for education majors, IBM clusters were provided for business majors, and computers were placed in classrooms, faculty offices, and laboratories. The most dramatic innovation—supplying each student with his or her own laptop computer and printer—came a little later.

Seeking to strengthen the faculty, the college began a loan program encouraging faculty members to seek doctorates in their fields, with the loans forgiven if they remained at Grove City. A few teachers chafed under the school's hierarchical structure. Kenneth F. Warren, an instructor in political science, resigned in the spring of 1974 and complained publicly in *The Collegian* that the administration imposed an intellectual "conformity" on the faculty. But Warren then admitted that no one at Grove City had ever told him "what I can or cannot say in the classroom. From my observation, this is true for the faculty as a whole." He insisted, nevertheless, that the college's reputation would be greatly improved if there were "a better ideological balance" in academic appointments. The young teacher clearly wanted more liberal appointments; he also complained about the absence of liberal speakers on campus. President MacKenzie contented himself with responding that Warren was entitled to his "dissenting point of view" that reflected "his experience as a student at a state university which has different presuppositions and policies from those which Grove City has utilized successfully through the years."[47]

In pursuit of academic excellence, the school created the Trustees' Academic Scholarships—full tuition to twelve outstanding freshmen to be renewed each year if they maintained a high grade average. A specially created fund brought to campus leading scholars like education editor Edward Fiske of the *New York Times*, Dr. Everett Koop of the University of Pennsylvania (later the U.S. surgeon general), and Dr. Armand Nicholi of Harvard University. And while most colleges and universities continued to drift farther and farther from any curricular consideration of faith and belief, Grove City held numerous workshops emphasizing the centrality of Christian values to learning.

It was noted that the president of Grove City College now often had a smile on his face; the reason lay far from the disposition of *Grove City College v. Bell*. Through trustee Louise Baird, in 1983 Dr. MacKenzie met Lavonne Rudolph Gaiser, the widow of a Methodist minister who had grown up in Grove City. Their friendship blossomed over the next two years, and in March 1985 they were married by Dr. Richard Morledge in Harbison Chapel. Vonnie was quickly accepted by the students and the townspeople, being elected president of the hospital's volunteers and president of the Shakespeare Club.

Under President MacKenzie's direction, Grove City College moved aggressively to prepare its students for the global village and economy that was clearly emerging. A course on international business was developed, and the board of trustees provided scholarship money for international students—in just one year, their number jumped from twelve to fifty. Courses in Chinese and Japanese were introduced, and a distinguished Japanese scholar was invited to teach.

The careful planning and implementation paid off. While other private colleges encountered difficulty in filling their classes, Grove City had 1,589 applications for 568 freshman openings in 1979–1980. And freshman SAT scores averaged 1,049, some 150 points above the national average. College guides now routinely gave Grove City College high ratings. *Peterson's Guide* described Grove City in 1983 as one of the three hundred "most competitive" schools in America, while *Barron's* called Grove City one of the 227 "most prestigious" colleges in the country.[48] In the fall of 1988 *U.S. News & World Report* for the first time listed Grove City College among the top twenty-five small "comprehensive" colleges in America.[49]

CHAPTER NINE

A Powerful Counterweight

Although many contributed to the ever increasing national prestige of Grove City College during the 1970s and 1980s, President MacKenzie praised one man above all others—Albert A. Hopeman, Jr., president of the board of trustees from 1972 (following J. Howard Pew's death) until February 1998, when he himself passed away. Together, Hopeman and Pew provided the college with sound, consistent leadership for sixty-seven years, an unprecedented example of continuity in American higher education. Al Hopeman gave "me new vision when I was weary," MacKenzie recalled, "courage when I was lonely and under attack," and "insight when I was perplexed. . . . I praise him as one of the finest Christian gentlemen I have ever known."[1]

Born in Rochester, New York, on October 3, 1911, Albert A. Hopeman graduated from the Massachusetts Institute of Technology in 1934 and joined the highly successful family manufacturing business—Hopeman Brothers has built ship interiors for almost a century. He rose steadily, eventually being named chairman of the board of AWH Corporation, the holding company for the several Hopeman companies. In 1953 he accepted the invitation of J. Howard Pew, an old friend and business associate, to become a trustee of Grove City College. Hopeman was devoted to the college, painstakingly analyzed its every aspect, and frequently conferred with MacKenzie and his successors. Hopeman was especially determined that the college live up to Joseph Newton Pew's admonition to make the college "beautiful." And so he insisted n financial policies to ensure that funds were available to do just that.

It is a measure of Albert Hopeman's sturdy character that he quietly accepted the challenge of succeeding the legendary J. Howard Pew, with whom he had worked professionally for some thirty years, and quickly demonstrated he was a worthy successor.

In June 1972, during his first annual talk to the faculty, Hopeman pledged to abide by the principles laid down by the Pews and the Ketlers before him. "I will always remember," Hopeman said, "Mr. Pew admonishing us to 'inculcate in the minds and hearts of the students an abiding faith in God and Country, a love for freedom, a respect for truth, an acceptance of personal responsibility, and a desire to contribute to the betterment of the human race.'" "What better advice," asked the new trustee president, "could we have?"[2]

The six-foot-five Hopeman was a man of few public words—he rarely talked for more than ten minutes at the annual faculty luncheons. But he would telephone MacKenzie and discuss a particular college policy for two or three hours. "Time meant absolutely nothing to the man," recalls fellow trustee Heath Larry. "Everybody else... thought we had dug as deep as you're going to get in this subject... [but] Al wasn't satisfied yet."[3] Albert Hopeman took special interest in the college's construction projects, leading trustee Richard Jewel to remark, "Albert was almost pouring the cement and dropping the plumb lines."[4]

Hopeman's was admittedly an unusually detailed management style, but MacKenzie welcomed the counsel of someone who had far more business experience than he. The two men and their talents, Larry says, were "just about the perfect complement."[5] While praising Hopeman's business acumen, MacKenzie never failed to stress the trustee president's adherence to principle. In the twenty years they worked together, recalled the college president, "I never heard him make a decision or advocate a decision... based on the pragmatic or the political. It [was] always, 'What's the right thing to do?'"[6]

Hopeman's decades-long commitment was all the more remarkable since he was not a graduate of Grove City College. But his deep admiration for J. Howard Pew and his uncle B. C. Hopeman, who had served as a trustee for many years, combined well with his conviction that Christian colleges like Grove City could make a profound difference in America's future. His annual talks were part report on the state of the college, part analysis of American education and culture, and part sermon. Many trustees, and preachers, talk longer and say less than Al Hopeman did when addressing the faculty each year.

In 1973, when discussing the new core curriculum that had just been introduced, Hopeman made it clear that as important as the new academic program was, Grove City's justification lay in building "the character of each student so that he or she will become a mature, responsible member of society." In contrast to the emotional immaturity seen so often in college graduates, he said, Grove City students must be infused with "a sense of personal responsibility, of integrity, and of self-discipline coupled with a love of freedom for the individual."[7] Let us not forget, he said the following year, that "we have the great advantage over state institutions of being able to reject indulgence as a way of life and teach self-discipline, loyalty and virtue as a fundamental part of the education we offer."[8]

In 1976 he began to report on Grove City's legal struggle against HEW's attempts to regulate the affairs of the college. He assured the faculty that Grove City would firmly resist regulation and went on to suggest that the school, especially its teachers, should help the students explore "the causes and implications of the massive increase in bureaucracy."[9] Two years later Hopeman declared that in order to succeed a small college like Grove City had to be strong in three areas: "fiscally, so that we may be independent; academically, so that we can continue to attract able students; and valuewise because... this is what justifies our existence as an independent institution." He spoke of "storm clouds on the horizon" and the Carter administration's efforts to force compliance with certain regulations. Such threats, he said, "would have been unthinkable a few decades ago."[10]

In retrospect, Hopeman maintained, America had regressed "from rule by laws enacted by our elected representatives to rule by edicts of bureau heads." There was only one possible response, he asserted: "independent colleges are going to have to fight for their freedom."[11]

In 1979, however, he was obliged to report that many independent colleges had chosen to surrender because they had become "so dependent on government funds that their administrations are afraid to stand up and fight." Grove City, on the other hand, would do all in its power to maintain its independence, he vowed, to be "an institution that is looked up to... a leader in our field."[12] The hands-on Hopeman was now on the phone to David Lascell, the college's attorney in the legal battle against the Department of Education, as often and as long as with Dr. MacKenzie. "He would call at five or six on Saturday afternoon," Lascell recalls, "and we would go over things for hours."[13]

In the spring of 1981, the first year of the Reagan administration, Hopeman was in good spirits and commented wryly on Reagan's announced intention to reduce federal spending on students and higher education in general. Noting that the media had immediately warned of the "privations which would result" from fewer federal funds, Hopeman wondered why the media had not suggested that our colleges and universities "lower the cost of their operations."

Hopeman also spoke of the late "student resistance" to the college's rules and regulations—Grove City had just decided to eliminate off-campus housing—but said the reaction was "natural and to be expected." Nevertheless, he asserted, there would be no compromise. The rules and the values on which they were based set Grove City College "apart from all public institutions and many private ones." "So," he said simply, "let us be true to our Christian beliefs."[14]

In 1983, the seventy-one-year-old engineer-businessman devoted a good part of his talk to the computer, predicting, correctly, that it would have as "profound an effect" on the lives of today's students as the airplane and the telephone had had on him and his generation. He revealed that his field of design and manufacture was "being completely revolutionized." Anticipating the college's later decision to give a laptop computer to every incoming freshman, Hopeman stated that Grove City's "future graduates are going to have to possess a technological awareness or skill that was not even thought of outside of engineering schools two decades ago."

He then turned to the matter of the ongoing legal dispute with the Department of Education, announcing that the Supreme Court would probably hear oral arguments in the fall. Hopeman expressed no second thoughts or regrets—although he was personally bearing a large part of the legal costs. He remarked that if the Department of Education obtained the right to regulate the college in any way, "we would be naive not to recognize that, ultimately, they would demand full control of every facet of our operation—much as, for example, the hospitals are regulated."[15]

In 1984, following the mixed but essentially adverse decision of the Supreme Court, Albert Hopeman stated emphatically at the annual faculty luncheon that there would be "no" change in college policy and that Grove City would continue to "shun all government handouts." He took time to explain yet again the principle underlying Grove City's opposition to government assistance: "We believe," he said, that "our strength lies in the fact that, being free from government entanglement, we are able to structure our organization quite differently from that of other institutions." At Grove City the trustees set the academic and moral policies, the administration carried out the policies, and the faculty concentrated on giving students "the best education possible." As a result, Hopeman stated, "our students receive more attention, care and affection than is customary at other colleges and universities."[16] By shunning government aid, he reiterated the following spring, "we have remained strong and our students graduate with a better understanding of personal responsibility"—a statement J. Howard Pew would have enthusiastically endorsed.

In the spring of 1987, in his thirty-fourth year as a member of the board of trustees, President Hopeman looked out over the assembled faculty members and trustees and talked about Grove City's "academic standing." He stated flatly that the college was failing "to attract very many able students from the higher quality secondary schools." While he and Dr. MacKenzie agreed the college was "superb" in some departments, he went on, it was poor in a few and mediocre in others, and it did not generate enough "creative intellectual excitement." He proceeded to out-

line some steps that would be taken, including improving the
school's cultural offerings and bringing more national lecturers
to campus. In early 1988, for example, immediately after he had
been denied a seat on the Supreme Court by a Democrat-
controlled U.S. Senate, Judge Robert Bork spoke at Grove City
College, drawing an enormous audience of more than four thousand. Hopeman also urged the faculty to think of "all possible
innovations" to stimulate their students and awaken in them a
deeper appreciation of the subjects they were teaching.[17]

To help galvanize the faculty, Hopeman and MacKenzie had
begun discussing who should succeed retiring Thaddeus Penar
as vice president for academic affairs and dean of the college.
Hopeman regarded the appointment as vital to the future of the
school and to what he called the national struggle between "secular humanism and Christian morality."

In 1988, Hopeman said that Grove City College could have
"a profound effect" on that struggle if "we come to be perceived as
an institution that, guided by Christian principles, conducts itself
honorably while at the same time providing a preeminent education."[18] The use of the word "preeminent" was significant. In the
past, college officials had been satisfied with the promise that
Grove City provided an "excellent" education. But in response to
the demands of the ever more competitive collegiate market,
Hopeman and MacKenzie were deliberately raising Grove City's
academic sights.

Hopeman, however, denied strongly there was any intention
of trying to make Grove City College "an elite institution." The
college was proud to be a middle-class, middle-income school
located in the heart of middle America. Rather, the school was
seeking to raise the competence of the average graduate and at the
same time, to inculcate in him or her "a deep sense of personal
responsibility" and a willingness "to work [throughout their

careers] for the betterment of all."[19] As they had been for more
than one hundred years, Grove City's leaders were determined to
maintain at the school the right balance of the mind, the body,
and the spirit. But that balance was far more difficult to achieve in
the late twentieth century than at the time Isaac Ketler had led the
college in the late 1800s.

In 1989, Hopeman pointed out that a century ago America
was "a God-fearing Christian society" in which transgressions
against the teachings of Christ were regarded as "sinful acts."
Today, he said, the college was charged with educating young
people "who have grown up in a secular society where such transgressions are accepted by many as normal, proper behavior." The
"swing to secularism" had received its great impetus after World
War II when most colleges and universities began accepting federal aid, and the faculties became dominated by radical activists.
The result in these schools, he added, was that "Christian ethics
and morals ... are given no more weight than the thoughts of a
teenager." But, he wondered, can a secular and endlessly diverse
society be a virtuous one?[20]

In such a society, Hopeman declared in a calm but firm
voice to the faculty and trustees, Grove City could have "a major
impact" on American higher education. It was up to Grove City to
remain a Christian school and teach "our students what it means
to be virtuous." It was up to Grove City to stress stewardship and
personal responsibility. It was up to Grove City to expose its students to "the knowledge and wisdom of the ages." And young
people across the country responded strongly to his message:
applications for the 1989–1990 academic year were 13 percent
above the previous year whereas most colleges and universities
were experiencing a decrease.[21]

Grove City, insisted Al Hopeman, did not have to grow
larger, only better by "improving our academic program" so that

the college would receive even more than the current three applications for each opening. When that began to happen, he exulted,
"the market place will cause others to follow our example, and
more people will then understand where the basic problem [of
our society] lies."[22]

A Scholar Administrator

President MacKenzie and the board of trustees decided that the
man to lead the college to a higher level of academic excellence was
forty-four-year-old Jerry H. Combee, the dean of the 1,200-
student School of Business and Government at Liberty University,
Lynchburg, Virginia; author and editor of seven scholarly and
popular books on government and civilization; former student of
the celebrated classical scholar Allan Bloom at Cornell University
(from which he had received his Ph.D. in government); and, in
MacKenzie's words, "a fiercely bright, well-organized scholar
administrator." Bloom, author of the nationally acclaimed *The
Closing of the American Mind*, described Combee as one of his best
graduate students in twenty-five years, someone "who knows not
only the tradition of Christian thought but also that of classical
political philosophy."[23]

Effective July 1, 1988, Combee was named vice president for
academic affairs and dean of the college, succeeding Thaddeus H.
Penar, who had served Grove City in a variety of important academic posts for thirty-five years. Over the next four years Combee
directed Grove City College through three important academic
processes—the 1990 reaccreditation by the Middle States Association; the ABET approval of the engineering department (an
unusual achievement for a small college from the nation's most
prestigious engineering accrediting organization); and the recer-
tification of the teacher training program by the Pennsylvania
Department of Education. Grove City's education students,

concluded a Pennsylvania report, "performed better than those at any other college or university in the state."[24]

With the unanimous backing of the faculty, Combee helped construct in 1989 a new general education and business curriculum that increased the core requirements from eighteen hours to 38–50 hours and included a foreign language and a laboratory science. In so acting, Grove City strengthened its liberal arts identity and responded to the concern expressed by the Middle States Association in 1980 about the balance between liberal arts and professional programs at Grove City College.

The school responded to the new technology reshaping America by computerizing the Buhl Library card catalogue, reorienting the computer center from a mainframe to a microcomputer system, and introducing telemarketing into the admissions process. The modernization was overdue: when Combee arrived at Grove City, there was only one Xerox machine for the entire school. The number of freshmen applications increased, and the SAT scores of enrolled students topped 1,100 for the first time. And yet, the cost of going to Grove City College remained almost the same.

The college had always been a good bargain, but in the 1990s it became an outstanding bargain—according to *Money* magazine Grove City ranked as the nation's fifth best buy among private colleges. The *National Review College Guide* named the school as among America's fifty best liberal arts colleges. And the Templeton Foundation placed Grove City on its honor roll of one hundred American colleges that stood for character and morality.

In any other field of endeavor, Grove City's success would have spawned a host of imitators, but it remained the exception rather than the rule in the American academy. Futurists predicted that mega-universities would continue to grow, private colleges would disappear or be absorbed into state systems, public institutions would multiply in number, and American higher education would become monolithic. It was conceivable, President MacKenzie suggested in a 1990 report to the trustees, that with the millennium Grove City might be "one of the few truly independent, truly Christian, truly free-market schools in the nation." But that was cause, the president argued, not for anxiety but for resolve. Grove City College was positioned for future greatness if it remained faithful to the "distinctive, unchanging values which gave her birth." He quoted what the chair of the Middle States' evaluation team had said to him that spring: "Your college has been building momentum which should propel Grove City into the very top echelon of private, undergraduate colleges."[25]

Grove City College was the beneficiary of its own steady rise in excellence and the equally steady decline of American higher education in the last decade of the twentieth century. The distinguished educator Jacques Barzun recounted that in 1991 a screening committee interviewed 150 top students who were competing for ten scholarships worth $60,000 each. Each candidate was asked to discuss briefly a book he had read in the last year that had not been assigned in class. "Only one student out of 150 was able to comply," Barzun said. Duke University professor Stanley Fish, often described as the "high priest" of political correctness, asserted that free speech was only a "political construct" and the First Amendment was "the first refuge of scoundrels." One of the most popular books used in college freshman composition classes—*Racism and Sexism*—defined racism as something that only white people could be guilty of and declared that sexism was "unique" to men.[26]

As the cost of going to college rose sharply—141 percent between 1980 and 1990, three times as fast as inflation—public dissatisfaction with higher education rose just as quickly. Pollster Lou Harris reported that in the 1960s, 61 percent of Americans placed a high degree of confidence in the "people running higher education." Three decades later, it had plummeted to 25 percent. And yet the education establishment continued to deny emphatically that anything was wrong. Journals like *Prospects*, *Innovative Higher Education*, *Liberal Education*, and *Change* were filled with self-congratulatory essays on the bright shining future of American higher education in the twenty-first century. "In its basic structure and degree configuration," wrote D. Bruce Johnstone, chancellor of the State University of New York, a sixty-four-campus system, "in the way professors teach and students learn, and in its prominent role within American society, colleges and universities at the turn of the millennium will look much as they did a decade or two earlier."[27] This was not simply cognitive dissonance but cognitive denial.

President Combee

At the May 1990 meeting of Grove City's board of trustees, Dr. MacKenzie announced that after twenty years of service, he intended to resign as president, effective the following year. Albert Hopeman warmly praised the retiring president for "a magnificent job... we are deeply in his debt." Trustee Richard G. Jewell later summed up that it was Sherry MacKenzie who had led Grove City College to "its unique place in American higher education... a school with true vision and values and with students and faculty that profess and practice those values."[28] To replace him, a special committee under Dr. Robert Lamont began a national search that ultimately considered more than 150 candidates. The board of trustees' choice as the school's sixth president was Jerry Combee, who had accomplished so much as vice president for academic affairs. "I am confident," said Sherry MacKenzie, "that Dr. Combee will prove to be not only an able leader, but a leader of great vision and insight." For his part,

trustee president Albert Hopeman stated, "We are indeed fortunate to have such a fine able person at the helm." "Grove City
College," promised Combee, "will continue to build upon its
Christian vision of excellence in education. The spirit of the
times has opened a window of opportunity for a college like this
that has never lost sight of what is good about America."[29] He
was formally inaugurated as president of Grove City College on
April 28, 1992.

President Combee got off to a fast start, playing Chuck
Berry's 1950s classic number "Johnny B. Goode" on the guitar at
his inaugural gala; suspending in his first week twenty-five students for underage drinking; placing attractive, double-page
advertisements in *US Air Magazine* and other national journals
(previous presidents had not been willing to spend money on
national advertising); increasing applications in his first academic
year by 15 percent and from forty-one states (compared with
thirty states the year before); raising the SAT average to 1,126;
improving the humanities core called the "civilization series";
launching publication of *Grove City College Alumni Magazine*, the
school's first alumni magazine; and hiring Dr. Garth E. Runion,
the dean of the school of education at Mississippi College, as vice
president for academic affairs and dean of the college—the position he had filled so capably. In his remarks at the opening convocation at the Harbison Chapel, Dr. Combee emphatically
denied that the values of work, family, freedom, and faith, in
which Grove City College believed, were "passé." Not only were
they "good for the past," he said, "they are also good for the
future."[30]

President Combee's lovely wife, Daneille, made her presence
felt as well. A gifted public speaker, she taught public speaking and
was deeply involved in the planning and programming of the new
FM radio station on campus. She also initiated a program to pre-

serve the college's history, collecting and categorizing unidentified memorabilia of previous administrations. In 1993, she received the Florence E. MacKenzie Campus-Community Award for her efforts on behalf of the college and the community. As the "first lady" of Grove City College, says Ruth Harker Mills, Daneille Combee "worked hard to raise student morale."[31]

New administrations are tested in different ways, and the school's fraternity students decided to find out how strict Combee and his new team would be about an old student custom, even at Grove City. One fraternity scheduled a ski trip and stocked a chartered bus with a variety of potables—beer, wine, and whiskey. Three young and very drunk men wound up in the hospital, and the student who organized the event was suspended for the rest of the semester, as was the fraternity. Grovers correctly concluded from the stiff penalties imposed for this and other alcohol infractions (such as a late evening keg party at the Meridian Vets Club that included thirteen women students) that the Combee administration would not hesitate to enforce its rules and the underage drinking laws of the Commonwealth of Pennsylvania.[32]

The fraternity groups chafed under what they regarded as the president's heavy hand, but the majority of the students who had come to Grove City to study, not to party, accepted—and even welcomed—the disciplinary action. "Student morale," Combee told the trustees, "appears quite positive."[33] As a practical matter, fraternity membership at the college had declined from 30.3 percent of the student body in 1984 to just over 20 percent in 1993. Sorority membership had also dipped, from 53.3 percent of the campus in 1984 to about 38 percent in 1993. The majority of students were satisfying their social needs outside the fraternity-sorority system. Fraternities, for example, once had tables in the cafeteria reserved for them, but no more.[34]

Grove City College continued to enjoy marked success over the next two years although some trustees noted the sharp rise in expenditures in several departments and expressed their concern. Charles MacKenzie had been known for pinching pennies— Jerry Combee seemed to delight in spending them. Still, there was no denying the school's rising academic stature: the incoming students' SATs—now called Scholastic Assessment (not Aptitude) Tests—went up twenty points in 1993 over the previous year, for an increase of seventy points since 1988. Construction of the new Joseph Newton Pew Memorial Dormitory proceeded smoothly. Chapel attendance increased as the students adjusted to and clearly approved the new schedule—twenty-minute convocations on Tuesday and Thursday mornings at 9 A.M. and a Sunday Vespers service at 6:30 P.M. The requirement of sixteen attendances per semester was retained.[35] A Catholic priest was invited to minister to the Catholic students on campus.

The school's athletic teams won 60 percent of their games in the fall of 1993; disciplinary violations by students dropped dramatically from 174 in 1991–1992 to 51 in 1992–1993; on August 27, 1994, all 624 of the incoming freshmen were given personal notebook computers and printers along with the usual orientation materials as the information age truly arrived at Grove City College; *U.S. News & World Report* and *Money* again described the college as one of the best educational "buys" in the country. And for the fifth consecutive year, in 1993 Grove City was named to the John Templeton Foundation Honor Roll for Character Building Colleges.

Eager to expand Grove City's academic reputation, Combee began publishing *Visions & Values*, which reprinted the remarks of nationally known speakers on the Grove City campus. A Washington internship program was started with Washington, D.C., insider and Grove City graduate Paul McNulty as the instructor. And Combee suggested to the board of trustees that an international study program based in London—perhaps at the University of London—would broaden the global outlook of Grove City students. He also proposed the creation of a communications major. Some trustees suggested things were moving too fast and asked about the costs of the proposed programs; the president replied the college could afford them.

Nor was that all. Combee decided to reform the teaching method of the humanities section—the Keystone core—of the school's Civilization Series. The six core courses had been taught in very large sections of 500–700 students, severely limiting interaction between teacher and student and drastically increasing the average class size of the entire college. Starting in 1994, four of the courses were reduced to a more normal class size of 40 to 50 students and offered each semester rather than yearly. But there was no change in the class size of HUMA 101 Civilization, taken by all first-year students and taught by President Combee himself, who used as a text his own book *Forward to Freedom*. One could question the unwieldy class size of 650—more common to a large university than a small college—yet be impressed by Jerry Combee's willingness to teach a course to every freshman. Not since Isaac Ketler in the early 1900s had a Grove City president undertaken such an academic responsibility.

Described by some educators as "the best kept secret in American higher education," Grove City College kept earning more and more national commendation.[36] In the fall of 1994 *U.S. News & World Report* ranked the college first among liberal arts colleges in the north as a "best value" and second in the region in the "most efficient" category. The *Princeton Review* gave Grove City a "desirability" rating of 91, tying it in the Middle States with Johns Hopkins University and besting Bryn Mawr College. An ever increasing number of applicants now came from outside the Pennsylvania-Ohio-New York region which had supplied most of Grove City's students for more than a century. Sophomore Daniel Brinker of Tucson, Arizona, explained that after "looking all over," he picked Grove City because of its quality academics, reasonable price, Christian atmosphere, and small size. Brinker had learned about the college from an ad in *Campus Life*.[37] It also made a difference that the campus remained essentially crime-free. Women students rarely locked their doors in the dormitories; as one young woman remarked to a visiting trustee, "Even your soap is safe."[38]

There was a demographic dip in the 1990s, and colleges, needing to fill beds and meet budgets, competed aggressively for the smaller pool of students. But unlike other schools, according to director of admissions Jeffrey C. Mincey, Grove City did not recruit more international students, nontraditional students (twenty-two years and older), or less qualified students. Nor did it try to "buy" students by discounting their tuition and other charges through financial aid. It relied instead on its proven formula of providing a very good education at a very good price in a Christian environment. "You get a lot for your money here," says Mincey.[39] The ever restless Combee now helped reverse a long-standing policy. Grove City offered its first graduate degree in nearly half a century—a Master of Science in Accounting starting in the fall of 1995. The school was reacting to the reality that a master's degree was almost mandatory for those entering public accounting. With the encouragement of trustee Richard Jewell, a 1967 graduate and managing vice president of a national accounting consulting firm, Grove City designed a thirty-semester-hour program of study.

The college had reached "a plateau of excellence," in the words of J. Paul Sticht, vice president of the board of trustees (and former chairman of R. J. Reynolds Industries). Where should it now go? At the November 1994 trustees meeting, Sticht asked Combee to bring to the board "his visions, goals, and concepts for the future of Grove City College."[40] Sticht tendered the request on behalf of Albert Hopeman, who had been ill for several months and could not be present. Combee took the trustees' invitation literally. Over the next six months he drew up a detailed plan for a new and greater Grove City College, contacting educators near and far, seeking advice from a prominent Pittsburgh law firm about the requirements for a Pennsylvania university, and trying to anticipate the inevitable questions and even objections to his unprecedented proposal.

He failed to touch base with the man who by custom and charter was primarily responsible for determining Grove City College policy—the president of the board of trustees, Albert Hopeman. Nor did he consult with other senior members of the board. Without advance warning, Dr. Combee was about to propose a radical departure from 115 years of Grove City College history. Under the best of circumstances his plan would have been skeptically received. But because he failed to involve Hopeman and other key trustees in the planning process, assuming an authority no Grove City College president had ever had, there was only one possible reaction to the proposal—and its author.

A College, Not a University

In his May 1995 president's report to the board of trustees, Combee proudly pointed out that student applications were up 3 percent, the number of companies visiting the campus and interviewing students for jobs had increased by 47 percent in the past year, the athletic teams in 1994–1995 had compiled an overall winning record of 58.7 percent, nationally known speakers like author Dinesh D'Souza, educator Diane Ravitch, and Berkeley law professor Phillip Johnson had visited the campus, and construction of the J. N. Pew Memorial Dormitory was complete. At the conclusion of his report, Combee submitted his plan for the college's future entitled "The Greater Grove City: A Five-Year Strategic Vision." Conceding that the plan was very ambitious and even startling with its recommendation that Grove City be converted into a university, Combee asked the thirty-six-member-board (including twelve new members solicited by the president) to give it their serious consideration.[41]

Pointing out that the school was about twice the size of a typical four-year college (usually around 1,200 students), Combee argued that Grove City College was already more like a small university than a "pure" small liberal arts school. The "University of Grove City" would, he assured the trustees, attract "the higher-achieving student" because it could boast "a level of quality, breadth, and seriousness" not always associated with a college.[42] He conceded that the transition would require certain changes—like offering at least five professional master's level programs, several master's programs in the arts and sciences, and at least one Ph.D. program. But the state of graduate education in America was so "disturbing," he argued, that Grove City had "a moral compulsion" not to turn over its undergraduates to graduate schools that would "systematically tear down what we have tried to build up."[43]

Combee acknowledged there would be additional costs such as hiring twenty-five additional faculty at $50,000 each, and integrating some two hundred graduate students into the campus community. Trying to reassure the trustees, Combee said that since the graduate students would live off campus, "they would have little or no contact with undergraduates." He did not address the quite likely negative consequences of a divided student population on a small campus like Grove City.

The president also suggested several undergraduate improvements, including new courses in environmental studies and the health professions. He then recommended spending $10 million over the next five years in building improvements, and he outlined a new loan program and an expanded merit scholarship program—financed by some $26 million in existing trust funds—based in large part on plans formulated during the MacKenzie years. The loan program would be administered by the PNC Bank of Pittsburgh. Pulling out all the stops, Combee used twenty-nine, single-spaced pages to present his audacious dream of a "greater" Grove City.

The executive committee, chaired by Albert Hopeman, did not take long to render its decision. The differences between the college president and the board of trustees over Grove City's future were too great to be reconciled: both the message and the messenger were rejected. Dr. Combee had already upset several trustees by what they regarded as his excessive spending—he didn't seem able to say "no." And succumbing to hubris, Combee had failed to keep the board, particularly its deeply committed president, fully informed of what he was doing and hoped to do. On June 20, 1995, Jerry Combee submitted his resignation as president of Grove City College, and the board, with one exception, accepted it. While they appreciated all that Combee had accomplished in his years at Grove City, the trustees simply did not share his vision of the future. They wanted Grove City to remain what it had always been—a small, independent, Christian college. Combee's idea of converting Grove City College into the University of Grove City was, in the words of one trustee, "too big a chunk [for the board] to swallow."[44]

Despite their fundamental differences, Jerry Combee left with the good wishes of the board. Trustee Phillip A. Smith publicly commended Combee for "upgrading the level of the faculty"

and creating a "palpable" vitality on campus. Heath Larry, a former vice chairman of the board, described Combee as "a man of
immense capability."[45]

In an interview with the author, Dr. Combee, who went on
to become president of Jamestown College in North Dakota,
spoke warmly about his years at Grove City and praised the board
of trustees. "Whatever was accomplished during my years at
Grove City College," Combee said, "are creditable to an outstanding board of trustees, led by Chairman Al Hopeman, who was
dedicated to following the principles of J. Howard Pew, and to
Vice Chairman J. Paul Sticht, a titan of corporate America. Mr.
Sticht's predecessor, R. Heath Larry, was also an honor to work
with." Credit should also go, he added, to the faculty that followed
the lead of the trustees. Asked to enumerate what he was most
proud of, Combee said: providing a notebook computer and
printer to every student—"there is a very short list of colleges that
has the information technology program Grove City has"; establishing a new general education curriculum that balanced professional and liberal arts and sciences programs; achieving ABET
accreditation for both electrical and mechanical engineering—
"we had to meet the same standards as Cal Tech and MIT"; and
carrying out major building projects like the renovated Pew
Memorial Dormitory.[46]

Combee also recalled proudly teaching the basic course in
humanities to the entire freshman class—"we wanted to ensure
that every Grove City graduate would have college level cultural
literacy." He had emphasized Western civilization but not in a
"Neanderthal" way—the other great world civilizations were
included. And he had required study of the Old and New
Testament, not for religious reasons, but because, he said, "How
can you be culturally literate without knowing the great stories of
the Bible?"[47]

Combee expressed optimism about the future of colleges like Grove City. While many schools were pricing themselves out of the market, Grove City and similar schools were continuing to offer quality education at a reasonable price—far below the annual $30,000 cost of a Swarthmore College. Too many colleges, Combee said, were focusing on educational gimmicks like "critical thinking." There was no substitute "for enabling students to master the subject matter. It is our reason for being." He predicted that small independent liberal arts colleges "will prosper in the next century" if they concentrate on the basics of education and stay current with the "leading edge of information technology."[48]

A National Leader

And so quite unexpectedly, in the summer of 1995, the trustees of Grove City College were tasked with a formidable duty—selecting a successor to Jerry Combee. The first six Grove City presidents had included ordained ministers, experienced educators, respected scholars, good managers, and skilled fundraisers. All of them had been inspired by the school's unofficial motto— "Faith and Freedom." They had carried out their duties in concert with and under the guidelines laid down by the board of trustees. They had worked closely with the faculty, constantly seeking to improve its quality and performance. And they had kept before them always the primary purpose of Grove City College—to graduate young men and women who would be successful in their chosen professions and as American citizens. The new president would have to honor the traditions and customs that Grove City College had accumulated for over a century and lead the college into a new century filled with manifold uncertainties and opportunities.

Many schools would have hurried the process to avoid any impression of indecision, but the trustees told the search committee, headed by Richard Larry, president of the Sarah Scaife Foundation, Pittsburgh, to take all the time it needed to find the best possible man. They were able to do so because Garth E. Runion, executive vice president and dean of the college, was there to keep the college running smoothly and efficiently. "Under his leadership," said Scott Powell, assistant to the president and a member of a management team that met every Monday morning, "all of us pulled together and worked to ensure that the college continued its advance."[49] And during the academic year of 1995–1996 following Combee's departure, Grove City did advance: receiving four applications for every dormitory opening; increasing the number of visits by recruiting companies; starting a home page on the World Wide Web; graduating the first class of the Master of Science in Accounting program; and racking up a .728 winning percentage in athletics. "Garth Runion," Albert Hopeman summed up, "stepped in and performed beautifully."[50]

In the spring of 1996, after an arduous nine-month search, the board of trustees named John H. Moore as the seventh president of Grove City College. The sixty-one-year-old Moore was a widely published economist and scholar, past deputy director of the National Science Foundation (receiving its Distinguished Service Award in 1990), a former senior fellow and associate director at the prestigious Hoover Institution at Stanford University, and a Distinguished Service Professor at George Mason University in northern Virginia who had served as director of its International Institute from 1990 to 1995. Moore received his bachelor of science degree in chemical engineering from the University of Michigan, a M.B.A. from Michigan, and his Ph.D. in economics from the University of Virginia where he collaborated with the highly respected economist Warren Nutter. He went on to positions at the University of Virginia, Emory

University, and the University of Miami. The board was impressed by the wide array of Moore's attributes: his proven management skills, his widespread national and international connections, his deep understanding of free market economics, and his strong personal faith. The college's "dedication to Christian values," Moore said in one of his first statements as president, "provides the foundation for a moral life for its students, both at Grove City and as members of society."[51]

Trustees from President Albert Hopeman to member Phillip Smith, who had initially questioned the method used to choose Jerry Combee's successor, were of a single mind about their new president. "We are very pleased," said Hopeman, "that a man of John Moore's caliber has agreed to serve as the next president of the college." "I am absolutely delighted," Smith said. "He clearly exhibits outstanding leadership skills." Heath Larry, a member of the board for nearly fifty years, remarked that the soft-spoken Moore reminded him of the renowned Weir Ketler, who had successfully guided the college through war, depression, and other crises of the times.[52] The trustees were also taken with the president's wife Sue, whose "innate sense of gentility and dignity," remarked one board member, "makes you glad you're with her. She's a considerable asset to John."[53]

President Moore went to work immediately at Grove City. In his first semester he helped the engineering department prepare for a visit from the Accreditation Board for Engineering and Technology (ABET), worked closely with the committee preparing for the Middle States Association's evaluation team scheduled to visit Grove City in the spring of 1998, kept the information technology initiative moving ahead (there were now 1,950 portable computer systems on campus), encouraged the internationalization of the school's curriculum (an international business major was offered for the first time), and noted that the incoming class of freshmen of 626 was the largest in the school's history, with an average SAT score of 1,239, well above the national average of 1,013. Summing up Moore's management style, Dr. Barbara Akin, chair of the history department for over twenty years, remarked, "He allows people to do their job."[54]

Grove City College was again singled out by *Money, U.S. News & World Report, The Princeton Review*, and *Peterson's Competitive Colleges Guidebook* as one of the best buys in higher education—tuition was 49 percent of the national average for four-year private colleges. Impressed with the high caliber of the students, more and more companies were interviewing graduating seniors on campus: almost one hundred companies conducted over 1,100 interviews in the 1995–1996 year (160 companies visited in 1999). And the percentage of graduates who found employment within three months was 81 percent. According to director of career services James T. Thrasher, corporate recruiters often described the students they interviewed at other campuses as "academic barbarians," unable to work with others. In contrast they found Grovers to be "team workers" with "high moral standards."[55] "The college," Moore states in his typically low-key way, "remains a faithful steward of its resources."[56]

Indeed, it seemed that in his leadership of Grove City College, John Moore was one of those stewards mentioned in the Bible who can be counted on to increase what he is given manifold. At the end of his first year as president, Dr. Moore reported to the trustees that *Time* had placed Grove City at the top of its select list of ten colleges and universities that offer "affordable, high-quality education." And among *Campus Life's* 275,000 Christian readers, Grove City had gone in the past decade from "no recognition" to a consistent top twenty position in the nation; they ranked the college number one in affordability and number four in academic reputation.[57] Amid all the glowing academic accomplishments, Moore was proud that 10 percent of the student body had spent their Easter break doing missionary work as part of the school's Inner-City Outreach program, with eighteen groups working in poverty-stricken areas in the Midwest, Northeast, and Southeast.

Grove City withdrew in October 1996 from the federal Stafford and PLUS loan programs. President Moore immediately assured the campus community that a student loan program, underwritten by the PNC Bank and comparable to the federal government's program, would be available to all interested students beginning with the fall 1997 semester. In fact, Grove City was able to accelerate the process and offer loans to forty-two students in the spring of 1997.

Another initiative was alumni relations. After years of being asked to do little for their alma mater, alumni were now being encouraged to form chapters and sponsor activities; they responded enthusiastically—almost four thousand people attended alumni events in 1996–1997. The stepped-up alumni activity would prove important in the school's first major fund-raising drive launched in the year 2000.

Grove City graduates have tended to go into business and often rise to the top—like J. Paul Sticht at R. J. Reynolds Industries, R. Heath Larry at U.S. Steel, Don Hayes at GTE, and Fred Fetterolf at Alcoa. But more recently, they can also be found in the nonprofit world or government. "I wouldn't be here," says Paul McNulty, who served as director of communications/chief counsel for the House Judiciary Committee during the impeachment trial of President Bill Clinton and is now chief counsel and director of legislative operations for House Majority Leader Dick Armey, "without my years at Grove City College." A 1980 graduate, McNulty credits the college for developing in him a sense of purpose about life. "It changed me," he says, "spiritually and intellectually."[58]

"The most important thing about Grove City," says Alejandro Chafuen, president of the Atlas Economic Research Foundation based in northern Virginia, "is the truth and character that the college imparts." A native of Argentina, Chafuen came to the college in 1978 under a scholarship program directed by economist Hans Sennholz. He learned at Grove City that "there is no contradiction between true science and true faith." He sees the college as "a shining light" for other schools to emulate in an era "when many think we're on automatic pilot regarding character and moral integrity."[59]

Lawrence W. Reed, president of the Mackinac Center for Public Policy in Midland, Michigan, and a 1975 graduate, says that Grove City College was "both a refuge and an inspiration." The school, he explains, was a refuge from "the radicalism and anti-intellectualism of the 1960s" and a place "where my instincts for a free society blossomed into a career commitment." With an annual budget of $2.7 million and a staff of twenty-eight, the Mackinac Center is the largest of some forty state-based conservative think tanks in America. Already enrolled as a freshman at the University of Pittsburgh, Reed transferred to Grove City after hearing Hans Sennholz speak at a conference about the importance of economic freedom—"he was and is a major inspiration to me."[60]

Demonstrating their personal commitment to the college, President Moore and his wife Sue have made it a point to have lunch frequently in the student cafeteria, standing in line with trays like everyone else. They occasionally invite students to have dinner with them in the President's House, giving Mrs. Moore an opportunity to display her culinary skills. Once four students were treated to a "Moroccan dinner," including black olives with harissa, coriander eggplant salad, fish chermoula, and Moroccan mint tea.[61] Like her predecessors as first lady of the college, Sue

Moore has been active on campus and in the community. She has served on the board of the Grove City YMCA and the Mercer County Bicentennial Commission (the county celebrated its 200th birthday on March 12, 2000). And she has helped organize campus blood drives and was mainly responsible for establishing Internet service for college retirees and the wives and children of current faculty.

Moore's second year at Grove City College was darkened by the death—at age eighty-six—of Albert A. Hopeman, Jr., who had served as president of the board of trustees for twenty-six years. Hopeman had directed Grove City's withdrawal from the federal Pell Grant Program following *Grove City College v. Bell* as well as its departure from the federal student loan program in 1996. "He embodied," Moore said, "the traits for which the college is admired—independence, integrity, and commitment to ideals of spirit and practice."[62] In recognition of Hopeman's many contributions to the college, the School of Science and Engineering was named after him in May 1997, and the alumni association at the same time conferred honorary alumnus status upon him. Hopeman, it will be recalled, had not attended Grove City College, although his uncle Bertram C. Hopeman had served as a trustee for eighteen years until his death in 1959.

Summing up Albert Hopeman's influence on the course of the college during the past quarter century, J. Paul Sticht, who had served on the board of trustees with him for over thirty years, stated that "Grove City College stands stronger and more respected than ever because of his leadership, because of his devotion to fulfilling the school's mission."[63] The board of trustees then ensured that the college would continue to benefit from principled and dedicated leadership by naming Sticht, a 1939 graduate of Grove City and former head of R. J. Reynolds Industries, as its new chairman.

The Need to Give Back

Asked why he was committed to Grove City's development, Sticht, looking a decade younger than his eighty-one years, explained, "If I had not been able to go to college, specifically Grove City College, I probably would have never had the opportunities that I have had throughout my life." Conceding it was a cliché, Sticht said simply, "Anybody who has gone through the experiences that I have gone through understands the importance of giving back... and I think the need to give back to Grove City College is becoming more important every day."[64]

In November 1999, President Moore informed the board of trustees that the class of 2003 was the brightest ever to matriculate at Grove City College. The 586 freshmen had an average SAT score of 1,258 and an average GPA (grade point average) of 3.70. Fifty-nine percent of them had graduated in the top 10 percent of their high school; seventy-six had been class valedictorians, twenty-six of them, salutatorians. And while Grove City remained primarily a teaching college, its professors were shining brighter in the field of academic achievement: English professor Janice Brown's book *The Seven Deadly Sins in the Work of Dorothy Sayers* was nominated for an Edgar Allen Poe Award; biology professor Fred Brenner was elected president of the National Association of Academies of Science; and psychology professor Peter Hill co-edited the *Baker Encyclopedia of Psychology and Counseling*. The college's rising reputation also lifted teacher's salaries: the average salary of a faculty member was now 7 percent above the average for baccalaureate institutions.[65] "The most frequent emotion I encounter from my colleagues on other campuses," says John A. Sparks, the longtime chairman of the Department of Business Administration, Economics, and International Management, "is envy."[66]

Almost automatically, in June 1998, the Middle States Association on Higher Education reaffirmed the accreditation of

Grove City College. After noting the considerable progress that
had been made since the last visit in 1990, the evaluation team
commented: "The Institution is entering another exciting phase
in its illustrious history and, in so doing, has an additional opportunity to strategically position itself, while maintaining the values
and goals that have undergirded its rich, successful past."[67] The
Intercollegiate Studies Institute's new college guide stated that "in
a day when public affiliation with a church and ardent defense
of tradition can cause the eyes of the literati to roll back in their
heads, Grove City has taken a courageous stand for the pursuit
of truth, and has done so with academic distinction."[68]

The guide was undoubtedly impressed that more than
twenty Christian groups (excluding independent Bible studies)
met regularly on campus. The largest was "Warriors for Christ"—
some five hundred students gathered in Harbison Chapel every
Thursday evening to sing, read scripture, and pray. "There are
more dedicated Christians among the students," says the dean of
students Nancy Paxton, who has been at Grove City since 1976,
"than there used to be."[69] These young Christians put their faith
into action. The Red Box Mission, established in 1976 to encourage international missionary work, has sent sixty volunteers to
countries in Latin America, the Caribbean, Europe, Asia, and
Africa.

Dean of the College Garth E. Runion stresses that what is
unique about Grove City is the blend of "high academics and
Christian emphasis—few Christian schools have our academic
quality."[70] The college also demonstrated its uniqueness in the
American academy by reinstituting 8 A.M. classes (without trig-
gering campus protests) to increase flexibility in course scheduling, reduce congestion in the dining halls, and eliminate many
late afternoon classes. One tradition did finally fall: At their fall
1999 meeting, the trustees eliminated Saturday classes (effective

in 2000–2001), persuaded that Grove City with its more geo-
graphically diversified student body would not become a phan-
tom campus on the weekends.

When a front-page article in a daily Pittsburgh newspaper
mocked Grove City students as a bunch of uptight squares who
would "rather crack a book than a beer," Grovers responded that
the reporter seemed to be suggesting that you could only have fun
if you drank alcohol. Pointing out that drinking was illegal for
anyone under twenty-one, one Grover said that the college made
no attempt to hide what it was—"a Christian liberal arts institution which staunchly upholds the promise of its founders and the
ideals of its charter."[71]

That did not mean never trying something new if it would
help the institution. And so for the first time in Grove City
College history, a major fund-raising program was approved.
Thomas J. Pappalardo was hired to fill a new position—vice president for institutional advancement—and to direct a five-year,
$60 million capital development program. Donors, once they
were convinced that neither J. Howard Pew nor any other Pew
had left Grove City with a large financial endowment, began coming forward: by the spring of 2000, more than one-third of the
goal had been reached in gifts and commitments. The public
kickoff was set for October 2000, coinciding with the school's
opening celebration of its 125th anniversary.

Looking ahead to the new millennium, President Moore
reflected on a meeting he had attended of college presidents,
deans, and faculty who shared the basic beliefs of Isaac Ketler,
J. N. Pew, and the other founders of Grove City College. It had
been exhilarating, he told Grove City alumni, to be among so
many like-minded educators, and yet he had been struck "by the
extent to which Grove City College is free of the problems that
afflict other colleges."[72]

While others worried about the ever escalating cost of higher education, Grove City's costs "remain among the lowest for selective private institutions"—the total cost of tuition, room, board, and books for the academic year 1999–2000 was just over $11,000. There was agreement among the conservative educators about the difficulty of maintaining a sound liberal education. Grove City's Humanities Core, Moore pointed out, represented "a strong, carefully planned, coherent [liberal arts] program." There was constant discussion by the other conservatives of alcohol and drug abuse. In contrast, Moore stated, Grove City students were committed, without apology, to the creation of a drug- and alcohol-free campus.

Many campus problems, Dr. Moore believed, could be traced to the general moral and spiritual decay in American society. Unfortunately, he pointed out, the moral relativism taught on many campuses reinforced the decay. Far from challenging students to think, Dr. Moore said, "attacks on traditional values... destroy their faith." Not so at Grove City College, he emphasized, where the central purpose of higher education is seen as preparing students "not only to make a living" but to live a life "that is consistent with the great traditions of Western civilization."[73] Through its students, Dr. Moore said proudly, Grove City acts as a powerful counterweight to the many negative and destructive forces that exist in American higher education and society.

But is the struggle too uneven? Are there too many destructive forces for one small college and a few kindred schools to resist? Indeed, the question must be asked: Is there a place for a small independent Christian college in the secular, bureaucratic, technologically drive modern world? What is the role of a college in America in the Twenty-first Century?

CHAPTER TEN

The Future of the American College

America is the most successful and enduring democracy in human history. While other nations have declined or fallen, America has survived foreign invasion, civil war, world wars, a great depression, not so small recessions, a cold war, assassinations, presidential scandals, malaise, an adversary culture, and the mass media.

What is the source of America's strength and endurance—its abundant natural resources? its hardworking, freedom-loving people? its fortuitous geographical location midway between Europe and Asia? its national will? Why do we Americans enjoy liberty, justice, and equality? Whence come our limited government, individual freedom, market economy, and fundamental values? Historian Russell Kirk, in *The Roots of American Order*, provides a persuasive answer: America is not only the land of the brave and the home of the free but a place of ordered liberty.

The roots of American order run deep in human history. They were planted, Kirk points out, nearly three thousand years ago by the Hebrews who perceived "a purposeful moral existence under God."[1] The Greeks strengthened the roots with their

281

philosophical and political self-awareness and were followed by the Romans who nurtured the roots with their law and social awareness. The roots, later intertwined with "the Christian understanding of human duties and human hopes, of man redeemed," were then joined by medieval custom, learning, and valor.[2] The roots were enriched, finally, by two great political experiments in law and liberty which occurred in London and then in Philadelphia.

It is a unique and inspiring story, but who will tell it to succeeding generations of Americans to ensure that America remains a land of liberty under God?

Clearly, a major part of the responsibility falls to our institutions of higher learning, particularly the subject of this history—the American college. And yet there is sharp disagreement among educators about the purpose of higher education in America. Progressives favor a generally utilitarian curriculum and traditionalists, a more philosophical one. There is of course nothing new about academic differences of opinion. Indeed, the greatest thinkers of Western civilization have debated the function of learning—and knowledge—in human society since the first "college" was founded in the Groves of Academe in Athens nearly 2,500 years ago.

The desire to know, Socrates said, is a cardinal virtue in a republic.[3] But to know what—and to what end? Plato's *Republic*, Russell Kirk maintains, is not a political treatise but "an inquiry into the real nature of spiritual and social harmony."[4] Like Socrates, Plato sought to renew Greek society by deepening its religious understanding. These ideas were early on embraced by American educators. In his last dialogue, *The Laws*, Plato affirms, "It is God who is, for you and me, the measure of all things."[5] The writings of the eminent Roman lawyer, senator, and orator Cicero were also at the core of the American curriculum in the seventeenth and eighteenth centuries. Cicero was ancient Rome's most eloquent spokesman for ordered liberty: "True law," he writes in *The Republic*, "is right reason in agreement with Nature." And God, he insists, is "the author of this law, its promulgator, and its enforcing judge."[6]

In the fourth century, St. Augustine asserted that all speaking is teaching, but that the response of the listener depends upon the teacher within him—Jesus Christ. The medieval humanist philosopher Vives was in turn eloquent about education qua education, writing that "there is nothing in life more beautiful than the cultivation of the mind through what we call the branches of learning."[7]

Others have argued that it is the heart rather than the head that should be cultivated. The eighteenth-century French political philosopher Montesquieu considered virtue to be the essential requirement of republics. He defined virtue as the love of law and of country, requiring "a constant preference of public to private interest." Everything, Montesquieu stated, depended "on establishing this love [of law] in a republic; and to inspire it ought to be the principal business of education."[8]

The American Founders, led by Thomas Jefferson, agreed that education was an essential ingredient of the new nation, but the virtue they wished to inculcate, political scientist Eva Brann says, was "a mean between the grand, selfless passion of ancient republics and the calculatingly enlightened self-interest of modern moralists."[9] They sought a benevolent and republican utilitarianism. Jefferson elucidated this notion in his "Rockfish Gap Report" on American education and made a clear distinction between citizen education (practical and aimed at private success) and higher education (theoretical and directed toward public service). But something crucial was missing in Jefferson's educational design—the Creator, so prominent in the Decla-

ration of Independence (which he drafted) and in the founding
charters of Harvard and America's other first colleges.

It is a critical point: If utilitarianism—always seeking the
greatest good for the greatest number—is the school's guiding
principle, the student can easily turn, Brann argues, "into the
socially adjusted individual willing to conform." Liberal education soon expands to include social education, and the teacher
becomes an ideologue. Individual students may demand the right
of self-expression, but in the ensuing struggle, there inevitably
ensues a relaxation of discipline and standards. This "complex of
educational dilemmas," Brann remarks, "is familiar enough" in
the modern era.[10]

The answer to the dilemma, educators Gene Edward Veith,
Jr., and Andrew Kern argue, is classical or genuine liberal arts
education. The classical school, they explain, is interested in "all
human knowledge from the arts to the sciences, history to mathematics."[11] It neither ignores nor idolizes the past. It seeks, rather,
to "inculcate wisdom and virtue" and to educate for citizenship.
Classical education, they say, is deeply personal, with teachers
gladly serving as mentors and students eagerly engaging in
Socratic dialogues.[12] A major influence on their thinking is the
nineteenth-century educator and churchman John Henry Newman, who wrote that the pursuit of truth for its own sake was
the purpose of the university, although he conceded the development of intellect and character had practical consequences.[13]

Even though its advocates insist that classical education has
always played a paradoxical role of preserving the past in order
to usher in change and improvement, they are accused of elitism
and anachronism. "Classical" is not a word that falls easily from
the lips of most Americans. We prefer to look ahead rather than
behind. "Progress is our most important product," the host
of television's most popular Sunday evening program declared

every week for eight years (the host later became our fortieth president).

The solution may be a golden mean between the two approaches—a prudential balancing of classical and practical education. A resolution to the dilemma is important because its results will extend far beyond the college campus. While a school is not *the* world, writes Brann, it is *a* world, "a small republic of the intellect within the political community."[14] And its inhabitants will one day lead the larger world. Alexis de Tocqueville believed that the survival of republican civilization depended upon the nature of the public associations of civil life. How then can one of America's most important associations—the liberal arts college—be sustained and in turn help sustain the vigor and virtue of the nation in the twenty-first century?

The View from the Establishment

The American college has a "bright" future if, in the words of the American Council on Education's president, Stanley O. Ikenberry, it maintains "a distinctive character that distinguishes its campus from the three thousand, six hundred other campuses."[15] And that character will be shaped by how the college deals with three current major challenges in higher education—technological uncertainty, economic uncertainty, and societal uncertainty.

So far, Ikenberry says, every area in American society has been more influenced by high technology than higher education. Second, higher education has been financed by a combination of the philanthropic and private sectors and state and federal government. But state governments over the last decade have pulled back, shifting more of the financial burden onto students. What, then, will be society's future capacity and commitment regarding institutions of higher learning? "We are in a period of substantial change," Ikenberry states, "and the community of higher education senses that." But in this fluctuating new world, "there is certainly a role for the small liberal arts college."[16]

A small "focused" college like Grove City College, Ikenberry believes, "can have the best of both worlds—to use technology to provide knowledge." Grove City's "dogged determination to remain distinctive," he adds, is "commendable.... We need more colleges like it."[17]

American higher education will be "fundamentally reshaped in the next five to ten years," says Peg Miller, president of the American Association for Higher Education. The traditional nonprofit school "is being challenged seriously" by proprietary and virtual providers like the online University of Phoenix, whose classroom is in the student's apartment or private home.[18] Another issue is how campuses make decisions: "Faculty want a major say, but are they competent" in the area of campus governance? At the same time, Miller reports, the importance of faculty tenure is being questioned across the country. "All it would take is for one key state [legislature] to break the mold and tenure would be gone."[19]

"We have become too self-congratulatory," Miller says of her profession, likening it to the steel and auto industries of the 1950s and 1960s. She welcomes the University of Phoenix and other developments, commenting that "competition is good for the soul." Some colleges "will live, some will die," which is regrettable, but, says Miller, we are now in "a new era of accountability."[20]

The most serious problems in higher education, according to David Warren, president of the Council of Independent Colleges (CIC), are what he calls the three "T's"—tuition, tenure, and technology. Tuition cannot continue to rise at the rate that it has since 1980. Tenure, Warren predicts, will be gradually phased out, except in the Ivy League schools, and be replaced by contracts. "The faculty," he says, "will have to demonstrate productivity." Technology will transform, perhaps radically, the curriculum. Already, 40 percent of CIC's nine hundred members send or receive courses over the Internet. At the same time, Warren says, colleges will be accepting "students unlike any others we have seen—students with little or no English."[21]

The residential college of the future, Warren maintains, will be competing with many different models including the University of Phoenix, "with its stripped down education," and the corporate universities which now number more than one thousand. "What if," he asks, the schools at Microsoft, IBM, and elsewhere "seek accreditation?"[22]

The image of higher education, according to Malcolm G. Scully, longtime editor at large of *The Chronicle of Higher Education*, is not as good as it once was because of "soaring prices" and "spending scandals" like the one at Stanford University several years ago. As a result, there is growing pressure on schools to be more concerned about the bottom line, "to act more and more like a corporation." That is understandable, says Scully, "but how are the humanities protected in such an environment?"[23] "Tenure is becoming an anachronism," agrees Scully. In public institutions particularly, "tenure will become harder and harder to get."[24]

The veteran *Chronicle* editor believes, however, that "the general press has exaggerated the high cost of higher education." More and more institutions are offering a "discount" so that the private school average is "closer to the Grove City College price than the Harvard price." Of the thirteen or fourteen million college and university students in America, only 250,000 to 300,000 pay "top dollar"—$20,000 to $30,000 a year. But the budgeting is a "mysterious" process, with administrators first determining what is "a reasonable price" and then charging students accordingly rather than the reverse.[25]

For all the problems, Malcolm Scully is optimistic about the future of higher education in America. He sees enormous potential in new technology like the Internet and is encouraged by the spread of "humanistic values" in our society. Stanley Ikenberry also thinks that higher education "is a pretty healthy enterprise." And, says David Warren, "I'm the house optimist." "Despite all the Chicken Little talk," Warren predicts that the CIC's nine hundred schools "will [still] be here in five, ten years."[26]

As to the perennial question of who should pay for higher education, these establishment figures share the conviction that government should play the same major role in the twenty-first century as it did in the late twentieth century. The federal government, says Ikenberry, "is the principal guarantor of student aid," and "there is a national bipartisan consensus that says this has been very sound [public] policy." While federal money is critical, adds Peg Miller, "most base funding comes from the states. You live inside the local political environment." Malcolm Scully believes that decades of government money have created "a sense of an entitlement to higher education among many parents."[27]

There are exceptions. "Grove City College," says David Warren, a former college president, "is a singular example" of an institution that declines to accept any federal funds whatsoever. Hundreds of independent colleges think that "the reach of the Department of Education—with its 7,000 regulations—is inappropriate and invasive." They "look longingly" at Grove City's independence but do not see how they can "imitate it."[28] Of the 3,600 institutions of higher learning in America, it would be difficult, says Warren, to name ten that have had the courage to reject all federal aid.

Is Grove City College, then, sui generis, or possibly a model for other American liberal arts colleges?

Other Voices, Other Views

In the spring of 1999, the author asked twenty prominent American educators who have often criticized the academic establishment to share their views about the role of an American liberal arts college in the twenty-first century and whether they were optimistic or pessimistic about the future of American higher education. They were also invited to comment on the educational path that Grove City College has chosen to follow.

Jacques Barzun, widely accepted for decades as the leading commentator on education in this country, believes that "the lower schools have forgotten what a school is, and that all the errors of the lower schools have finally crept up into higher education." Those in charge of the educational system, says Barzun, "have busied themselves with everything and everybody but students and their needs."[29]

The most serious problems facing higher education today, according to Harvard sociologist David Riesman, are "a general loosening of standards since 1963, even at the top"; "political correctness"; and the failure of the leadership to lead. He remains pessimistic about the future of education because he does not "see a cohort of leaders who are courageous enough to risk their positions in order to uphold a standard."[30]

The purposes of a liberal arts education, says Stanley Rothman, professor of government emeritus at Smith College, are to "enlighten the student about his/her cultural heritage and the cultural heritages of other civilizations"; raise questions about how to deal with the present and the future "and how to change it if necessary"; help the student develop "a moral compass" which enables him/her to develop "into a full human being"; and encourage the development of skills in thinking, writing, and speaking. Unfortunately, Rothman adds, this is not what is taking place in all too many American colleges and universities.

Instead, education is increasingly "dumbed down," the notion of "transcendent moral values" is discounted, decadence is encouraged, and "America's traditional culture and its values are constantly attacked."[31]

The author of several books about American culture, Rothman is pessimistic about the future of higher education because of the general decline of American society. He singles out "a corrupt mass media," "the [continuing] breakdown of marriage and the family," and the substitution of "a cult of personal narcissism" for the liberal ideology of self-restraint and discipline "upon which this country was built."[32]

Ideally, says retired Harvard professor Nathan Glazer, a liberal arts college "should serve to transmit some reasoned summary of our intellectual, cultural, and scientific achievements and heritage." But in reality "it mostly serves as preparation for professional careers." As to the major problems confronting the college and university, Glazer lists preserving the idea and practice of knowledge "for its own sake," dealing with diversity in a moral way, and justifying a core curriculum.

The true liberal arts college, argues John Agresto, former president of the Sante Fe campus of St. John's College, does far more than just serve the individual student—it preserves "the whole legacy of the West that makes the continuance of civilization possible." Such an objective is exceedingly difficult when there is "a total loss of understanding of the meaning of liberal education, including a view that 'diversity' somehow equals excellence." And when there is "an inability to see that the moral virtues need to be as healthy on a campus as the intellectual virtues." Agresto admits to pessimism about the future because he sees "no one and no institution in higher education talking about what an educated culture would/could look like.... All the rhetoric ('cutting edge research,' 'skills,' 'training for the future,' 'inclusion,' 'multiculturalism') is totally on the other side."[33]

"A liberal arts college," says Harvard professor of government Harvey C. Mansfield, "should provide a liberal education, one that frees you from ignorance and prejudice, and that introduces you to things worth learning for their own sake." Working against such a liberal education in the American college and university of today, Mansfield maintains, are "a decline of standards resulting from the belief in self-esteem," the "politicization of academic disciplines," and "meek and incapable leadership." The iconoclastic Mansfield (an authority on Machiavelli) is ambivalent about higher education: optimistic "because I hope for rebellion, perhaps from a new generation of students," and pessimistic because "I do not think the system is self-correcting."[34]

Yet despite their often dark predictions, Mansfield, Agresto, Rothman, and Riesman all concede at least one encouraging sign—the existence of small liberal arts colleges like Grove City. "They serve as exemplars," remarks Mansfield, "of how to educate, and more generally, of how to use freedom wisely." Riesman admires Grove City College for accepting no federal funds whatsoever, "showing that it is possible to survive and even prosper without succumbing to federal regulations." Christian schools like Grove City, says Agresto, have "a higher regard" for liberal education than vaunted colleges like Middlebury and Oberlin. "They take the issues of liberal education—God, man, nature, language, philosophy—often more seriously. They also know the importance of moral development." Endorsing Grove City College's refusal to accept "federal largesse" in order to retain its independence, Rothman adds: "May they flourish."[35] While arguing that Grove City and similar institutions can be "a saving cultural remnant," Steven Balch, president of the influential National

Association of Scholars, argues that they must "become more outgoing in mission than is generally true now."[36]

Regarding the most serious problems facing higher education, Paul Hollander at the University of Massachusetts, Amherst, is concerned about the "influence of left-over 1960s values" in the American academy. George Marsden at the University of Notre Dame laments the application of "technological-scientific ideas" to all knowledge resulting in "absurd fragmentation in scholarship and overspecialization in teaching." Jeffrey D. Wallin, head of the American Academy for Liberal Education, points to "the failure of most faculties to make clear, mandatory curricular demands," and President John Jacobson of Hope College criticizes the "lack of clarity of mission in many institutions."[37]

Along with several other respondents, Candace de Russy, a trustee of the State University of New York, singles out "the prevalence on most campuses of an increasingly extreme and invidious moral relativism." Professor emeritus John M. Ellis at the University of California, Santa Cruz, sees "a humanities faculty poorer in quality, knowledge, and attitudes to[ward] knowledge than at any time in my lifetime." And according to Paul R. Gross at the University of Virginia, a central problem "is the politicization of all academic life."[38]

Looking back over a lifetime of fighting against governmental intrusion into higher education, former president John A. Howard of Rockford College bemoans the "failure to understand that the foremost purpose of education in every society is to train the young in the ideals and responsibilities of living in their own society." The college and university presidents, says Howard, who mobilized the first campaign against federal funding of education back in 1961, used "to lead their institutions." Now, too often, "the president is fund-raiser, mediator, and public relations person." Highly to be praised are Christian colleges like Grove City that are "keeping alive the tradition of graduating responsible citizens, spouses, parents, neighbors and children of God."[39]

The "Ideal" College*

If we were asked to describe the kind of small independent college we would like our children or grandchildren to attend, what would we say? Many of us, I believe, would respond along the following lines:

It should be an *American* college—idealistic and pragmatic, individualistic and communitarian, secular and sacred.

It should teach its students the things necessary for good character, a successful career, responsible citizenship, and a moral life.

It should excel in academic pursuits. Its students—men and women—should be among the brightest and the best with a passion for learning and understanding.

Its curriculum should be balanced between liberal arts and professional studies. It should study the most enduring ideas of the past and consider the most pressing problems of the present.

It should be reasonably priced, with parents and students not required to assume vast debt to pay for tuition, room, board, and books.

It should be apart from the distractions and temptations of the city—an oasis in the countryside where the mind can reflect and the spirit flourish.

It should have teachers who like to teach and are readily available in class or in their offices to talk about the lesson of the day or a trend of the millennium.

It should have department heads and deans who are efficient but not officious. And a president who spends more time on

---

* The following description applies to the small independent college, not a university, which has different requirements, such as a topflight research capability.

campus managing the affairs of the college than on the road raising money.

It should have a board of trustees who are not absentee
landlords but concerned overseers. And alumni who are proud
of their alma mater and willing to support it generously with
their time and treasure.

It should have a well-maintained physical plant, with comfortable housing for every student, modern classrooms and lab
equipment, a first-class library, and an up-to-date information
and technology program.

It should be a temple of the body, as well as of the mind and
the spirit. There should be varsity and intramural teams, exercise
and physical training rooms, a football stadium and outdoor field
track, a basketball gym, a swimming pool, and tennis courts.

It should be beautiful. It should have lofty trees, bright flow-
ers, and a broad open quadrangle, handsome stone and brick
buildings, and a chapel with a graceful spire and stained glass
windows that shimmer in the sun.

It should be steadfast in its commitment to the mission of
the school regardless of any inducements to deviate offered by
government, foundation, corporation, or individual.

Colleges remarkably similar to the above do exist. This work
is the history of one of them.

Not that Grove City College is perfect. Not every Grove
City student is above average—some even flunk a course. Not
every teacher is always brilliant—some have been known to have
a bad lecture-day. Not every trustee comes to every meeting.
Not every alumnus contributes to the endowment campaign.
Sometimes a student steps on the grass, sometimes a meal in
the dining room is less than mouth-watering, sometimes youth-
ful passion gets out of control, and sometimes a beer can or two

wind up in the trash behind a dorm. Grove City College is, after all, a human institution.

Yet it has remained faithful to its mission—to provide an excellent education in a thoroughly Christian environment at an affordable cost. Why? Because above all else, it has been blessed in its leadership. In the beginning there was Isaac Ketler, the college's founding president, who wrote, "The God of the Bible requires that His followers will never rest on their past laurels but will press on to fulfill their high calling to be the best they can be in scholarship, character and piety."

There was J. Howard Pew, the college's most generous benefactor and the head of its board of trustees for forty years, who urged the school "to inculcate in the minds and hearts of the students an abiding faith in God and Country, a love for freedom, a respect for truth, an acceptance of personal responsibility, and a desire to contribute to the betterment of the human race."

And there was Albert A. Hopeman, Jr., trustee president for twenty-six years, who declared that it was up to Grove City to teach "our students what it means to be virtuous," to stress stewardship and personal responsibility, and to expose the students to "the knowledge and wisdom of the ages."[40]

The present leaders of Grove City College have a formidable assignment. Because of the impact of the technological revolution and the demands of the global economy, higher education in America is undergoing a radical transformation. The existence of the independent American college is being called into question. But President John H. Moore, trustee chairman Paul Sticht, and their colleagues have an enormous advantage over other schools—they can look to Ketler, Pew, Hopeman, and the school's other past leaders for guidance and inspiration as they face the myriad challenges of an ever changing world.

Grove City College's success and its independence are not a coincidence, but go hand in hand. They proceed naturally from the school's historic mission founded on the tenets of faith and freedom. They enable Grove City to refuse all federal funds, direct or indirect; keep costs down by running the college as much like a business as possible; integrate Christian principles and truths in the curriculum; seek out the best possible students; and hire the best possible faculty. Looking about at the nation and the world and noting the widespread confusion, self-indulgence, and callousness, the school's president remarked, "We take the less traveled path at Grove City College."[41]

Traveling that different and yet rewarding path has made all the difference in the lives of the many thousands of students, teachers, administrators, trustees, and alumni of Grove City. It prompts them to echo proudly the words of Daniel Webster, who, defending his alma mater Dartmouth against an attempted government takeover 180 years ago, said: "It is, sir, as I have said, a small college, and yet there are those that love it."[42]

Acknowledgements

I am doubly indebted to President John H. Moore and the trustees of Grove City College for asking me to write the 125-year history of their school. First, because they enabled me to become acquainted with a group of extraordinary men—like Grove City's founding president Isaac Ketler and the longtime head of the board of trustees J. Howard Pew—who believed it was possible for a college to provide a quality education in a Christian atmosphere at an affordable price. Many other American colleges started out with the same mission but sooner or later compromised on the quality, the atmosphere, or the price—and sometimes on all three. Grove City College never has.

Second, in the course of my research and writing, I was obliged to study the history of higher education in America over the last century or so. It is a history filled with fascinating and often disturbing contradictions—of ever rising student registration and ever declining standards; of universities that are the envy of the world and yet are filled with students who are little more than a number in a computer; of students who do not know how to learn, teachers who do not want to teach, and administrators whose major concern is neither the performance of the student body nor the commitment of the faculty but how much money they raised last year. One would be tempted to make baleful predictions about the future of the American academy if it were not for the existence and the example of colleges like Grove City. And yet one is compelled to ask—why aren't there more Grove City Colleges?

In my conversations with leaders of the education establishment, I often heard the same explanation: They would praise Grove City for its rejection of government money and regulations, for keeping tuition and other charges low, for raising the academic standards of its students and faculty, for remaining faithful to its mission for well over a century. But then they would always shake their head and add, "It's too bad other colleges can't follow their example, but it's just not possible."

I hope this history of a once obscure school in western Pennsylvania that has become one of the best small colleges in America shows that it *is* possible for other colleges to follow—if trustees, administration, faculty, student body, and alumni agree to break the cycle of government aid and dependence and take the less traveled and more exhilarating path of independence.

Among the many at Grove City College who helped me in the writing of this history, I want to begin with President Moore, who always took time from an always busy schedule to answer questions and provide guidance. Next comes Rhoda Mathias, Dr. Moore's always cheerful executive assistant, who provided the right answers to a thousand of my questions. I also wish to thank Scott Powell, Diane Grundy, Garth Runion, Lee Wishing, John Van Til, and Richard Morledge for their help and counsel. Among the trustees, I am especially grateful to J. Paul Sticht, David Lascell, Richard Larry, Elizabeth Gilger, Richard Jewell, and trustee emeritus Heath Larry for their insights.

Indispensable to my research was David Dayton's earlier history, '*Mid the Pines*, and Charles S. MacKenzie's reminiscences of his twenty years as president of Grove City. Other helpful sources included Hans Sennholz's account of the first eighty years of the college, Fred Kring's sprightly memoir of his days as dean, and Mary Sennholz's biographical sketch of J. Howard Pew.

I was fortunate to have the research assistance of Dan Barnes, Sarah Simmons, and William Connery, as well as that of Andy Hromyak who helped ensure a high response to my higher education questionnaire. As usual, my wife Anne accompanied me on visits to Grove City, plowed through dusty minutes and correspondence at the school library and Crawford Hall, and provided me with invaluable editorial advice.

I wish to thank the Pew Charitable Trusts and the Glenmede Trust for allowing me to research the J. Howard Pew and Sun Oil Company Papers at the Hagley Museum and Library in Wilmington, Delaware, and for giving me access to interviews conducted for their oral history project. Joel Gardner expertly conducted those interviews as well as the interviews for the oral history project of the Grove City College Alumni Association.

I wrote much of this history in my office at the Heritage Foundation in Washington, D.C., and I am grateful to Edwin J. Feulner, Jr., for the foundation's continuing and generous support of my work.

The last chapter of this work considers the future of the American college. Because of schools like Grove City College, I can honestly say I believe there is one, and an encouraging one.

Lee Edwards
Alexandria, Virginia
April 2000

Bibliography

INTERVIEWS

Barbara M. Akin • Edwin P. Arnold • Louise S. Baird • Steven H. Balch • Daniel F. Barnes • Jack R. Behringer • Paul Bonacelli • Dale R. Bowne • Alejandro Chafuen • Jerry Combee • Laura Conner • Michael Coulter • Peg Curry • Anne Harker Dayton • David M. Dayton • Matthew Donnelly • Ross A. Foster • Jon W. Fuller • Lynn Gibson • Elizabeth Gilger • Joseph F. Goncz, Jr. • Diane H. Grundy • Stanley O. Ikenberry • Richard Jewell • Robb M. Jones • Paul Kengor • Alice Ketler • Bruce William Ketler • Hilda Kring • R. Heath Larry • Richard M. Larry • David M. Lascell • Charles S. MacKenzie • Rhoda K. Mathias • Marian McConkey • Paul McNulty • Harvey A. Miller, Jr. • Peg Miller • Ruth Harker Mills • William Mills • Jeffrey C. Mincey • John A. Moore • Sue Moore • Richard A. Morledge • John Moser • Elizabeth Nix • Nancy Paxton • William W. Pendleton, Jr. • Scott K. Powell • Walter Ransom • Garth E. Runion • Hans Sennholz • Mary Sennholz • Robert W. Smith • John A. Sparks • Leo Stevenson • Kim Stetson • J. Paul Sticht • Malcolm G. Scully • Karen L. Swenson • Robert Swezey • James T. Thrasher • William

Anderson • Andrew Toncic • L. John Von Til • Cynthia A. Walters • Thomas Wall • David Warren • Bradford Wilson

BOOKS AND ARTICLES

Anderson, Martin. *Imposters in the Temple: American Intellectuals Are Destroying Our Universities and Cheating Our Students of Their Future* (New York: Simon & Schuster, 1992).

Barnes, Harry E. *The New History and the Social Sciences* (New York: The Century Co., 1925).

Bennett, Ralph Kinney. "Colleges Under the Federal Gun," *Reader's Digest*, May 1976.

Bishop, Morris. *A History of Cornell* (Ithaca, NY: Cornell University Press, 1962).

Bloom, Allan. *The Closing of the American Mind: How Higher Education Has Failed Democracy and Impoverished the Souls of Today's Students* (New York: Simon and Schuster, 1987).

Bloustein, Edward J. *The University and the Counterculture* (New Brunswick, NJ: Rutgers University Press, 1972).

Brann, Eva T. H. *Paradoxes of Education in a Republic* (Chicago: University of Chicago Press, 1979).

Brubacher, John S. and Willis Rudy. *Higher Education in Transition: An American History: 1636:1956* (New York: Harper & Brothers, 1958).

Burrell, Sidney A. "The GI Bill and the Great American Transformation, 1945–1967," *Boston University Graduate Journal* 15 (Spring 1967).

Chambers, Whittaker. *Cold Friday* (New York: Random House, 1964).

Cleaveland, Bradford. "A Letter to Undergraduates." in *The Berkeley Student Revolt: Facts and Interpretations*, Seymour Martin Lipset and Shelden S. Wolin, eds. (New York: Anchor Books, 1965).

Commager, Henry S., ed. *Documents of American History* (New York: Appleton-Century-Crofts, 1962).

Connell, Christopher. "Providing the Leaders and the Decision-Makers," *Change*, July/August 1982.

Dayton, David M. *'Mid the Pines: A History of Grove City College* (Grove City, PA: Grove City College Alumni Association, 1971).

Dobbins, Charles G., ed. *Higher Education and the Federal Government: Papers Presented at the 45th Annual Meeting of the American Council on Education*, October 1962.

D'Souza, Dinesh. *Illiberal Education: The Politics of Race and Sex on Campus* (New York: The Free Press, 1991).

Edwards, Lee. *The Conservative Revolution: The Movement That Remade America* (New York: The Free Press, 1999).

Feuer, Lewis S. *The Conflict of Generations* (New York: Basic Books, 1969).

Giddens, Paul H. *Early Days of Oil: A Pictorial History of the Beginnings of the Industry in Pennsylvania* (Princeton, NJ: Princeton University Press, 1948).

Gladieux, Lawrence E. and Thomas R. Wolanin. *Congress and the Colleges: The National Politics of Higher Education* (Lexington, MA: D. C. Heath & Company, 1976).

Goodman, Paul. *Growing Up Absurd: Problems of Youth in the Organized Society* (New York: Vintage Books, 1962).

Goulden, Joseph. *The Best Years, 1945–1950* (New York: Atheneum, 1976).

Graham, Hugh Davis. "The Storm Over Grove City College: Civil Rights Regulation, Higher Education, and the Reagan Administration," *History of Education Quarterly*, 38, no. 4, Winter 1998.

Hayden, Tom. "Two, Three, Many Columbias," *University Crisis Reader*, 2.

Hamby, Alonzo L. *Beyond the New Deal* (New York: Columbia University Press, 1973).

―――. *The New Deal* (New York: HarperCollins, 1997).

"Harvard in 1898 and 1998," *Harvard Magazine*, November-December 1998.

Hawkins, Hugh. *Pioneer: A History of the Johns Hopkins University, 1874–1889* (Ithaca, NY: Cornell University Press, 1960).

Hirsch, E. D., Jr. *Cultural Literacy: What Every American Needs to Know* (Boston: Houghton Mifflin Company, 1987).

Johnson, Arthur M. *The Challenge of Change: The Sun Oil Company, 1945–1977* (Columbus, OH: Ohio State University Press, 1983).

Johnson, Paul. *A History of the American People* (New York: HarperCollins, 1997).

―――. *Modern Times: The World from the Twenties to the Eighties* (New York: Harper & Row, 1983).

Johnstone, Bruce D. "Higher Education in the United States in the Year 2000," *Prospects*, XXI, 3, (1991).

Kazin, Alfred. *On Native Grounds* (New York: Harvest Books, 1995).

Ketler, Weir C. *An Adventure in Education: 75 Years of Grove City College (1876–1951)* (New York: The Newcomen Society in North America, 1953).

Kerr, Clark. *The Uses of the University* (New York: Harper Torchbook, 1977).

Kimball, Roger. *Tenured Radicals: How Politics Has Corrupted Our Higher Education* (New York: Harper & Row, 1990).

Kirk, Russell. *The Conservative Mind from Burke to Santayana* (Chicago: Henry Regnery Company, 1953).

―――. *The Intemperate Professor and Other Cultural Splenetics* (Peru, IL: Sherwood Sugden & Company, 1965).

———. *The Roots of American Order* (LaSalle, IL: Open Court, 1974).

Kring, Frederick S. *One Day in the Life of Dean Fred: Autobiography or Legend* (New Wilmington, PA: Globe Printing Company, 1988).

Lee, Calvin B. T. *The Campus Scene, 1900–1970* (New York: David McKay Company, 1970).

Lippmann, Walter. "The Permanent New Deal," *Yale Review*, 24 (1935).

Lyons, Eugene. *The Red Decade* (New Rochelle, NY: Arlington House, 1970).

Lucas, Christopher J. *American Higher Education: A History* (New York: St. Martin's Press, 1994).

———. *Crisis in the Academy: Rethinking Higher Education in America* (New York: St. Martin's Press, 1996).

Manchester, William. *The Glory and the Dream: A Narrative History of America 1932–1972*, volume one (Boston: Little, Brown and Company, 1974).

Marsden, George M. *The Outrageous Idea of Christian Scholarship* (New York: Oxford University Press, 1997).

———. *The Soul of the American University: From Protestant Establishment to Established Nonbelief* (New York: Oxford University Press, 1994).

McCandless, Lee C. "History of Grove City College," a master's thesis submitted April 25, 1925, Grove City College.

MacKenzie, Charles S. "Just Say No to Uncle Sam's Money," *Christianity Today*, September 2, 1988.

———. "Reminiscenses of the Hopeman-MacKenzie Era at Grove City College (1971–1991).

McKinney, William W., ed. *The Presbyterian Valley* (Pittsburgh: Davis & Warde, 1958).

Miller, William J. "A Little School Against the Big Bureaucracy," *Reader's Digest*, August 1980.

Morison, Samuel Eliot. *Three Centuries of Harvard 1636–1936* (Cambridge, MA: Harvard University Press, 1946).

———. *The Oxford History of the American People, Vols. 1 & 3*, (New York: New American Library, 1972).

Nielsen, Waldemar A. *The Golden Donors: A New Anatomy of the Great Foundations* (New York: Truman Talley Books, 1985).

Palmer, R. R. and Joel Colton. *A History of the Modern World* (New York: Alfred A. Knopf, 1958).

Patterson, James T. *Grand Expectations: The United States, 1945–1974* (New York: Oxford University Press, 1996).

Perkinson, Henry J. *Two Hundred Years of American Educational Thought* (New York: David McKay Company, 1976).

Pew, J. Howard. "Rip Van Winkle, Wake Up!" *Manufacturers Record*, August 1935.

———. "What the Future Holds for the American System of Free Enterprise," address at the 44th Congress of American Industry, December 6, 1939, published by the National Association of Manufacturers.

———. "Which Road to Take?" Institute of Public Affairs, University of Virginia, July 12, 1935. (Distributed by the American Liberty League, Washington, D.C.)

Phillips, Charles F. "The Private College and Federal Aid," *Association of American Colleges Bulletin*, May 1949.

Pulliam, John D. and James J. Van Patten. *History of Education in America*, 7th ed. (Upper Saddle River, NJ: 1999).

Ramsay, W. M. *An Estimate of the Educational Work of Dr. Isaac Conrad Ketler* (London: Hodder and Stoughton, 1915).

Ravitch, Diane. *The Troubled Crusade: American Education 1945–1980* (New York: Basic Books, 1983).

Reeves, Thomas C. *The Life and Times of Joe McCarthy: A Biography* (New York: Stein and Day, 1982).

Roche, George. *The Fall of the Ivory Tower* (Washington, D.C.: Regnery Publishing, 1994).

Roosevelt, Theodore. *The New Nationalism*, William E. Leuchtenburg, ed. (Englewood Cliffs, NJ: Prentice-Hall, 1961).

Rudolph, Frederick. *The American College and University: A History* (Athens, GA: University of Georgia Press, 1990).

Sennholz, Hans. *The First Eighty Years of Grove City College: The Ketler Era* (Grove City, PA: American Book Distributors, 1993).

Sennholz, Mary. *Faith and Freedom: The Journal of a Great American J. Howard Pew* (Grove City, PA: Grove City College, 1975).

Smith, Page. *America Enters the World: A People's History of the Progressive Era and World War I* (New York: McGraw-Hill Book Company, 1985).

———. *The Rise of Industrial America: A People's History of the Post-Reconstruction Era* (New York: McGraw-Hill, 1984).

Sowell, Thomas. *Inside American Education: The Decline, The Deception, The Dogmas* (New York: The Free Press, 1993).

Spalding, Matthew. "The Trouble with TR," *National Review*, February 23, 1998.

———. "Sun Oil," *Fortune*, February 1941.

Sykes, Charles J. *The Hollow Men: Politics and Corruption in Higher Education* (Washington, D.C.: Regnery Gateway, 1990).

Truman, Harry S. *Memoirs by Harry S. Truman, Volume One, Year of Decisions* (Garden, City, NY: Doubleday & Company, 1955).

———. *An Uncommon Man—J. Howard Pew* (Grove City: Grove City College, 1982).

Van Til, L. John. "The Legacy of J. Howard Pew: A Personal View." Private Papers of L. John Van Til.

Veith, Gene Edward, Jr., and Andrew Kern. *Classical Education: Towards the Revival of American Schooling* (Washington, D.C.: Capital Research Center, 1997).

Wechsler, James. *Revolt on the Campus* (New York: Covici-Friede Publishers, 1935).

Wilson, James Q. *American Government: Institutions and Policies* (Lexington. MA: D. C. Heath and Company, 1980).

Notes

PREFACE

1   David M. Dayton, *'Mid the Pines: A History of Grove City College* (Grove City, PA: Grove City College Alumni Association, 1971), 145.

2   R. Heath Larry, a longtime trustee of Grove City College, so described J. Howard Pew, saying, "Whenever I think of the Prudential rock, I think of him." Reminiscences of R. Heath Larry, interviewed by Joel Gardner, July 1, 1998, Grove City College Oral History Project. I am indebted for the ensuing description to L. John Van Til, a longtime professor at Grove City College, who was a research assistant to Pew during the last four years of his life.

3   Mary Sennholz, *Faith and Freedom: The Journal of a Great American J. Howard Pew* (Grove City, PA: Grove City College, 1975), 171.

4   J. Howard Pew, Remarks on Parents' Day, May 1, 1971, Grove City College.

5   Bill Foster, "J. Howard Pew 1882–1971," *The Collegian*, December 7, 1971.

6   Robert G. Dunlop, foreward to *Faith and Freedom: The Journal of a Great American J. Howard Pew* by Mary Sennholz, ix.

7   Ibid., 171–172.

CHAPTER ONE

1   Samuel Eliot Morison, *The Oxford History of the American People,* vol. 3 (New York: New American Library, 1972), 50.

2   Page Smith, *The Rise of Industrial America: A People's History of the Post-Reconstruction Era* (New York: McGraw-Hill, 1984), 927.

3   Samuel Eliot Morison, *The Oxford History of the American People,* vol. 2 (New York: New American Library, 1972), 113.

4   Ibid., 114.

5   Christopher J. Lucas, *American Higher Education: A History* (New York: St Martin's Press, 1994), 104.

6   John S. Brubacher and Willis Rudy, *Higher Education in Transition: An American History: 1636–1956* (New York: Harper & Brothers, 1958), 9.

7   Besides the aforementioned Harvard, William and Mary, and Yale, the others were the College of Philadelphia, 1740, renamed the University of Pennsylvania; the College of New Jersey, 1746, renamed Princeton College; Kings College, 1754, renamed Columbia University; the College of Rhode Island, 1764, renamed Brown University; Queen's College, 1766, renamed Rutger's College; and Dartmouth College, 1769.

8   Lucas, *American Higher Education*, 112.

9   Frederick Rudolph, *The American College and University: A History* (Athens, Georgia: University of Georgia Press, 1990), 18.

10 Ibid., 113.

11 Henry J. Perkinson, *Two Hundred Years of American Educational Thought* (New York: David McKay Company, 1976), 6, 44.

12 Brubacher and Rudy, *Higher Education in Transition*, 15.

13 Ibid., 117.

14 William W. McKinney, ed., *The Presbyterian Valley*, (Pittsburgh: Davis & Warde, 1958), 359.

15 Rudolph, *The American College and University*, 242.

16 Much of the following narrative is drawn from David M. Dayton's indispensable history of Grove City College, *'Mid the Pines*.

17 Ibid., 18.

18 Ibid., 19.

19 Weir C. Ketler, *An Adventure in Education: 75 Years of Grove City College (1876–1951)* (New York: The Newcomen Society in North America, 1953), 8.

20 Ibid., 9.

21 Ibid., 10–11.

22 Select School at Pine Grove, PA, flyer; Offical Records of Grove City College, Grove City, PA.

23 Herman Rodgers, "Interesting Highlights in the History of Grove City College," *The Collegian*, February 19, 1936.

24 *Grove City College Bulletin 1914–1915* (Grove City, PA: Grove City College, 1914), 15.

25 Hans Sennholz, *The First Eighty Years of Grove City College: The Ketler Era* (Grove City, PA: American Book Distributors, 1993), 22–23.

26 Ibid., 28.

27 *Catalogue of Pine Grove Normal Academy* (Pine Grove, PA: Pine Grove Normal Academy, 1879), 22.

28 *Catalogue of Pine Grove Normal Academy* (Pine Grove, PA: Pine Grove Normal Academy, 1878), 10.

29 Weir Ketler, *An Adventure in Education*, 13.

30 Lee C. McCandless, "History of Grove City College" (Master's thesis, Grove City College, 1925), 21.

31 *Catalogue of Pine Grove Normal Academy* (Pine Grove, PA: Pine Grove Normal Academy, 1880), 28–29.

32. Dayton, *'Mid the Pines*, 31.

33 Ibid., 33.

34 *Catalogue of Grove City College* (Grove City, PA: Grove City College, 1884), 1.

35 R. R. Palmer and Joel Colton, *A History of the Modern World* (New York: Alfred A. Knopf, 1958), 431.

36 Harry E. Barnes, *The New History and the Social Sciences* (New York: The Century Co., 1925), 589.

37 Hugh Hawkins, *Pioneer: A History of the Johns Hopkins University, 1874–1889* (Ithaca, NY: Cornell University Press, 1960), 132, 272–273.

38 Lucas, *American Higher Education*, 147.

39 George M. Marsden, *The Soul of the American University: From Protestant Establishment to Established Nonbelief* (New York: Oxford University Press, 1994), 3.

40 "Harvard in 1898 and 1998," *Harvard Magazine*, November–December 1998, 50.

41 Lucas, *American Higher Education*, 145.

42 Brubacher and Rudy, *Higher Education in Transition*, 159.

43 Morris Bishop, *A History of Cornell* (Ithaca, NY: Cornell University Press, 1962), 234.

44 Lucas, *American Higher Education*, 165; Brubacher and Rudy, *Higher Education in Transition*, 107.

45 Lucas, *American Higher Education*, 166; Rudolph, *The American College and University*, 298.

46 Rudolph, *The American College and University*, 305.

47 Brubacher and Rudy, *Higher Education in Transition*, 111.

48 Rudolph, *The American College and University*, 271.

49 Ibid., 275.

50 Marsden, *The Soul of the American University*, 155.

51 Ibid., 177.

52 Lucas, *American Higher Education*, 168.

53 Bishop, *A History of Cornell*, 38.

54 Lucas, *American Higher Education*, 170.

55 W. M. Ramsay, *An Estimate of the Educational Work of Dr. Isaac Conrad Ketler* (London: Hodder and Stoughton, 1915), 23.

56 Isaac, Ketler. "A Sure Foundation," Baccalaureate Sermon June 17, 1894, *Grove City Collegian*, June 1894, 1–7.

57 Dayton, *'Mid the Pines*, 41.

58 Marsden, *The Soul of the American University*, 40.

59 Ketler, *An Adventure in Education*, 17.

60 Ibid., 15. The statement was authored by James B. McClelland, a longtime friend and colleague of Isaac Ketler.

61 Dayton, *'Mid the Pines*, 43.

62 Ibid., 44.

63 Ketler, *Adventure in Education*, 18.

64 Ibid., 18.

65 Dayton, *'Mid the Pines*, 53.

66 Ibid., 72.

67 Rudolph, *The American College and University*, 406.

68 Ibid., 414–415.

69 Dayton, *'Mid the Pines*, 48.

70 "Historical Sketch of Grove City: Advantages for Home Seekers. Business Outlook," Grove City, 11.

71 Dayton, *'Mid the Pines*, 49.

72 "Grove City College: Character and Aims," 50, Grove City College.

73 Marian McConkey, interview with the author, October 2, 1998.

74 Dayton, *'Mid the Pines*, 79.

75 Rudolph, *The American College and University*, 146.

76 Ibid., 147.

77 Dave Huffman, "College Boys Expelled," *The Collegian*, February 29, 1980.

78 Dayton, *'Mid the Pines*, 126.

79 Rudolph, *The American College and University*, 373–374.

80 Dayton, *'Mid the Pines*, 50.

Chapter Two

1   Samuel Eliot Morison, *The Oxford History of the American People*, vol. 3 (New York: New American Library, 1972), 132.

2   Theodore Roosevelt, *The New Nationalism*, William E. Leuchtenburg, ed. (Englewood Cliffs, NJ: Prentice-Hall, 1961), 36; Samuel Eliot Morison, *Oxford History of the American People*, 137.

3   Page Smith, *America Enters the World: A People's History of the Progressive Era and World War I*, vol. 7 (New York: McGraw-Hill Book Company, 1985), 99.

4   Ibid., 5.

5   Matthew Spalding, "The Trouble with TR," *National Review*, February 23, 1998, 32.

6   Ibid.

7   Henry J. Perkinson, *Two Hundred Years of American Educational Thought* (New York: David McKay Company, 1976), 208; Page Smith, *America Enters the World*, 849–850.

8   Gene Edward Veith, Jr., and Andrew Kern, *Classical Education: Towards the Revival of American Schooling* (Washington, D.C.: Capital Research Center, 1997), 52.

9   George Marsden, *The Soul of the American University* (New York: Oxford University Press, 1994), 267.

10 Dayton, 'Mid *the Pines*, 63.

11 Ibid., 76–77.

12 Hans Sennholz, *The First Eighty Years of Grove City College* (Grove City: American Book Distributors, 1993), 17.

13 Ibid., 15.

14 Ibid., 17.

15 Dayton, 'Mid *the Pines*, 71.

16 Ibid., 79.

17 "How Dr. I. C. Ketler Treated Chicken-Hearted Students," *The Collegian*, May 6, 1936.

18 Dayton, 'Mid *the Pines*, p. 81.

19 Marian McConkey, interview with the author, October 2, 1998.

20 Arthur M. Johnson, *The Challenge of Change: The Sun Oil Company, 1945–1977* (Columbus: Ohio State University Press, 1983), xiii.

21 Much of the following is taken from "The Sun Company: A Brief History," The Sun Company Collection, Hagley Museum, Wilmington, Delaware.

22 Dayton, 'Mid *the Pines*, 54–55.

23 Paul H. Giddens, *Early Days of Oil: A Pictorial History of the Beginnings of the Industry in Pennsylvania* (Princeton, NJ: Princeton University Press, 1948), 92.

24 Dayton, 'Mid *the Pines*, 83.

25 McKinney, William W., ed. *The Presbyterian Valley* (Pittsburgh: Davis & Warde, 1958), 358.

26 Babcock, Frederick R. "Dedicatory Address," *The Collegian*, February 1913, 3–5.

27 Ketler, *An Adventure in Education* (New York: The Newcomen Society in North America, 1953), 22.

28 Ibid., 22.

29 Dayton, 'Mid *the Pines*, 86–87.

30 Sennholz, *The First Eighty Years of Grove City College*, 22.

31 W. M. Ramsay, *An Estimate of the Educational Work of Dr. Isaac Conrad Ketler* (London: Hodder and Stoughton, 1915), 31.

32 Alexander Ormond, "Extracts from the Inaugural Address," *The Collegian*, December 13, 1913, 4.

33 "Our New President," Robert Scott Calder, *The Collegian*, October 1913, 4.

34 "President Wilson's Letter," *The Collegian*, December 1913, 7.

35 Alexander Ormond, "Inaugural Address," *The Collegian,* December 1913, 5.

36 Sennholz, *The First Eighty Years of Grove City College*, 34.

37 Marian McConkey, interview with the author, October 2, 1998.

38 Dayton, 'Mid *the Pines*, 99.

39 Bruce Ketler, interview with the author, November 19, 1998.

40 *Grove City College Friends and Alumni Monthly*, December 1913, 7.

41 *Grove City College Friends and Alumni Monthly*, September 1914, 3–4.

42 Minutes of the Board of Trustees, Grove City College, November 16, 1914.

43 Dayton, 'Mid *the Pines*, 97.

44 Christopher J. Lucas, *American Higher Education: A History* (New York: St. Martin's Press, 1994), 188.

45 "President Ketler's Speech," *The Collegian*, March 4, 1916.

46 The student and faculty figures used by David Dayton and Hans Sennholz do not agree with each other nor with the statistics provided by Grove City College. The confusion arises because the college did not provide a detailed breakdown of student enrollment— so many in music, so many in teaching, so many in preparatory classes. My figures are a consensus of all three sources.

47 Frederick Rudolph, *The American College and University: A History* (Athens, GA: University of Georgia Press, 1990), 442.

48 Samuel Eliot Morison, *Three Centuries of Harvard 1636–1936* (Cambridge, MA: Harvard University Press, 1946), 390.

49 Rudolph, *The American College and University*, 451–452.

50 Ibid., 452.

51 Ibid., 455.

52 Samuel Eliot Morison, *Three Centuries of Harvard*, 444.

53 "An Appeal," *The Collegian*, January 29, 1916.

54 Minutes of the Grove City College Board of Trustees, January 16, 1917; Dayton, 'Mid *the Pines*, 104; "Military Training," *The Collegian*, April 21, 1917.

55 Dayton, 'Mid *the Pines*, 103.

56 "Editorial Column," *The Collegian*, May 5, 1917.

57 Weir Ketler, "The College and the War," President's Report to the Trustees, June 1917.

58 John S. Brubacher and Willis Rudy, *Higher Education in Transition* (New York: Harper & Brothers, 1958), 222.

59 Dayton, 'Mid *the Pines*, 107.

60 Morison, *The Oxford History of the American People*, vol. 3, 205.

61 "Students Walk Out," *The Collegian*, October 30, 1917; "Men Are Reinstated," *The Collegian*, November 6, 1917.

62 *Catalogue of Grove City College 1918–1919*, 91.

63 Ibid., 105.

64 President Ketler's Report to the Board of Trustees, January 20, 1920.

65 Ibid.

66 Ibid.

67 Christopher J. Lucas, *American Higher Education*, 193.

Chapter Three

1   Morison, *The Oxford History of the American People*, vol. 3, 220.

2   Ibid., 227.

3   Ibid., 239.

4   Ibid., 258.

5   Ibid., 245.

6   Alfred Kazin, *On Native Grounds* (New York: Harvest Books, 1995), 150.

7   Whittaker Chambers, *Cold Friday* (New York: Random House, 1964), 93, 99.

8   Eugene Lyons, *The Red Decade* (New Rochelle, NY: Arlington House, 1970), 107.

9   Rudolph, *The American College and University*, 470.

10 Ibid., 472.

11 Dayton, 'Mid *the Pines*, 120. Many of the figures in this section are taken from Dayton's scrupulously researched history. For the Ketler quote, see President Ketler's Report to the Board of Trustees, June 15, 1922.

12 Minutes of Grove City College Faculty, July 27, 1920.

13 Russell Kirk, *The Conservative Mind from Burke to Santayana* (Chicago: Henry Regnery Company, 1953), 8; President Ketler's report to the board of trustees, January 16, 1923.

14 President's Report to the Board, January 16, 1923.

15 Ibid.

16 Dayton, 'Mid *the Pines*, 125.

17 Ibid., 129.

18 *Ouija*, 1923, 131.

19 Dayton, 'Mid *the Pines*, 124.

20 "Forty-fourth Year Opens with Record Enrollment—Marks Beginning New Era," *The Collegian*, October 8, 1923.

21 *Ouija*, 1922, 108.

22 R. Heath Larry, interview by Joel Gardner, July 13, 1999, Grove College Oral History Project.

23 Rudolph, *The American College and University*, 438.

24 "Twenty-five Things That a College Course Should Give," *The Collegian*, November 19, 1923.

25 President Ketler to the Board of Trustees, January 10, 1928.

26 Ibid.

27 President Weir Ketler's annual report to the board of trustees, June 1929.

28 Morison, *The Oxford History of American People*, 290. For a crisp summary of the 1929 Crash and the Great Depression, 286–293.

29 J. Howard Pew to William L. Clause, Papers of J. Howard Pew, Hagley Museum & Library, Wilmington, Delaware.

30 Dayton, 'Mid *the Pines*, 137.

31 "Dedication Exercises Harbison Chapel, The Hall of Science, Frances St. Leger Babcock Memorial Organ," Grove City College, October 8, 1931, 35.

32 Ibid., 16.

33 *Grove City College Bulletin*, September 1932, 3–4.

34 "Dedication Exercises," 17.

35 William Manchester, *The Glory and the Dream: A Narrative History of America 1932–1972*, vol. 1 (Boston: Little, Brown and Company, 1974), 95.

36 Walter Lippmann, "The Permanent New Deal," *Yale Review* 24 (1935), 649–67.

37 Quoted in George F. Will, *The Woven Figure: Conservatism and America's Fabric* (New York: Scribner, 1997), 108.

38 Manchester, *The Glory and the Dream*, vol. 1, 105.

39 Ibid.

40 Henry S. Commager, ed., *Documents of American History*, vol. 2 (New York: Appleton-Century-Crofts, 1962), 280, 283.

41 Alonzo L. Hamby, *The New Deal* (New York: Weybright and Talley, 1969), 8.

42 Paul Johnson, *A History of the American People* (New York: HarperCollins, 1997), 764.

43 Brubacher and Rudy, *Higher Education in Transition*, 227.

44 Manchester, *The Glory and the Dream*, vol. 2, 154.

45 Rudolph, *The American College and University*, 480.

46 President's Report to the Board of Trustees, December 14, 1936.

47 Adele M. Armstrong to J. Howard Pew, January 25, 1940; J. Howard Pew to Weir C. Ketler, January 29, 1940, J. Howard Pew Papers, Hagley Museum & Library, Wilmington, Delaware.

48 Weir Ketler to J. Howard Pew, January 18, 1939, J. Howard Pew Papers, the Hagley Museum and Library, Wilmington, Deleware.

49 J. Howard Pew to Weir C. Ketler, February 6, 1939, J. Howard Pew Papers, Hagley Museum & Library, Wilmington, Delaware.

50 Allan MacLachlan Frew to Weir C. Ketler, May 16, 1939; J. Howard Pew to Allan MacLachlan Frew, May 17, 1939, J. Howard Pew Papers, Hagley Museum & Library, Wilmington, Delaware.

51 J. Howard Pew to James E. Marshall, June 17, 1940, J. Howard Pew Papers, Hagley Museum & Library, Wilmington, Delaware.

52 Weir C. Ketler to J. Howard Pew, September 6, 1939; J. Howard Pew to Weir C. Ketler, September 8, 1939, J. Howard Pew Papers, Hagley Museum & Library, Wilmington, Delaware.

53 Dayton, 'Mid *the Pines*, 151.

54 Ibid.

55 "Students Take Chapel Roll of Faculty," *The Collegian*, October 31, 1934.

56 J. Howard Pew to Weir C. Ketler, May 26, 1944, J. Howard Pew Papers, Hagley Museum
& Library, Wilmington, Delaware.

57 Minutes of the Board of Trustees, June 4, 1934.

58 *Grove City Catalogue for 1931–32*, 104.

59 "The Cross and Crown," *The Collegian*, November 30, 1938.

60 Calvin B. T. Lee, *The Campus Scene, 1900–1970* (New York: David McKay Company,
1970), 60.

61 James Wechsler, *Revolt on the Campus* (New York: Covici-Friede Publishers, 1935),
432, 452.

62 "A Verbal War to End War," *The Collegian*, November 11, 1936.

63 "Scholarship Offered," *The Collegian*, January 26, 1936.

64 "May Pageant Program," *The Collegian*, May 14, 1938.

65 Dayton, '*Mid the Pines*, 157–158.

66 *Grove City College Catalogue for 1939–40*, 41.

67 Alice Ketler, interview by author, May 13, 1999.

68 Tuxedo advertisement in *The Collegian*, December 11, 1935.

69 *Campus and Dormitory Customs and Standards Observed by Women Students of Grove
City College*, circa 1935.

70 Alice Ketler interview at Grove City, May 13, 1999.

71 "Maine 'Takes a Walk,'" *The Collegian*, November 4, 1936.

72 Dayton, '*Mid the Pines*, 163, 165.

73 *Grove City Reporter-Herald*, June 12, 1931.

74 "Ahead," *The Collegian*, March 22, 1939.

75 *Grove City Reporter-Herald*, June 30, 1939.

Chapter Four

1   Morison, *Oxford History of the American People*, vol. 3, 368.

2   Ibid., 366–367.

3   Ibid., 368.

4   Manchester, *The Glory and the Dream*, vol. 1, 302–303.

5   Ibid.

6   Minutes of Grove City College Faculty, September 24, 1940.

7   Ibid.

8   "...And All Shall Make a Sacrifice," *The Collegian*, April 1, 1941.

9   "Dr. Ketler's Chapel Message," *The Collegian*, December 10, 1941; Minutes of the
Board of Trustees, Grove City College, December 14, 1941.

10 President's Report to the Board of Trustees, June 9, 1942.

11 Manchester, *The Glory and the Dream*, 343.

12 "Torpedoed in Mid-Atlantic..." *The Collegian*, February 17, 1943.

13 Dayton, '*Mid the Pines*, 171.

14 President's Report to the Board of Trustees, June 9, 1942.

15 *QST*, "The Navy Trains Radio Technicians," November 1942, 17.

16 Sennholz, *The First Eighty Years of Grove City College*, 50.

17 Brubacher and Rudy, *Higher Education in Transition*, 223.

18 Robert A. Taft, Grove City College Commencement Address, May 22, 1943, Grove City College Archives.

19 Ibid.

20 Ibid.

21 Ibid.

22 Minutes of the Faculty of Grove City College, October 5, 1943.

23 "Alumni Write Vivid Letters of Service Life Here and Abroad," *The Collegian*, February 24, 1943.

24 Manchester, *The Glory and the Dream*, 344.

25 President's Report to the Grove City College Board of Trustees, December 11, 1944.

26 J. Howard Pew to Weir C. Ketler, June 23, 1944, J. Howard Pew Papers, Hagley Museum & Library, Wilmington, Delaware.

27 Morison, *The Oxford History of the American People*, vol. 3, 408.

28 Harry S. Truman, *Memoirs by Harry S. Truman*, vol. 1, *Year of Decisions* (Garden City, NY: Doubleday & Company, 1955), 419.

29 Editorial, *The Collegian*, May 5, 1945.

30 "Letters to the Editor," *The Collegian*, March 29, 1945.

31 Sidney A. Burrell, "The G.I. Bill and the Great American Transformation, 1945–1967," *Boston University Graduate Journal* 15 (Spring 1967), 3.

32 Brubacher and Rudy, *Higher Education in Transition*, 228.

33 Ibid., 229.

34 George Roche, *The Fall of the Ivory Tower* (Washington, D.C.: Regnery Publishing, 1994), 56.

35 Dayton, '*Mid the Pines*, 180.

36 Sennholz, *The First Eighty Years of Grove City College*, 52.

37 J. Howard Pew to Weir C. Ketler, February 4, 1946, J. Howard Pew Papers, Hagley Museum & Library, Wilmington, Delaware.

38 President's Report to the Board of Trustees, May 18, 1945.

39 Ruth Harker Mills, "Alva John Calderwood," on the dedication of Calderwood Hall, October 26, 1958.

40 Ibid.

41 Remarks by J. Howard Pew at a Grove City College alumni luncheon, June 5, 1948, Grove City College Archives.

42 President's Report to the Board of Trustees, December 14, 1949.

43 Lucas, *American Higher Education*, 232.

44 Brubacher and Rudy, *Higher Education in Transition*, 230.

45 Diane Ravitch, *The Troubled Crusade: American Education 1945–1980* (New York, Basic Books, 1983), 15–17.

46 Ibid., 17.

47 Brubacher and Rudy, *Higher Education in Transition*, 232.

48 Ibid.

49 Lawrence E. Gladieux and Thomas R. Wolanin, *Congress and the Colleges: The National Politics of Higher Education* (Lexington, MA: D. C. Heath & Company, 1976), 456.

50 Joseph Goulden, *The Best Years, 1945–1950* (New York: Atheneum, 1976), 257.

51 Alonzo Hamby, *Beyond the New Deal* (New York: Columbia University Press, 1973), 245.

52 For the March 1946 Gallup Poll, see page 13 of the author's *The Conservative Revolution: The Movement That Remade America* (New York: The Free Press, 1999). For the college presidents' position regarding communists on the faculty, see page 42 of the same work.

53 Roche, *The Fall of the Ivory Tower*, 32.

54 Lucas, *American Higher Education*, 235.

55 Charles F. Phillips, "The Private College and Federal Aid," *Association of American Colleges Bulletin*, May 1949, 283.

56 William F. Buckley, Jr., "Hillsdale Rejects Federal Cash—and Control," *Detroit Free Press*, May 24, 1991.

57 Nathan M. Pusey, "The Carnegie Study of the Federal Government and Higher Education," in *Higher Education and the Federal Government: Papers Presented at the 45th Annual Meeting of the American Council on Education*, ed. Charles G. Dobbins (October 1962), 19.

58 Christopher Lucas, *American Higher Education*, 236.

59 Ibid., 237.

60 Minutes of the Board of Trustees, June 3, 1949.

61 President's Report to the Board of Trustees, December 1, 1952.

62 Thomas C. Reeves, *The Life and Times of Joe McCarthy: A Biography* (New York: Stein and Day, 1982), 439.

63 Minutes of the Board of Trustees, June 4, 1948.

64 Ravitch, *The Troubled Crusade*, 93.

65 Ibid., 97.

66 Ibid., 111.

67 Richard G. Jewell, interview by Joel R. Gardner, July 14, 1999, Grove City College Oral History Project.

68 Minutes of the Board of Trustees, January 27, 1956.

69 J. Howard Pew, remarks upon the retirement of Weir C. Ketler, June 9, 1956, Grove City College Archives.

70 *The Collegian*, May 19, 1956.

CHAPTER FIVE

1   Lewis S. Feuer, *The Conflict of Generations* (New York: Basic Books, 1969), 438.

2   Much of the following is drawn from the chapter, "The Polarized Sixties: An Overview," in James T. Patterson, *Grand Expectations: The United States, 1945–1974* (New York: Oxford University Press, 1996), 442–457.

3   Ibid., 452.

4   Johnson, *Modern Times* 641.

5   Diane Divoky, "A Loss of Nerve," *Wilson Review*, Autumn 1979.

6   Clark Kerr, *The Uses of the University* (New York: Harper Torchbook, 1977), 101.

7   Ravitch, *The Troubled Crusade*, 311.

8   Kerr, *The Uses of the University*, 103–104.

9   Christopher J. Lucas, *Crisis in the Academy: Rethinking Higher Education in America* (New York: St. Martin's Press, 1996), 18.

10 Russell Kirk, *The Intemperate Professor and Other Cultural Splenetics* (Peru, IL: Sherwood Sugden & Company, 1965), 57.

11 John A. Howard, *Widening Horizons*, Rockford College, Illinois, April 1963, 3.

12 Ruth Harker Mills, interview by author, November 19, 1998; Leo Stevenson, interview by author, October 2, 1998.

13 Anne Harker Dayton, interview by Joel R. Gardner, May 4, 1999, Grove City College Oral History Project.

14 President's Report to the Board of Trustees, November 8, 1956.

15 "An Evaluation Report, Submitted by the Commission on Higher Institutions, Middle States Association of Colleges and Secondary Schools," February 1957.

16 "Confidential Report for Grove City College of an Evaluation conducted by the Middle States Association of Colleges and Secondary Schools," February 21–24, 1960.

17 President's Report to the Board of Trustees, June 5, 1959.

18 Sara K. Naegele, interviewed by Joel R. Gardner, September 16, 1998, Grove City College Oral History Project.

19 Dayton, 'Mid *the Pines*, 210; Richard Jewell, interview by author, March 7, 2000.

20 President's Report to the Board of Trustees, June 8, 1962.

21 Dedication Program of Calderwood Hall, October 26, 1958.

22 Hans Sennholz, "Memoir" (Grove City, PA), 37.

23 Frederick S. Kring, *One Day in the Life of Dean Fred: Autobiography or Legend* (New Wilmington, PA: Globe Printing Company, 1988), 73–74.

24 I have based the following narrative on public and private sources, including "Academic Freedom and Tenure: Grove City College," *AAUP Bulletin*, vol. 49 no. 1 1962, and notes of meetings between President Harker, Dean Swezey and Professor Gara.

25 J. Stanley Harker to Mrs. Ronald P. Rose, April 9, 1962, President's Files, Grove City College; "Academic Freedom and Tenure: Grove City College," *AAUP Bulletin*, vol. 49 no. 1 1962, 22.

26 Harker to Rose, April 9, 1962.

27 Ibid.

28 Sennholz, "Memoir," 39.

29 AAUP, "Academic Freedom and Tenure: Grove City College," 23.

30 Ibid.

31 Sennholz, "Memoir," 40.

32 AAUP, "Academic Freedom and Tenure: Grove City College," 15.

33 President's Report to the Board of Trustees, June 8, 1962.

34 Ibid.

35 Ibid.

36 Jordan E. Kurland to John H. Moore, November 6, 1998, Grove City College Archives.

37 Ravitch, *The Troubled Crusade*, 186–187.

38 Paul Goodman, *Growing Up Absurd: Problems of Youth in the Organized Society* (New York: Vintage Books, 1962), 14–15.

39 Diane Ravitch, *The Troubled Crusade*, 191.

40 Bradford Cleaveland, "A Letter to Undergraduates," in *The Berkeley Student Revolt: Facts and Interpretations*, eds. Seymour Martin Lipset and Sheldon S. Wolin (New York: Anchor Books, 1965), 72, 80.

41 Ravitch, *The Troubled Crusade*, 192.

42 Ibid., 196.

43 Ibid., 203.

44 Tom Hayden, "Two, Three, Many Columbias," *University Crisis Reader*, 2, 163–164.

45 Ravitch, *The Troubled Crusade*, 205.

46 Ibid., 207, 209.

47 Patterson, *Grand Expectations*, 455.

48 Edward J. Bloustein, *The University and the Counterculture* (New Brunswick, NJ: Rutgers University Press, 1972), 95.

49 Patterson, *Grand Expectations*, 456.

50 John Sparks and Dick Jewell, "Neff, Mendenhall, and Kauffmann 'Teach-in' on Vietnam Question," *The Collegian*, November 19, 1965.

51 Dayton, *'Mid the Pines*, 236.

52 Kring, *One Day in the Life of Dean Fred*, 148.

53 From a speech by John Howard Pew at Grove City College in 1967, Grove City College Archives.

54 R. Heath Larry, interviewed by Joel R. Gardner, January 13, 1999, Grove City College Oral History Project; Richard G. Jewell, interview by Joel R. Gardner, July 14, 1999, Grove City Oral History Project.

55 President's Report to the Board of Trustees, June 7, 1968; Anne Harker Dayton, interview by Joel R. Gardner, August 25, 1999, Grove City College Oral History Project.

56 Anne Harker Dayton, interview by Joel R. Gardner, May 4, 1999; Sara K. Naegele, interview by Joel R. Gardner, September 16, 1998, Grove City College Oral History Project.

57 "Baird reviews abortion, incites GCC involvement," *The Collegian*, May 7, 1971.

58 "Report to the Faculty, Administration, Trustees of Grove City College by An Evaluation Team representing the Commission on Higher Education of the Middle States Association," 32; Kring, *One Day in the Life of Dean Fred*, 70.

59 President's Report to the Board of Trustees, June 4, 1971.

60 Charles S. MacKenzie, "Reminiscenses of the Hopeman-MacKenzie Era at Grove City College (1971–1991)," Grove City College files.

61 Ross A. Foster, interview by author, September 25, 1998.

62 "Reminiscenses," 3.

63 Ibid., 1.

64 Ibid., 2.

65 Ibid.

66 Ibid.

67 Ibid., 4.

68 Ibid.

69 Ibid., 38.

70 Bill Foster, "Pew Influences all aspects of GCC," *The Collegian*, December 7, 1971.

Chapter Six

1 "Sun Oil," *Fortune*, February 1941, 112.

2 J. Howard Pew, talk at the first annual dinner of the Marcus Hook Refinery Sapphire Club, November 21, 1946.

3 Ibid.

4 "J. Howard Pew—Sidebar," Sun Oil Co. Papers, Hagley Museum & Library, Wilmington, Delaware.

5 Sennholz, *Faith and Freedom*, 22.

6 Ibid., 22.

7 J. Howard Pew, remarks to Grove City College alumni, May 1949, in Pittsburgh, *Grove City College Magazine*, Fall/Winter 1996, 8.

8 Sennholz, *Faith and Freedom*, 6.

9 Ibid.

10 Isaac Ketler, "Joseph Newton Pew In Memoriam," remarks delivered at a memorial service at the Pew homestead, Mercer, Pennsylvania, October 14, 1912.

11 Ibid.

12 Ibid.

13 Sennholz, *Faith and Freedom*, 14.

14 Ibid., 15.

15 "The Sun Company: A Brief History," Sun Company Collection, Hagley Museum & Library, Wilmington, Delaware.

16 Sennholz, *Faith and Freedom*, 11.

17 Ibid., 15.

18 Ibid.

19 Ibid., 17.

20 Ibid.

21 Ibid., 19.

22 Ibid.

23 Hans Sennholz, "J. Howard Pew—An Entrepreneur par Excellence," in *An Uncommon Man—J. Howard Pew* (Grove City: Grove City College, 1982), 22.

24 J. Howard Pew, "Preserving the Free Enterprise System" (delivered at the 45th annual Congress of American Industry, December 12, 1940), *Vital Speeches of the Day*, February 1, 1941, 244–247.

25 "Sun Oil," *Fortune*, February 1941, 51.

26 Ibid., 52.

27 Sennholz, "J. Howard Pew," 23.

28 "Sun Oil," *Fortune*, 112.

29 J. Howard Pew, "Governmental Planning and Control as Applied to Business and Industry: A Common Sense Plea by an American Citizen" (an address before Princeton University in the Cyrus Fogg Brackett Lectureship in Applied Engineering and Technology, April 12, 1938).

30 Ibid.

31 Sennholz, "J. Howard Pew," 25.

32 Ibid., 25–26.

33 Mary Sennholz, *Faith and Freedom*, 27.

34 Ibid., 32.

35 J. Howard Pew, talk to Grove City College Alumni, June 1932, Grove City College Archives.

36 J. Howard Pew, "Which Road to Take?" Institute of Public Affairs, University of Virginia, July 12, 1935, an address distributed by the American Liberty League, Washington, D.C.

37 J. Howard Pew, "Which Road To Take?" Institute of Public Affairs, University of Virginia, July 12, 1935.

38 J. Howard Pew, "Rip Van Winkle, Wake Up!" *Manufacturers Record*, August 1935, 18–19.

39 J. Howard Pew, "The Fallacy of Economic Planning by Government" (remarks before the Princeton Theological Seminary, January 24, 1939).

40 Ibid.

41 J. Howard Pew, "What the Future Holds for the American System of Free Enterprise" (an address at the 44th Congress of American Industry, December 6, 1939), National Association of Manufacturers.

42 Ibid.

43 Ibid.

44 John Moser, interview by author, March 4, 1998.

45 J. Howard Pew, remarks on the dedication of the Mary Anderson Pew Dormitory, June 1937, Grove City College Archives; R. Heath Larry, "Reminiscences of R. Heath Larry," interview by Joel Gardner, July 1, 1998, Grove City College Oral History Project.

46 J. Howard Pew, talk to Grove City College alumni, June 1932, Grove City College Archives.

47 J. Howard Pew, remarks at the dedication of the Mary Anderson Pew Dormitory, Grove City College, June 1937, Grove City College Archives.

48 Ibid.

49 J. Howard Pew to Weir Ketler, July 2, 1940, J. Howard Pew Papers, Hagley Museum & Library, Wilmington, Delaware.

50 Reminiscences of R. Heath Larry, July 1, 1998, interview by Joel Gardner, Grove City College Oral History Project.

51 J. Howard Pew, remarks at Grove City College alumni luncheon, June 7, 1947, Hagley Library & Museum, Wilmington, Delaware.

52 J. Howard Pew to Weir Ketler, January 18, 1939, and September 8, 1939, J. Howard Pew Papers, Hagley Library & Museum, Wilmington, Delaware.

53 Robert Dunlop, interview by Joel Gardner, May 8, 1989, Oral History Project of the Pew Charitable Trusts.

54 Morison, The Oxford History of the American People, vol. 3, 381.

55 J. Howard Pew, "Initiative Will Win the War," an address before the War Congress of American Industry, December 2, 1942, Grove City College Archives.

56 Ibid.

57 Ibid.

58 Manchester, The Glory and the Dream, 362.

59 J. Howard Pew, remarks at Grove City College Alumni luncheon, June 15, 1946, GCC Archives.

60 J. Howard Pew, remarks at Grove City College Alumni luncheon, June 7, 1947, GCC Archives.

61 Robert McClements, Jr., "J. Howard Pew—An Uncommon Man," An Uncommon Man—J. Howard Pew (Grove City: Grove City College, 1982), 14.

62 Waldemar A. Nielsen, *The Golden Donors: A New Anatomy of the Great Foundations* (New York: Truman Talley Books, 1985), 173–174.

63 J. Howard Pew to Weir Ketler, July 15, 1948, J. Howard Pew Papers, Hagley Museum & Library, Wilmington, Delaware.

64 J. Howard Pew, address at the commencement exercises of Grove City College, June 4, 1955.

65 J. Howard Pew to Weir C. Ketler, July 3, 1956, J. Howard Pew Papers, Hagley Museum & Library, Wilmington, Delaware.

66 Sennholz, "J. Howard Pew," 28.

67 Mary Sennholz, *Faith and Freedom*, 149, 152.

68 Charles S. MacKenzie, "J. Howard Pew—His Contribution to the Spiritual Life of the Nation," in *An Uncommon Man—J. Howard Pew* (Grove City: Grove City College, 1982), 47. Also see the article, "Clergy Outvoted Us, 10 to 1," *U.S. News & World Report*, February 3, 1956, 47–48, based on J. Howard Pew's letter of December 15, 1955, that prefaced the final report of the National Lay Committee.

69 Mary Sennholz, *Faith and Freedom*, 33–34.

70 Ibid., 34.

71 J. Howard Pew to J. Stanley Parker, April 29, 1959, J. Howard Pew Papers, Hagley Museum and Library, Wilmington, Delaware.

72 Charles MacKenzie, "J. Howard Pew," 48.

73 Excerpted from remarks by J. Howard Pew before the faculty of Grove City College, June 6, 1970, J. Howard Pew Papers, Hagley Library & Museum, Wilmington, Delaware.

74 MacKenzie, "J. Howard Pew," 49.

75 Larry, interview by Joel Gardner, 77, July 2, 1998, Grove City College Oral History Project.

76 L. John Van Til, "The Legacy of J. Howard Pew: A Personal View," Private Papers of L. John Van Til.

77 MacKenzie, "J. Howard Pew," 50.

78 Mary Sennholz, *Faith and Freedom*, 171–172.

79 Ibid., 29.

80 Van Til, "The Legacy of J. Howard Pew."

81 Ibid.

82 MacKenzie, "J. Howard Pew," 45.

Chapter Seven

1 MacKenzie, "Reminiscences."

2 Ralph Kinney Bennett, "Colleges Under the Federal Gun," *Reader's Digest*, May 1976, 126.

3 William F. May, "Boards, Trustees and University Governance" (delivered at the College of Education, University of Rochester, September 23, 1978), *Vital Speeches of the Day*, October 15, 1978.

4 Roche, *The Fall of the Ivory Tower*, 112.

5 William J. Miller, "A Little School Against the Big Bureaucracy," *Reader's Digest*, August 1980, 3.

6 Bennett, "Colleges Under the Federal Gun," 129; Gerald L. Paley to Albert Hopeman, November 8, 1977, David Lascell Private Papers, Rochester, N.Y.

7 "Will Government Secularize Christian Colleges?" Charles S. MacKenzie, April 1978, Grove City College Archives.

8 In the Supreme Court of the United States, October Term, 1982, Petition for a Writ of Certiorari to the United States Court of Appeals for the Third Circuit, *Grove City College v. T.H. Bell*, November 9, 1982, 5.

9 Charles S. MacKenzie, notes on Grove City College's opposition to the HEW compliance form, circa 1980, Grove City College Archives.

10 "*Grove City* v. *HEW*: It's a matter of decree," *Jamestown* [New York] *Post-Journal*, July 7, 1978.

11 Ibid.

12 Hugh Davis Graham, "The Storm Over Grove City College: Civil Rights Regulation, Higher Education, and the Reagan Administration," *History of Education Quarterly* 38, no. 4 (Winter 1998), 411.

13 Ibid., 412.

14 Ibid., 413.

15 Bennett, "Colleges Under the Federal Gun," 127.

16 Ibid., 128.

17 Ibid.

18 Ibid., 130.

19 Albert A. Hopeman, Jr., to David Lascell, September 4, 1979, David Lascell Private Papers, Rochester, N.Y.

20 Miller, "A Little School Against the Big Bureaucracy," 4.

21 Plaintiffs' Reply Memorandum, *Grove City College v. Patricia R. Harris*, October 24, 1979, 22.

22 Decision of the United States District Court—Western District of PA—March 10, 1980, in *Grove City College v. Patricia R. Harris*, 17.

23 Ibid., 18.

24 "Sundae Punch," *Time*, March 24, 1980, 70.

25 Press release of Grove City College, December 22, 1980, Grove City College Archives.

26 Graham, "Storm Over Grove City College," 416.

27 Kathy Kiely, "U.S. To Pursue Grove City Sex Bias Case," *Pittsburgh Press*, January 13, 1982.

28 Martin Linsky, *Impact: How the Press Affects Federal Policymaking* (New York: W. W. Norton & Company, 1986), 101.

29 Ibid.

30 Charles R. Babcock, "Education Secretary Loses a Round," *Washington Post*, January 15, 1982.

31 "Education official defends reversal of anti-bias rule," *St. Louis Globe-Democrat*, May 20, 1982.

32 Christopher Connell, "Providing the Leaders and the Decision-Makers," *Change*, July/August 1982, 55.

33 Brief for Plaintiffs-Appellants in the United States Court of Appeals for the Third Circuit, *Grove City College* v. *Patricia R. Harris*, December 15, 1980, 42–43.

34 Ibid.

35 Cheryl M. Fields, "Even Colleges that Get Only Indirect Aid Must Obey U.S. Bias Laws, Court Says," *Chronicle of Higher Education*, September 1, 1982, 1.

36 Curtis J. Sitomer, "College asks high court to halt government meddling," *Christian Science Monitor*, January 28, 1983.

37 Ibid.

38 James Q. Wilson, *American Government: Institutions and Policies* (Lexington, MA: D. C. Heath and Company, 1980), 376.

39 According to the Public Information Office of the Supreme Court in November 1999.

40 Wilson, *American Government*, 395.

41 Stuart Taylor, Jr., "Court Case Yanks on the Whole Ball of Federal-Aid Strings," *New York Times*, September 25, 1983.

42 Ibid.

43 Brief for Petitioners, *Grove City College* v. *T. H. Bell*, June 7, 1983, 9.

44 Taylor, "Court Case Yanks on the Whole Ball of Federal-Aid Strings," *New York Times*.

45 Robb Jones, interview by author, September 17, 1999.

46 Wilson, *American Government*, 396.

47 Brief Amicus Curiae of Wabash College, *Grove City College* v. *T. H. Bell*, 7, 12.

48 Brief Amicus Curiae of Hillsdale College in support of Petitioners, *Grove City College* v. *T. H. Bell*, 19.

49 Brief Amicus Curiae for the Mexican American Legal Defense and Educational Fund, et. al., *Grove City College* v. *T. H. Bell*, 4.

50 Jim Mann, "College Seeks to Remain Independent of U.S. Rules," *Los Angeles Times*, November 30, 1983.

51 David Lascell, interview by author, September 15, 1999.

52 Transcript of Oral Argument, November 29, 1983, *Grove City College* v. *T.H. Bell*, 3.

53 Ibid., 5.

54 Ibid., 8–9.

55 Ibid., 11.

56 Ibid., 14, 16.

57 Ibid., 21.

58 Ibid., 31, 27.

59 Ibid., 29–30.

60 Robb Jones, interview by author, September 17, 1999; David Lascell, interview by author, November 10, 1998.

61 Charles S. MacKenzie, "Why Grove City College Won't Take the Pledge," *Wall Street Journal*, December 14, 1983.

62 Mary H. Purcell, "Fighting for Fairness in Education," *Newsday*, December 15, 1983.

63 Linda Greenhouse, "Grove City case limits bias rule," *Pittsburgh Post-Gazette*, February 29, 1984.

64 *Grove City College* v. *Terrel H. Bell, Secretary of Education*, in *The United States Law Week*, February 28, 1984, Supreme Court Opinions, 4, 6.

65 Ibid., 6.

66 Ibid., 7.

67 Ibid., 7–8.

68 Ibid., 8, 14.

69 Graham, "The Storm over Grove City College," 416.

70 Barbara Gubanic, "College president vows to avoid government control," *Pittsburgh Post-Gazette*, February 29, 1984.

71 Robert Smith, interview by author, March 18, 2000.

72 Ibid.

73 William Robbins, "A College Proud of Its Independence," *New York Times*, March 1, 1984.

74 " 'Grove City' Rights Bill Shelved by Senate," *Congressional Quarterly Almanac*, vol. XL, 1984, 239.

75 "Dr. MacKenzie Testifies before House Committee," *Allied News*, March 6, 1985.

76 MacKenzie, "Reminiscences," 30.

77 Graham, "The Storm over Grove City College," 420.

78 Ibid., 426–427.

79 Ibid., 427.

80 Ibid., 428.

81 "College decision receives positive response from press," *Grove City College Magazine*, Fall/Winter 1996, 5; Graham, "The Storm over Grove City College," 428.

82 Charles S. MacKenzie, "Just Say No to Uncle Sam's Money," *Christianity Today*, September 2, 1988, 12.

CHAPTER EIGHT

1 Ravitch, *The Troubled Crusade*, 225.

2 Lucas, *American Higher Education: A History*, 270.

3   Ravitch, *The Troubled Crusade*, 319.

4   Lucas, *American Higher Education*, 294, 270.

5   John D. Pulliam and James J. Van Patten, *History of Education in America*, 7th ed. (Prentice Hall, Upper Saddle River, NJ, 1999), 243.

6   Allan Bloom, *The Closing of the American Mind: How Higher Education Has Failed Democracy and Impoverished the Souls of Today's Students* (New York: Simon and Schuster, 1987), 22, 345. Also see Lucas, *American Higher Education*, 295, for his comments about C. P. Snow's 1959 Cambridge lecture, The Two Cultures.

7   Lucas, *American Higher Education*, 296.

8   E. D. Hirsch, Jr., *Cultural Literacy: What Every American Needs to Know* (Boston: Houghton Mifflin Company, 1987), 10.

9   Lucas, *American Higher Education*, 296.

10 Dinesh D'Souza, *Illiberal Education: The Politics of Race and Sex on Campus* (New York: The Free Press, 1991), 2, 5, 8, 13.

11 Ibid., 230.

12 Ibid., 23.

13 Ibid., 23.

14 Lucas, *American Higher Education*, 274.

15 Roger Kimball, *Tenured Radicals: How Politics Has Corrupted Our Higher Education* (New York: Harper & Row, 1990), xviii; Charles J. Sykes, *The Hollow Men: Politics and Corruption in Higher Education* (Washington, D.C.: Regnery Gateway, 1990), 68.

16 Martin Anderson, *Imposters in the Temple: American Intellectuals Are Destroying Our Universities and Cheating Our Students of Their Future* (New York: Simon & Schuster, 1992), 194–196.

17 Ibid., 206–210.

18 Thomas Sowell, *Inside American Education: The Decline, The Deception, The Dogmas* (New York: The Free Press, 1993), 300.

19 Bradford P. Wilson, "The Culture Wars in Higher Education" (paper prepared for the National Association of Scholars, Princeton, New Jersey, 1997).

20 Ibid.

21 Christopher J. Lucas, *Crisis in the Academy: Rethinking Higher Education in America* (New York: St. Martin's Press, 1996), 220.

22 MacKenzie, "Reminiscenses," 9.

23 Ibid., 10.

24 President's Report on the State of the College, Grove City, PA, May 1976, 1.

25 MacKenzie, "Reminiscences," 10.

26 Ibid., 11.

27 President's Report to the Board of Trustees, November 15, 1971, Grove City College Archives.

28 Minutes of the Board of Trustees, June 2, 1972.

29　President's Report to the Board of Trustees, May 18, 1973; Charles S. MacKenzie, interview by author, October 2, 1998.

30　MacKenzie, *Reminiscences*, 12.

31　Ibid., 12–13.

32　Ross Foster, interview by author, September 25, 1998.

33　Charles S. MacKenzie, "Reminiscences," 13.

34　President's Report to the Board of Trustees, May 1975.

35　President's Report on the State of the College May 1978, 1; President's Report on the State of the College May 1979, 1.

36　Foster interview.

37　MacKenzie, "Reminiscences," 13.

38　Ibid., 15.

39　Ibid., 21.

40　Ibid., 15–16.

41　Dale R. Bowne, interview by author, May 13, 1998.

42　MacKenzie, "Reminiscences," 18.

43　Ibid., 25.

44　Mary Ellen McGinty, "Origin of the 'Gedunk' provides imaginative responses from students," *The Collegian*, March 27, 1973.

45　Report to the Faculty, Administration, Trustees, Students of Grove City College, by an Evaluation Team representing the Commission on Higher Education of the Middle States Association of Colleges and Schools, prepared after a campus visit, April 13–16, 1980.

46　MacKenzie, "Reminiscences," 25–26.

47　Kenneth F. Warren, "Why I am resigning," The Collegian, March 26, 1974.

48　Minutes of the Board of Trustees, November 7, 1983.

49　"America's Best Colleges," *Grove City College Alumni News*, November 1988.

Chapter Nine

1　MacKenzie, "Reminiscences," 42.

2　Albert C. Hopeman, Jr., Address to the Faculty, June 1972.

3　R. Heath Larry, interview by Joel R. Gardner, July 1, 1998, 56, Grove City College Oral History Project.

4　Richard G. Jewell, interviewed by Joel R. Gardner, July 14, 1999, Grove City College Oral History Project.

5　Ibid., January 13, 1999.

6　Charles S. MacKenzie, interview by Joel R. Gardner, October 1, 1990 Pew Charitable Trusts/Glenmede Trust Oral History Project.

7　Albert A. Hopeman, Jr., Grove City College faculty luncheon, May 18, 1973.

8　Albert A. Hopeman, Jr., Grove City College faculty luncheon, May 17, 1974.

9 Albert A. Hopeman, Jr., Grove City College faculty luncheon, May 16, 1975.

10 Albert A. Hopeman, Jr., Grove City College trustee-faculty luncheon, May 20, 1977.

11 Ibid.

12 Albert A. Hopeman, Jr., Grove City College trustee-faculty luncheon, May 18, 1979.

13 David Lascell, interview by author, November 10, 1998.

14 Albert A. Hopeman, Jr., Grove City College trustee-faculty luncheon, May 15, 1981.

15 Albert A. Hopeman, Jr., Grove City College trustee-faculty luncheon, May 13, 1983.

16 Albert A. Hopeman, Jr., Grove City College trustee-faculty luncheon, May 18, 1984.

17 Albert A. Hopeman, Jr., Grove City College trustee-faculty luncheon, May 15, 1987.

18 Albert A. Hopeman, Jr., Grove City College trustee-faculty luncheon, May 14, 1988.

19 Ibid.

20 Albert A. Hopeman, Jr., Grove City College trustee-faculty luncheon, May 12, 1989.

21 Ibid.

22 Ibid.

23 "Leadership in academic ranks undergoing change," *Grove City College Alumni News*, March 1988, 1.

24 MacKenzie, "Reminiscences," 35.

25 Ibid.

26 Roche, *The Fall of the Ivory Tower*, 194, 196, 202.

27 Bruce D. Johnstone, "Higher education in the United States in the year 2000," *Prospects* XXI, no. 3 (1991), 441.

28 MacKenzie, "Reminiscences," p. 39; Richard G. Jewell, interview by Joel R. Gardner, July 14, 1999, Grove City College Oral History Project.

29 "Dr. Jerry H. Combee Named Sixth Grove City College President," Grove City College news release, April 17, 1991; Albert A. Hopeman, Jr., "Sailing the Steady Course," *Grove City College Alumni Magazine*, June 1992, 6.

30 "Back to the Future, Combee Begins Chapel," *The Collegian*, September 10, 1993.

31 Ruth Harker Mills, interview by author, November 19, 1998.

32 President's Report to the Board of Trustees, May 1992, 36–38.

33 Ibid., 39.

34 Matthew Donnelly, interview by author, September 25, 1998.

35 President's Report to the Board of Trustees, May 1993, 23.

36 "Grove City College—No longer the 'best kept secret,'" *Grove City College Alumni Magazine*, Spring/Summer 1993, 7.

37 Ibid.

38 Louise S. Baird, interview by author, September 23, 1998.

39 Jeffrey C. Mincey, interview by author, September 25, 1998.

40 Jerry H. Combee, "The Greater Grove City: A Five-Year Strategic Vision," report to the Board of Trustees, May 1995.

41 Minutes of the Board of Trustees, May 13, 1995.

42 Combee, "The Greater Grove City."

43 Ibid.

44 R. Heath Larry, interview by Joel R. Gardner, January 14, 1999, Grove City College Oral History Project.

45 Brian P. David, "President of Grove City College ousted," *The Herald*, June 21, 1995; R. Heath Larry, interview by Joel R. Gardner, January 14, 1999, Oral History Project of Grove City College.

46 Jerry H. Combee, interview by author, September 1, 1999.

47 Ibid.

48 Ibid.

49 Scott Powell, "Full speed ahead," *Grove City College Magazine*, Spring/Summer 1996, 7.

50 Rebecca Beinlich, "New president: Drawn by GCC's strengths," *Allied News*, May 8, 1996.

51 John H. Moore, message to the alumni, *Grove City College Magazine*, Spring/Summer 1996.

52 Beinlich, "New president: Drawn by GCC's strengths;" R. Heath Larry, interview by Joel R. Gardner, January 13, 1999, Grove City College Oral History Project.

53 R. Heath Larry interview by Joel R. Gardner, July 14, 1999, Grove City College Oral History Project.

54 Barbara M. Akin, interview by author, September 22, 1998.

55 James T. Thrasher, interview by author, September 21, 1998.

56 John H. Moore, "Report to the Board of Trustees," November 1996, 1.

57 John H. Moore, "Report to the Board of Trustees," May 1997, 9.

58 Paul McNulty, interview by author, September 2, 1999.

59 Alejandro Chafeun, interview by author, September 13, 1999.

60 Lawrence W. Reed, telephone interview by author, March 15, 2000.

61 Steve DeCaspers and Andy Hromyak, "President and wife treat reviewers," *The Collegian*, December 6, 1996.

62 John H. Moore, letter to the alumni, *Grove City College Magazine*, Spring/Summer 1998, 2.

63 J. Paul Sticht, "Memorial tribute to Mr. Hopeman," *Grove City College Magazine*, Spring/Summer 1998.

64 "J. Paul Sticht directs board of trustees," *Grove City College Magazine*, Winter 1999, 7.

65 According to Dr. Paul Kengor of Grove City College's political science department, the range of faculty salaries in the humanities in western Pennsylvania are assistant professor, $30,000–35,000; associate professor, $35,000–40,000; and full professor, $40,000–45,000. Paul Kengor, interview by author, September 22, 1998.

66 John A. Sparks, interview by author, May 13, 1998.

67 Report to Grove City College by a Middle States Evaluation Team, May 1998, 4–5.

68 John H. Moore, "Report to the Board of Trustees," November 1998, 13.

69 Nancy L. Paxton, interview by author, May 11, 1998.

70 Garth E. Runion, interview by author, May 16, 1998.

71 Lisa Fabian, "Angry students react to misrepresentation of college," *The Collegian*, October 31, 1997.

72 John H. Moore, letter to the alumni, *Grove City College Magazine*, Winter 1999, 2.

73 Ibid.

CHAPTER TEN

1   Russell Kirk, *The Roots of American Order* (LaSalle, IL: Open Court, 1974), 672.

2   Ibid.

3   I have depended upon Eva T. H. Brann's superb work, *Paradoxes of Education in a Republic* (Chicago: University of Chicago Press, 1979) as well as Russell Kirk's *The Roots of American Order*, for much of the succeeding analysis.

4   Kirk, *The Roots of American Order*, 82.

5   Ibid., 75.

6   Ibid., 108.

7   Brann, *Paradoxes of Education*, 6.

8   Ibid., 52.

9   Ibid., 53.

10 Ibid., 45.

11 Veith, and Kern, *Classical Education: Towards the Revival of American Schooling*, 77.

12 Ibid., 78.

13 Ibid., 51.

14 Brann, *Paradoxes of Education*, 146.

15 Stanley O. Ikenberry, interview by author, December 8, 1998.

16 Ibid.

17 Ibid.

18 Peg Miller, interview by author, December 8, 1998.

19 Ibid.

20 Ibid.

21 David Warren, interview by author, January 7, 1999.

22 Ibid.

23 Malcolm G. Scully, interview by author, December 7, 1998.

24 Ibid.

25 Ibid.

26 Scully, interview, December 7, 1998; Ikenberry, interview, December 8, 1998; Warren, interview, January 7, 1999.

27 Ikenberry, Miller, and Scully, interviews.

28 Warren, interview.

29 Jacques Barzun to the author, June 21, 1999.

30 David Riesman to the author, February 26, 1999.

31 Stanley Rothman to the author, July 4, 1999.

32 Ibid.

33 John Agresto to the author, August 11, 1999.

34 Harvey C. Mansfield to the author, February 26, 1999.

35 Mansfield, Riesman, Agresto, and Rothman all to the author.

36 Steven Balch to the author, December 20, 1999.

37 Paul Hollander to the author, February 18, 1999; George Marsden to the author, June 22, 1999; Jeffrey D. Wallin to the author, April 2, 1999; John Jacobson to the author, March 19, 1999.

38 Candace de Russy to the author, March 11, 1999; John M. Ellis to the author, February 18, 1999; Paul R. Gross to the author, February 13, 1999.

39 John A. Howard to the author, February 17, 1999.

40 Isaac Ketler, quoted by Charles S. MacKenzie, President's Report on the State of the College, May 18, 1990; J. Howard Pew, quoted by Albert A. Hopeman, Jr., address to the faculty, June 1972; Albert A. Hopeman, Jr., Grove City College trustee faculty luncheon, May 12, 1989.

41 John H. Moore, "Life on Mars and Life on Earth," *Grove City College Magazine*, Fall/Winter 1996, 12.

42 Rudolph, *The American College and University*, 210.

Index